HOW TO LIVE BETTER AND SPEND 20% LESS

Third Edition

Also by This Author

How to Earn a Fortune and Become Independent in Your Own Business

Merle E. Dowd

HOW TO LIVE BETTER
AND SPEND 20% LESS

Third Edition

PARKER PUBLISHING COMPANY, INC.
West Nyack, New York

© 1979,1972,1967, by

MERLE E. DOWD

Library of Congress Cataloging in Publication Data

Dowd, Merle E.
  How to live better and spend 20% less.

  Includes index.
  1. Saving and thrift. 1. Title.
HG7931.D6 1979 332'.024 79-10019
ISBN 0-13-415133-X

Printed in the United States of America

To my wife, Anne, and our four boys, Jerry, Stephen, Richard, and Timothy—five ever-present incentives to develop and practice the precepts found in this volume.

HOW YOU WILL BENEFIT
FROM READING THIS BOOK

How would you like to count $1,000 in a special savings account one year from the day you are reading this book? You can, if you are now taking home at least $10,000 after taxes. That means $1,000 is only 10 percent of your spendable dollars. Readers of the First and Second Editions of this book have written to me in uncounted numbers to report they have saved the full 20 percent—double the 10 percent needed to put an extra $1,000 in cash at your fingertips within one year. Think what you could do with an extra $1,000-$2,000—or $3,000—possibly more! The key point of this book is not how to save money. The key point is this— You learn to spend less for those goods and services that are relatively unimportant to you, and spend more on things and activities you enjoy. Managing your money can be dull without a purpose. This book tells you how to have more fun with your money. To do that, this book emphasizes these elements:

● You learn how to be an uncommon consumer. Rather than follow the crowds, you can buy for half what others are paying, learn how to buy out of season, earn discounts for cash while others fritter away precious dollars on credit, and generally spend less on practically everything you and your family need.

● You learn how to recognize value among alternatives and how to buy cost effectively—greatest value for least cost. Price can be a confusing guide to value, as you will discover in learning how to be an "agressive spender," one who challenges the usual or commonplace and looks for the true bargain—equal or greater value at a lesser price. But, paying too little may also lead to low cost-effective buys, hence the emphasis on value. Value or purchase analysis, as used by professionals in business, means to spend only the minimum necessary to get the value you need—but no more.

● You discover how to choose effectively. Living today is more complex than even a few years ago. Every person, every family faces many more buying decisions today. So, every family needs to develop more and better skills necessary to cope with the myriad decisions that must be made daily. Only when you can choose from a range of alternatives will your choices be consistently "right on." Learning to

7

develop alternatives through aggressive spending will get you more for your money.

● You develop motivation for managing your resources. Motivation to cut expenses in one category comes from the benefits you receive when spending in another. You will be absolutely amazed at the benefits you can gain by tying one goal to another and "making it all happen."

● Commuting cost and housing are tied together, as moving to the suburbs commits one or more persons to transportation expense to get to jobs and activities in the city. In this book you will learn how to cut the cost of commuting and/or housing by considering them together.

This Third Edition emphasizes energy conservation—saving money on heating oil or natural gas and spending those dollar savings on steaks, evenings out, a new boat, or—the list is endless. Yet, these necessities soak up a pile of after-tax dollars. The technique for cutting your food bill each week is different, for example, than for reducing commuting expenses—or car insurance. This Third Edition tackles major spending one category at a time.

Specifically, you will find in this Third Edition completely new material, updated prices and information on market facts that have changed, and a number of savings ideas reported by readers of the First and Second Editions. Look for these features in this Third Edition—

● An entirely new Chapter 4, Conserving Energy and Pocketing the Cash Savings, is added. Energy saving has become a national priority. By saving energy, you not only aid our country's efforts toward energy independence, you conserve cash in a category of spending that has been increasing faster than the overall inflation.

● Specific examples in each chapter name names, dollar amounts, and unique techniques readers used to make 20%, 40%—up to 95% savings. You can learn from these readers' experiences and gain the same benefits they did from using the techniques that are actually expanded in this Third Edition.

● Two completely new sections within Chapter 3 aid in controlling car operating costs. Everything relative to tires for your car has changed, and this book brings you right up to date on all the new types of tires.

● Truth-in-lending, Equal Credit Opportunity Act, and other anti-discriminatory legislation became the law of the land since the First and Second Editions were published. In this Third Edition, you will learn how to make credit work for you—saving you hundreds of dollars in interest and other charges.

● A key element in any family's control of money is the Spending Plan, and this Third Edition expands the explanation of this all-important tool. A number of questions arose from readers indicating the original treatment was too brief and left a number of important points obscure. The expanded chapter on how you can develop and use a Spending Plan in this edition is a direct outgrowth of reader feedback from letters.

● "Two decisions—one choice" is a principle important in all family decisions. The First Edition only hinted at this point, but it is paramount to your full understanding of money management as a way to more tax-free income.

● All of the numerical examples, charts, price schedules, and comparisons are updated to reflect higher prices common in nearly all spending categories.

● Much more data are provided on how you can use the consumer protection agencies functioning at the city, state, and Federal levels. Specific Federal agencies, such as the Federal Trade Commission, U.S. Department of Agriculture, Federal Reserve System, Food and Drug Administration, and the Interstate Commerce Commission are only a few of such agencies.

● Better ways to compare prices and values have appeared in the form of improved unit-price computers developed since the appearance of the First Edition. One of the best is unit pricing. This is just one of the new techniques detailed throughout this Third Edition.

● Automobile insurance alternatives are far more important today. The differences between the "no fault" and "tort" systems are explained in the car insurance section.

● Along with inflation came high interest rates, a particular problem for homeowners. This Third Edition tells you how to cope with these higher rates.

    If you don't save the cost of this book with ideas you find in each chapter, you're not really trying. Consider 10% or 20% savings as a minimum—then try to beat them. As you become more and more goal-oriented, you'll find yourself discovering more and more techniques, tricks, and gimmicks to cut your spending.

    Finally, you may have wondered, how can you "live better and spend 20% less"? The answer: Because you spend 20% less in certain kinds of spending, you discover more dollars left to live better. You can do it too. These are techniques followed by thousands of readers of my two syndicated newspaper columns and hundreds of students in my university classes. The results are proved. So—why don't you, too, live better because you learned to spend 20% less? I challenge you!

Merle E. Dowd

WHY THIS THIRD EDITION?

When the First Edition of this book first appeared in 1967 the United States was in a fast-developing period before much of the turmoil that affected families and pocketbooks in the early 1970s. I thought then that pocketbook economics was critical. But getting along, "making ends meet,"—simply surviving in the money-oriented world, is even tougher today than when I first discovered how many families were living on the brink of desperation and how difficult they found handling their money was.

Inflation has become a creeping catastrophe. While the cure for inflation is well known, most politicians believe that it would be worse than the disease; so, inflation continues. Individuals cannot hope to cope with inflation by reading or worrying about what is happening in Washington. But, you as an individual can cope with your personal inflation—and that's one reason for updating the strategies and coping techniques added to this Third Edition.

For example—

Energy is much on the minds of politicians, individuals, and families concerned about the price of keeping their home warm or of being able to drive to work. The emphasis on energy, its conservation, and how to save money in using it were not important in either the first or second editions. But, energy is critical, and this Third Edition deals with it in specific terms you can do something about.

Super income is a concept I had not developed in the First or Second Editions Super income represents those benefits you gain that are not subject to income tax. As dollar incomes have expanded due to inflation, so have taxes as we move steadily into higher and higher income-tax brackets. Thus, the federal government effectively collects more taxes without actually raising the rate schedule—workers simply grow into the higher brackets. How we use our resources to expand our standard of living with super income is another important way of coping with inflation. So—a Third Edition takes the tack of developing more super income.

For the past eight years I have written a syndicated newspaper column, "Managing Your Family's Money," that appears twice a week in newspapers across the United States. In one column each week I answer questions of general interest from readers. I hope that the thousands of readers who have responded to my invitation to ask a money question have learned a bit more about the sometimes confusing world of money. I know that I have learned much about what has been on their minds. I learned that many were concerned about family debt and how they were slipping into it deeper and deeper. They were concerned about bankruptcy. A new chapter on getting out of dept appeared in the Second Edition to answer those queries. This and many of the other sections have been completely rewritten to respond to the full range of letters with one major exception. Many letters asked about personal investing strategies and techniques. Space limitations prevented a treatment of investment opportunities. Besides, many excellent books have addressed the problems of investing in almost every area. But, these books assume the reader is sitting on a pot of money looking for an investment opportunity. I learned that many persons who wrote to me would like to be investors, but they had no cash. Gaining money to invest for the future can be a great motivator—but how?

Regardless of the reason for stretching one's income, including investment, you need a system. The "Howgozit Chart System" was introduced in the First Edition. It was expanded and explained in more detail in the Second Edition. In this Third Edition, not only are the elements highlighted, but examples are available to simplify your use of this "miracle system," as one reader called it. She used the "Howgozit Charts" to control her spending and found a whole new standard of living.

Finally, in addition to the detailed updating in every chapter to bring prices into line and to recognize an entirely new level of government regulation of the market place, I am encouraged by the success of previous readers to gain control of their life. Letter after letter has reported, "We are now taking charge of our lifestyle instead of letting money boss us around. We're calling the shots!" I feel good about these kinds of reports because they indicate that my system works. Few things are as important as the money we use to get what we want out of life.

Merle E. Dowd

CONTENTS

HOW TO LIVE BETTER
AND SPEND 20% LESS

Third Edition

1

WHY YOU AND YOUR FAMILY SHOULD "BOTHER" WITH MONEY

When anyone suggests that we should change our ways, we usually ask—"Why?" Here you'll learn "why" you should bother with money and discover the real advantages of learning how to manage your money. When you "bother" with money, you can—

- Discover aggressive spending.
- Spend more cash for fun.
- Enjoy a better life.
- Stop fighting over money.
- Save cash at income-tax time.
- Develop confidence in your ability to handle money.

Are you interested in spending $8 instead of the $10 you have been spending? It's as simple as that—save $2 out of every $10 (20%) while buying what used to cost you $10. The $2 you save provides you with 25% more purchasing power to live better—the way you really want to live—on your present earnings.

Or look at it another way. Could you use a 20% hike in salary or wages? If your salary is $500 per month, could you use another $100 to pay off doctor bills, fix up the house, buy new clothes, or spruce up your home with new furniture? Or, even better, would an extra $100 per month help you and your family have more fun, take a long vacation trip, buy a new car, trade in your black-and-white TV for color, buy a boat, give more to your church, or send your children to college? You can spend more by managing your money. That's the whole purpose of this book.

WHAT IS YOUR *DOLLAR PERSONALITY?*

Do you know your *dollar personality* (DP)? We all have one whether we know or care to admit it or not. You have probably seen the headline that read: "Lonely Recluse Dies in Dump Shack—$100,000 Found in Mattress." Often, these oldsters die from malnutrition because they wouldn't spend cash for good food. Obviously, their DP was as mixed up as a kaleidoscope. Not so unusual, though, is the wife who spends money as if she were the Federal Government. She spends cash on the frailest impulse and runs up credit charges in every store. She never considers where the money comes from—only that there's never enough to buy all the things she "needs."

Between the tightwad (savers) who squirrel away every nickel they can lay their hands on and the spenders who are always broke and in debt, there is the middle group of persons with a different DP. They are the worriers. They may spend money logically—not too much, not too little—but they worry excessively. They worry when they spend, and they worry when they don't spend.

Nobody's DP can be judged "OK." For, who's to judge? The point is, you should know your DP and make allowances for it. Analyze whether your DP is causing friction in your marriage, delaying your progress on the job, or interfering with your social life. Here's how you can determine your *dollar personality*.

Savers—Do you know to the penny how much money is in your pocket, make special trips to bargain sales, pay cash for a new car, read a restaurant menu from right to left, stash away money or travelers' checks in different places, and really use an organized budget? Such behavior marks you as a money saver. Misers, on the other hand, deprive themselves of even small comforts to accumulate money. Savers exercise firm control over their dollars, but, they sometimes find it difficult to spend money and enjoy it.

Worriers—Whether he puts money in the bank or spends it, the worrier frets and stews about his decision. After awhile the worrier, knowing he will worry later, finds it difficult to make up his mind, and spends too much time deciding whether to make a purchase or not. The worrier in a restaurant not only looks at the prices but worries about what his wife or a friend may think if he picks the ground sirloin instead of the New York steak. A worrier considers both sides—whether he is spending enough to make an impression (and scuttling his budget) or too little (and depriving himself of some enjoyment he could easily afford). He may end up spending more than he should—then worrying about it for days. The worrier may spend hours shopping for a dress, then buy the one she saw at the first store. Or, at Christmas time, the worrier decides on an appropriate inexpensive gift for his wife, then at the last minute buys another more expensive gift, with the result that he spends more than he intended and gives two so-so gifts instead of one really good one.

Spenders—Most likely to be in money trouble are the persons who never consider costs. If you pick out the one item you can't do without from the restaurant menu without considering its price, go overboard for presents at birthdays and Christmas, buy the car you want—not the car you can afford—are chronically in hock to the finance company, seldom use a shopping list at the supermarket, and make up menus as you roam through the aisles, then you are probably a spender. Impulse buying and a lack of goals cause spenders to fritter away their resources. A spender may push aside the problem of which creditor to stave off for another month by taking his wife out to dinner at an expensive restaurant.

Psychologically, there are reasons behind each of these dollar personalities. Chronic savers may have grown up in a family atmosphere where money was constantly a problem. Or a saver may have faced a crisis without money. The shock of not having money may have left such a mark that he vowed never to be broke again. Basically, savers are insecure. Money in the bank is something they can count on.

A person's DP may reflect an outward look or an inward look. Outward-looking persons use money to impress their friends, to achieve a status they may or may not deserve. Such persons are likely to insist on new cars and a home in a neighborhood that tells the world of their position. Outward-looking persons derive pleasure from associating with people, to satisfy an inner need to "belong."

Inward-looking people, on the other hand, spend their money on libraries of good books, expensive stereo sound systems, and cultural activities that satisfy themselves. However, these inner-directed activities are sometimes a cover-up for basic insecurities and a reluctance to meet and associate with a broad range of people.

Suppose you are a *spender*. To get more out of your life, you need to work at a planned spending program rather than continue your succession of impulsive purchases. Look at your many installment bills to see if the repayment discipline is substituting for planning you should be doing yourself. Resolve to "sleep" on ideas before rushing into major purchases such as a new house, a new car, or a vacation. Look more closely at the true costs and all the angles, before diving into a real estate "deal," for example. Spenders need to slow down the rate of their money outgo long enough to catch their breath—then go ahead on a rational plan.

If you are a *saver*, an opposite tack may be desirable. If you make a point of "not keeping up with the Jonses," you may be depriving yourself and your family of many pleasures you could easily afford. With so many built-in safeguards in our economy, social security, unemployment insurance, medical care plans, etc., you may be banking excessive cash as insurance against catastrophes that are unlikely to happen. Any family needs reserves, but savers usually go overboard to insure themselves against every conceivable catastrophe. Savers are already good budgeters, but they need to change the mix of their budget to channel more money for fun, for getting more out of life than the pleasure of watching a mounting total in a savings account passbook.

Suppose you are a *worrier*. Instead of spending so much effort worrying whether you should or should not spend money one item at a time, set up a plan, study it with your wife and family, establish goals you can all agree on, then follow through—without worry. Once you have worked out an overall plan, you know that money spent for a good used car, for example, conforms to your pattern and won't deprive you of some other desired activity later.

Sick Dollar Personalties—Money quirks can achieve such excesses as to need outside treatment. The man who gambles compulsively, for example, may be as sick as the alcoholic—only the medium is different. A wife who keeps the family broke by "saving money on bargains," or who frequents auctions to buy goods at improbably low prices also needs help. Numerous community service organizations are available to help these persons who are frequently unable or unwilling to help themselves. Fortunately, the number of these persons is relatively small. More numerous are the husbands and wives who are in trouble financially but are unwilling to take a close look and then do something about their problems.

What happens when a man and women with different dollar personalities marry? Without considering worriers who may lean either toward overspending or oversaving, three combinations are possible—two savers, two spenders, or a spender and a saver. When two spenders marry, results can be catastrophic with neither party applying discipline or exercising responsibility for money. A marriage of two savers may be solid financially, but little fun. Probably the best combination is a marriage of a spender and a saver. Whether the saver happens to be the man or woman, that person assumes responsibility for money management, pays the bills, keeps the bankbook balanced, and generally keeps a wary eye out financially. The spender, again either male or female, insists that they enjoy life as they live it.

Please do not interpret from all of the above that dollar personalities are forever cast in concrete from an early age. Personalities and your approach to managing money can change. A modern technique of behavior modification can be adapted to change your money manners.

STOP FIGHTING YOUR WIFE (HUSBAND) OVER MONEY

Marriage counselors agree that while money is a major cause of quarrels between husbands and wives, most money quarrels are only a surface symptom of deeper problems. If a husband, for example, neglects to notice his wife's appearance or "forgets" to compliment her on her housekeeping or cooking, she nips back at him for failing to earn more money. The opposite is also true—if a couple is happily in tune with each other, money problems, real and imaginary, seldom develop into a full-fledged monetary war.

Basic differences in outlook and differences in their dollar personalties (DP) frequently fan a couple's financial problems into major quarrels. Unless these basic differences can be resolved or at least understood, only temporary cures to the symptoms can be expected. Let's look at one case.

John and Mary (the names have been changed to protect the guilty) fought constantly over money. John had grown up in a family that actively participated in clubs, school, sports, and group activities. His personality was outer-directed—he belonged to a bowling league, attended club parties, and played golf incessantly. He liked to "live it up" with a new car every year, membership in a golf club, and frequent dinners out. Money was a way to do all of these things *away from home*. Since a restricted income limited these activities, he was constantly pressing Mary to reduce expenses on food, the children's clothes, and the house.

Mary, on the other hand, had lived closely with her mother after her father's death. Her nesting instinct and basic security were centered in her home. Outside activities were a diversion. She preferred to spend money on carpeting, good food (she could spend hours in the kitchen cooking), and a sewing machine that allowed her to make dresses for her daughters, as her mother had done for her.

Money simply meant different things to John and Mary. Quarrels over money reflected their priority differences. Mary kept harping about how little their house was. John was equally bitter about the money Mary spent on such "unimportant" items as payments for the sewing machine. He accused her of poor management of the household funds. When their monetary war finally forced John and Mary to see me for counseling, I patiently pointed out the cause of their disagreements over money. Once the causes were fully understood, the symptoms gradually disappeared. Sometimes, as in this case, an outsider is needed to first analyze the underlying problems and then create an awareness of each partner's *dollar personality*.

Equally trying are the open or hidden attempts of each marriage partner to "one up" the other. Henry and Alice were always in debt, frequently behind in payments, and completely irresponsible in their spending. When a garnishment of his check forced Henry to divulge his problems to a counselor at the plant, a spending pattern quickly stood out from the background. Henry was an outdoorsman; Alice was a homebody. But, though quiet and soft-spoken, she had spunk. Whenever Henry bought a fishing pole or an outboard motor or took off for a fishing trip with his buddies, she retaliated by buying an expensive coat, a new hat, or a new chair for the living room. When the new chair appeared, Henry figured he was entitled to buy something for his boat. Each selfishly wanted to make sure he or she spent an equal share of Henry's income. When the counselor was able to show Henry and Alice how their defensive spending was wrecking any chance to develop a true marriage relationship, they set about developing a plan each could live with.

Defensive spending becomes even more complicated when both husband and wife work. The quarrels over "my" money and "our" money and the tendencies to make sure the other doesn't spend more than his or her "share" disclose an immature approach to marriage. Such a couple should toss all money earned into one teapot. How the money is taken out should not be figured on the basis of how much each contributed but on what is to be spent to satisfy goals both can agree on.

Another frequent cause of marital money muddles is the desire of newly married couples to start off with the same standard of living their parents took 20 years to achieve. A couple immediately wants a ranch house in a socially desirable suburban neighborhood, all new furnishings in keeping with the accepted social position, a new car of course, and a level of continuous entertainment all out of proportion to the salary earned by a junior executive with his foot barely on the bottom rung of the corporate ladder. If the couple immediately plunges into debt to buy all of these things at once, they may find finance charges and monthly payments leave them strapped for enough cash to eat on. When money is short during the first year or two, before a harmonious accommodation is firmly established, short tempers result and their marriage sinks to a marital battleground. Once established, the pattern is hard to break.

YOUR PLAN FOR SPENDING MONEY

Plan for spending money the way you *really* want, but *spend* it *all!* You may have heard, "You can't take it with you!" But, spending all you make doesn't mean spending it as fast as it comes in. Consider "all you make" over a period longer than a week, month, or even a year. A workable spending plan may call for borrowing today (spending more than you make) and spending less at a later date when you pay back what you borrowed—plus interest. Another spending plan may call for saving today to permit you to spend more later. The important thing is to spend according to some kind of plan.

Spending Plan, as used in this book, should not be confused with a budget. If you are typical, the word "budget" calls forth a string of negative thoughts and images. Using the Spending Plan is a positive approach; you plan how to spend money, not how to save it.

Only exceptional families, the Kennedys, Rockefellers, and the like, can plan their living patterns without considering limitations on their resources. Most families, companies, organizations, and governments find their wish list exceeds their resources. So, we are all faced with the "tyranny of choice." How to decide? One finding is painfully clear—you can't make one decision at a time. Whenever you decide to do something or buy some article, you really make two decisions. You decide to buy something and, at the same time, you decide not to buy something else, because the money is spent. Learning how to manage your money means learning how to choose amoung various alternatives. Decision making is much more complex these days than it used to be when most of a family's food and all of its entertainment were homegrown.

WHY MANAGE MONEY?

Ask nearly any family about money and invariably they will tell you they need some. You know how hard it is to make more money, to get a raise out of the boss, to earn additional commissions, or for your union to negotiate a contract calling for increased pay. A surprising number of family heads moonlight at a second job to earn more money. Or, wife and husband both work to increase income. But, how much time does either spend in planning how to spend their money? Does it make sense to work and worry constantly about making more money and then spend no more time deciding how to spend it than it takes to balance a checkbook?

Consider this idea for a moment. You spend 40 hours a week on a job plus an additional 5 to 10 hours in round-trip transportation and lunch time. You have already invested a substantial part of an irreplaceable item—your time, big-size chunks of your life. Doesn't it make sense then to spend an hour or two a week examining how the profits from your invested time (wages, salary) can be spent to get the most out of life?

So, as long as you work hard for your money, why not spend some time managing it? Remember, the extra purchasing power you squeeze out of the dollars you now have are "after tax" dollars. You have already paid income taxes on the money you have. If you were to "moonlight" at a second job evenings or weekends, the government would take its 16-50% right off the top. Newly earned dollars, then, produce no more than 84¢ of purchasing power. If you use the money you have already more effectively, you spend a full dollar for every dollar you save.

MANAGING MONEY LIKE A BUSINESS

How often have you heard the comment, "Why don't you run the house like a business?" or "If a business ran it finances like this family, it would fold up in a month!" More often than not, a business *would* fail if finances were as loosely controlled as in most households. Over the years, business has developed a number of techniques to keep a company's checkbook balanced. Let's look at some that have proven their worth in business.

Pinching the Big Bucks—Benjamin Franklin is credited with the saying, "Watch the pennies and the dollars will take care of themselves." But dollar watchers in business prefer watching the big expenditures or sales rather than the piddling sums. They reason thusly: If, by careful control, they can reduce an annual $100,000 cost item by 1%, the company's profit goes up $1000. Just as much effort may be required to cut 5% from an annual $1000 cost item to net a profit of only $50. In other words, the potential gain from the same effort spent on controlling big sums far outdistances the gains from cutting costs that are already small.

How can you use this idea? First, consider which are your "big buck" items. You can tick off food, housing, transportation, and clothing. Suppose you spend $25 out of every $100 of your after-tax income on food. If, by thrifty shopping, you can save $1 out of every $25, that's a reduction of about 4%. Suppose too that you spend $5 of the same $100 take-home pay on recreation and fun. Adding the $1 you save on food to your recreation fund increases your allowance for fun from $5 to $6—an increase of 20 per cent.

Watching the Regular Bucks—Paying a few cents more on a regular item can mount, over a year's time, to much much more than a big increase on something that hits the bank account only once or twice a year. Saving 3 to 5¢ a gallon on gasoline, for example, can save you much more than shopping for the last possible dollar saving when buying seat covers for your car. The same idea applies to such foods as milk that you buy two or three times a week.

Watching the Fixed Costs (Facilities Analysis)—Capital expenditures for everything from a new building to new tools and equipment are checked thoroughly from every angle in a well-managed business, because, once a decision is made, the company must live with it for many years. A mistake in facilities expenditures hangs around a company's neck for a long time.

You have the same problem when you consider buying a home vs. renting an apartment, or, buying a second car vs. taking a cab for occasional trips around town when the first car is in use. Once you incur a fixed expense, it continues to take a regular bite out of your take-home pay.

Watching All Dollars—Every business, regardless of size, keeps records. Taxes, employee records, and knowing whether the business is making or losing money all require a business to keep detailed books. Similar planning or budgeting can help you. Adopting a businesslike attitude toward family finances is probably one of the best ideas you can borrow from the business world to help you get the most out of your dollars.

Planning—Basically, planning is an organized forward look. Business planners estimate income expected over a future period, figure existing assets (money in the bank, value of inventories, etc.), and determine manpower available. Managers are constantly juggling these resources in an attempt to get the most return or profit.

As manager of your family's resources, you are a planner of a small business. So, you plan how you can get the most living for your money— today and tomorrow. Your family should consider possible trade-offs just like a business. Too much effort you say? Why should you spend your time "sweating the small stuff"? Or you think, "It doesn't make any difference how I plan, the money's all gone anyway!" A common reaction, but one that leaves little hope.

But, let's look at it this way. Over a lifetime, an average high school graduate will earn nearly half a million dollars. A college graduate can reasonably expect to earn from three-quarters to a million dollars or more. Isn't it reasonable to develop a plan for spending this money—one of your lifetime resources?

HOW DO YOU RATE?

Have you wondered, "How come the Smiths next door can buy a new car every two years?" Or, "Why can't I buy as many new clothes as that salesman's wife across the street?" Many times salaries or wages are common knowledge, as on a military post, among government agency employees, or among teachers where each rank carries a known income. Comparisons of spending patterns among families in these neighborhoods can be vicious. Housing costs and car expenses are easily compared. But, furnishings, personal clothing, good times on the town, vacation trips, and cultural expenditures are more difficult, mainly because comparisons of personal effects are wrapped up in emotions.

Even more difficult are comparisons among neighbors when incomes are known to vary widely. Often, the actual difference in income is likely to be less than some families are willing to admit. "John must really be rolling in it," a husband will comment to his wife when John and his wife return from a vacation in Bermuda. If the facts were known, John probably isn't "rolling in it." John may simply be a better money manager than his neighbor.

Comparisons of affluence among neighbors are almost certainly off-hand, emotionally biased comparisons. Seldom will a husband or wife set down facts and figures on their own expenditures and attempt to compare these figures with objective estimates liberally laced with known facts about their neighbors' affairs. Income-tax investigators are known to be quite successful at working backward to find a family's income by analyzing expenditures. Only a cool appraisal of all facts is likely to yield a meaningful comparison.

ESCAPING THE FIXED-INCOME TRAP

Tax rates since World War II have leveled off many medium to high incomes. Minimum wage laws and wage negotiations have raised the floor of other incomes. These two actions have created a much bigger middle-income class. The continuing increase in government employment and industrywide bargaining by labor unions contribute to a further loss of income flexibility. Take the Federal Government Salary grade scale, for example. Numerical levels control income for literally millions of Federal employees. Rigid job evaluation and salary scales impose similar limitations on earnings in many industries. Except for moonlighting or getting your wife a job, there's little you can do to expand your income in these situations. If you are caught in such a bind, consider aggressive spending as a means of expanding your buying ability from a relatively fixed income.

Suppose you are employed in a government bureau with a fixed income. Your neighbor works in the same bureau in the same salary grade. If you both take home let's say $20,000 yearly, you can spend $4000 more each year for fun (or some worthwhile purpose) than your neighbor. Where does the additional $4000 come from? Out of your $20,000 income, as detailed in the following chapters.

"DOING IT YOURSELF" AND YOUR INCOME TAX

Since World War II, families have been building, painting, and fixing up at a rate reminiscent of pioneer days when families were completely self-sufficient. For example, almost 90% of the paint applied inside homes is rolled or brushed on by do-it-yourselfers. Some families have even built an entire house from the ground up. Aside from the satisfaction many gain from doing something constructive, there's a real benefit at income-tax time.

Suppose your house needs a complete paint job inside. A painter estimates the job will cost $600. You can probably buy the paint for $60— the rest is labor. To have $600 left after paying out 25% income tax, you must earn $800. If you do the job yourself, you pay $60 for the paint. The value of your labor is tax free. By painting your own house you have boosted your income by $740. According to the Internal Revenue Service, a penny saved is *not* a penny earned; that is, you don't pay income tax on the money you save. So, rather than taking a second job to earn money to pay for having a job done—and giving the government 16-40% or more of your earnings—you might consider doing the job yourself.

Let's take another example. Suppose you are living in a small house and your growing family demands more room. For $1,000 materials and your own time on weekends and evenings, you add on another bedroom. If your house was worth $30,000 before, the additional room may increase its value to $35,000. Do you pay income tax on the value added by your own labor? Not until you sell it! But, suppose you do sell it for $35,000. Since the house sold for $5,000 more than its value before the addition, you would ordinarily expect to pay a capital-gains tax on the difference. Again, the government gives the homeowners and the do-it-yourselfer a break. If you buy another house within 18 months that costs at least $35,000, you pay no tax on the increase in value, so your labor tax is free. Even if you did not buy another house right away, the value of your labor is taxed at only 40 percent of the usual rate as a long-term capital gain.

IT'S UP TO YOU

Consider for a moment the battle of wits that is going on week-in, week-out between retailers and wily shoppers. The shopkeeper appears to have all the big guns. He uses advertisers skilled in the psychology of attracting your eye and softening your resistance. He knows better than you the actual cost and quality of the goods he offers for sale. His salespersons are practical psychologists skilled in the art of closing a sale. Manufacturers enter the contest to support the retailer. In the face of such competition some shoppers simply withdraw from the contest, and the markets win by default. Despite such formidable opposition, you *can* win. You are still the buyer, the one who, by choice or default, picks an item off the shelf and buys it. But, you must plan ahead, study the facts available, analyze the trade-offs, and improve your shopping skills. How well you fare in managing your money and way of life, once you master the fundamentals, is strictly up to you.

SUMMING UP

To make any real personal improvement that calls for changing our ways, we must be motivated; that is, we must find a good reason for changing. The detailed advice on buying wisely, spending aggressively, and knowing when and how to get the most for your money, that you'll find in succeeding chapters, will be scarcely noticed unless you are interested. A few of the ideas covered in this chapter were—

- Finding your *dollar personality*.
- Examining whether money problems are the real cause of fights between you and your husband (wife) or merely symptoms.
- Planning, when you begin to manage your money, you learn to spend it all effectively.
- Borrowing proved ideas from business to help you and your family get more for your money.
- Understanding that how you spend your money probably makes a bigger difference in your standard of living than how much you earn.

- Learning how to escape the fixed-income trap by spending your money aggressively.

- Analyzing the income-tax effects of buying or doing it yourself.

- Remembering, you're still in charge. It's your money you're spending. Learn the skills you need to bargain and compete in the marketplace.

2

SAVE HUNDREDS OF DOLLARS
WHEN YOU SHOP THE SUPERMARKETS

Food, being the prime necessity of life, takes a big chunk out of your income. Where you spend the most, you have the biggest opportunity for saving. Savings of 20% on food are commonplace. You can save even more than 20% by—

- Cutting the cost of "big dollar items"—meat, milk, cereals, and desserts.

- Shopping the specials—systematically and aggressively.

- Using convenience foods—to save both money and time.

- Sharpening your "shopping tactics."

- Learning to buy nutrition, a balanced diet, rather than just food.

Buying, cooking, and serving food for the family presents a housewife with a whopping big opportunity for saving money. No other item in a family's total spending pattern offers the housewife so many alternatives.

There's absolutely no question about it—you can cut spending for food by 20%—at least. Let's suppose your family includes four persons— you and your husband, a 12-year old son, and a 9-year-old daughter. According to U.S. Dept. of Agriculture (USDA) figures, a middling figure for food for your family comes to $71.80 per week (at the price level for October, 1978)—that's $3,733.60 for the year. Twenty per cent cut off that figure amounts to $746.72—enough to pay for a vacation trip, a big chunk of a new car, savings for college, a start on a down payment on a new home, or new furniture.

Biggest savings must come out of the big food items—meat, milk, and dessert purchases. Together, these items account for almost 60% of your purchases. A small saving on a big item amounts to more than a big saving on a small item. If you stopped buying crackers, you might save 50¢ per month. But, changing your meat buying habits can easily save you $5 to $12 per month.

20% Savings Idea

Here's how Emma Frain cut her family's food bill—and nipped in her and husband Arby's waistlines too. She began measuring food portions and serving less. For example, instead of serving two pork chops, Emma served one large one apiece plus a half for Arby and her teen-age son. On one meal she saved $1.40, the difference between $3.60 for ten chops and $2.20 for six chops. Over a week's time, Emma figured she saved an average of $2.80 per day simply by serving less food. Over a year's time; such savings cut the Frain's expenditures for food by $803. And—both she and Arby slimmed down to a more healthy, energetic weight.

A quick way to save money on food is—eat less. Whoo-ee—some advice! Actually, almost everyone in the United States eats more food than he or she needs, can use, or should have. Every serious nutritionist states flatly that most people—and particularly fat people—simply eat too much.

Too many families overload a plate with huge servings and then hammer away at the kids to clean up their plates. So serve smaller portions, but keep seconds available.

One caution—don't get snared into the "diet food" practice to reduce overeating. Buying these more costly "diet foods" puts you in the uneasy position of paying more money for less food.

Your family's attitude and philosophy also affect your food planning, of course. There's the old saw, "Some people eat to live—others live to eat." Families who love good food in great variety willingly spend more of their resources on food than average families. For these gourmets, food is both a necessity and a luxury. But the difference between a tasteful, nutritious diet and meals that include luxurious, unusual items should be recognized for what it is—a way of life. These families literally "live to eat."

Several books have appeared recently about feeding a family for less with far more detail than is possible in this chapter. They are: *How I Feed My Family of Five on $135 a Month* by Jean Gaffin, Creation House, Carol Stream, Illinois; *How I Feed My Family on $16 a Week (And Have Meat, Fish or Poultry on the Table Every Night)* by Jo Ann York, Coward, McCann & Geoghegan, Inc., New York; *Penny Pincher's Cook Book* by Sophie Leavitt, Lancer Books, New York; *Eat Well on a Dollar a Day* by Bill and Ruth Kaysing, Chronicle Books, San Francisco; and *The Waste Not, Want Not Cookbook* by Helen McCully, Random House, New York.

MEAT

To save on meat costs, plan a whole week's menus around that week's specials, but stay flexible (see "Shopping the Specials," page 45.) If pork is on sale one week, eat pork, whether it's ham, loin roasts, picnics, or chops. Over a period of six weeks you won't have to repeat a single item unless you want to, and you'll still be buying at reduced prices.

Lean parts of beef, lamb, pork, and poultry provide about the same food value. So, practice your creative cookery. Instead of plopping a luscious sirloin on a charcoal grill and spending $1.00 to $1.50 per serving, check one of the women's magazines that are handy at most supermarket checkout stands for 35¢ to 50¢. Any issue will have dozens of ways to doll up a pound of ground beef or slices from a chunk of beef, lamb, or veal to make a culinary delight at a cost of 15 to 20¢ per serving. Rice, noodles, spaghetti, and macaroni are all good extenders for meat and canned fish for a "cheapie" meal.

Lean meat is what you pay for in a market. Prices for specific cuts of meat vary according to how much bone, gristle, and fat are combined with lean. One simple way to compare meat costs is to price the cost of an individual serving of lean meat in various cuts and kinds of meat. The USDA figures a 3-oz. serving of lean meat as "right" for one meal for one person. A 3-oz. serving of meat ordinarily provides 15 grams of protein or about one-fourth of the daily adult requirement.

Table 2A helps you compare meat alternatives on the basis of 3 oz. cooked lean meat. Use Table 2A several ways—to locate those meats that generally cost less per serving, to compare the cost of a ham, for example, "with the bone in" to a ham priced higher "with the bone out," and as a guide for quantities needed for a meal to serve a set number. Here's how—

22% Savings Idea

Mary Anne Mower picked up the idea from Table 2A in the original edition of this book. Recognizing that meat was the biggest single item in her food basket, she decided never to buy meat unless it was on special. From her records, she found she had spent $2,644 on food for her family of five during the past year. Meat purchases represented $861 of that. So, for one year, she bought only meats on special at an average reduction of 22% for a saving of $189.42. The family enjoyed steak just as often as they had before; Mary Anne simply waited until it was on sale before serving a sirloin or New York cut. The same with the other meats.

● Ground beef, ham with the bone in, boneless round steak, boneless rump roast of beef, and ham slices are generally at the low end of the meat cost range when figured on a cost/serving basis. T-bone steak, rib lamb chops, club beef steaks, and short ribs are generally at the high cost end. Even though short ribs may cost only 80 cents/pound, waste in the form of bone and fat push the cost/serving to 47 cents.

● Compare the cost of ham with the bone in at 35 cents/serving, and you'll be paying $1.00/pound at the store. For a comparable 35 cents/serving, you could pay $1.35/pound for boneless ham. That is, you could pay 35 percent more for boneless ham than for ham with the bone in, and your cost/serving would be the same.

● Planning quantities can be confusing until you work backwards from the cost/serving. For example, if you plan to serve a ham slice to five persons and the price is $1.50/pound, check Table 2A and find the cost of a 3-oz. serving is 47¢. Multiply 47¢ by 5 persons and you'll need to buy 1⅔ pounds.

● Compare different meats at varying prices. For example, a beef chuck is priced at 95¢/pound, cost/serving is 42¢. Other meats that would deliver one serving for 42¢ would be round steak with the bone in at $1.25/pound, ground beef at $1.60/pound, fresh boneless pork chops at 95¢/pound, a boneless pork loin roast at $1.20/pound, or a picnic ham with the bone out at $1.20/pound.

Alternatives to red meat can supply needed protein at prices to help you keep food expenditures in line. Table 2B helps you compare various meat and nonmeat sources of protein on the basis of a 20-gram serving. Market prices will obviously vary with location and time. You can make your own comparison by using the data in the table. For example, if dry beans should be priced at 49 cents rather than the 29 cents noted in the table, simple multiply 49 cents by .24 and come up with a cost of 12 cents for 20 grams of protein rather than the 7 cents noted.

MEAT SUBSTITUTES

When meat prices shot out of sight a few years ago and came down only a bit since, homemakers looked around for meat substitutes. When they switched to fish, the price of fish escalated along with meat. The same thing happened to beans that increased in price by a factor of five, and cheese that doubled in price. Another meat substitute that had been around for years gained new friends—protein concentrates from soybeans. The soybean protein is now available in many more forms in two

TABLE 2A: Cost of a 3-oz. serving of cooked lean meat from selected kinds and cuts of meat at specified retail prices/pound

Kind & cut of meat	.95	1.00	1.05	1.10	1.15	1.20	1.25	1.30	1.35	1.40	1.45	1.50	1.55	1.60	1.65	1.70	1.75	1.80	1.85	1.90	1.95
	Cost of a 3-oz. serving (cents)																				
Beef, roasts																					
Brisket	.49	.52	.55	.57	.60	.62	.65	.68	.70	.73	.76	.78	.81	.83	.86	.89	.91	.93	.96	.99	1.01
Chuck, bone in	.42	.45	.47	.49	.51	.54	.56	.58	.60	.62	.65	.67	.69	.71	.74	.76	.78	.80	.83	.85	.87
Chuck, bone out	.33	.35	.36	.38	.40	.42	.43	.45	.47	.49	.50	.52	.54	.56	.57	.59	.61	.62	.65	.67	.69
Ribs—7th, bone in	.42	.45	.47	.49	.51	.54	.56	.58	.60	.62	.65	.67	.69	.71	.74	.76	.78	.80	.83	.85	.87
Round, bone in	.32	.33	.35	.37	.38	.40	.42	.43	.45	.47	.48	.50	.52	.54	.55	.57	.59	.60	.61	.63	.65
Round, bone out	.30	.31	.33	.34	.36	.38	.39	.41	.42	.44	.45	.47	.48	.50	.52	.53	.55	.56	.58	.59	.61
Rump, bone in	.41	.44	.46	.48	.50	.52	.55	.57	.59	.61	.63	.66	.68	.70	.72	.74	.76	.79	.81	.83	.85
Rump, bone out	.32	.34	.36	.38	.39	.41	.43	.44	.46	.48	.49	.51	.53	.55	.56	.58	.60	.61	.63	.65	.66
Beef, steaks																					
Chuck, bone in	.42	.45	.47	.49	.51	.54	.56	.58	.60	.62	.65	.67	.69	.71	.74	.76	.78	.80	.83	.85	.87
Chuck, bone out	.33	.35	.36	.38	.40	.42	.43	.45	.47	.49	.50	.52	.54	.56	.57	.59	.61	.62	.65	.66	.68
Club, bone in	.54	.57	.60	.62	.65	.68	.71	.74	.77	.80	.82	.85	.88	.91	.94	.97	.99	1.02	1.05	1.08	1.11
Porterhouse, bone in	.49	.52	.55	.57	.60	.62	.65	.68	.70	.73	.76	.78	.81	.83	.86	.89	.91	.94	.96	.99	1.01
Round, bone in	.32	.33	.35	.37	.38	.40	.42	.43	.45	.47	.48	.50	.52	.54	.55	.57	.59	.60	.61	.63	.65
Round, bone out	.30	.31	.33	.34	.36	.38	.39	.41	.42	.44	.45	.47	.48	.50	.52	.53	.55	.56	.58	.59	.61
Sirloin, bone in	.40	.43	.45	.47	.49	.51	.53	.55	.57	.60	.62	.64	.66	.68	.70	.72	.74	.77	.79	.81	.83
Sirloin, bone out	.37	.39	.41	.43	.45	.47	.49	.51	.53	.55	.57	.59	.61	.62	.64	.66	.68	.70	.72	.74	.76
T-bone, bone in	.52	.55	.58	.61	.64	.66	.69	.72	.75	.77	.80	.83	.86	.88	.91	.94	.97	.99	1.02	1.05	1.07
Ground beef, lean	.25	.26	.27	.29	.31	.33	.34	.36	.38	.39	.41	.43	.44	.46	.48	.49	.51	wait			
Beef short ribs	.56	.58	.61	.64	.67	.70	.73	.76	.79	.82	.85	.88	.91	.94	.96	.99	1.02	1.05	1.08	1.11	1.14
Pork, fresh roasts																					
Loin, bone in	.48	.51	.53	.56	.58	.61	.63	.66	.69	.71	.74	.76	.79	.81	.84	.86	.89	.91	.94	.97	.99
Loin, bone out	.33	.36	.36	.38	.40	.42	.43	.45	.47	.49	.50	.52	.54	.56	.57	.59	.61	.63	.65	.66	.67
Picnic, bone in	.51	.53	.56	.59	.62	.64	.67	.70	.72	.75	.78	.80	.83	.86	.88	.91	.94	.96	.98	1.01	1.04
Chops, loin	.42	.45	.47	.49	.51	.54	.56	.58	.60	.62	.65	.67	.69	.71	.74	.76	.78	.80	.83	.85	.87
Chops, rib	.48	.51	.53	.56	.58	.61	.63	.66	.69	.71	.74	.76	.79	.81	.84	.86	.89	.91	.94	.97	.99
Pork, cured roasts																					
Butt, bone in	.34	.36	.38	.40	.42	.43	.45	.47	.49	.51	.52	.54	.56	.58	.60	.61	.63	.65	.67	.68	.70
Ham, bone in	.33	.35	.36	.38	.40	.42	.43	.45	.47	.49	.50	.52	.54	.56	.57	.59	.61	.63	.65	.66	.68
Ham, bone out	.25	.26	.27	.29	.30	.31	.33	.34	.35	.36	.38	.39	.40	.42	.43	.44	.46	.47	.48	.49	.51
Picnic, bone in	.43	.46	.48	.50	.53	.55	.57	.59	.62	.64	.66	.68	.71	.73	.75	.78	.80	.82	.85	.87	.89
Picnic, bone out	.34	.35	.37	.39	.41	.42	.44	.46	.48	.49	.51	.53	.55	.57	.58	.60	.63	.64	.65	.67	.69
Ham slices	.30	.31	.33	.34	.36	.38	.39	.41	.42	.44	.45	.47	.48	.50	.52	.53	.55	.56	.58	.59	.61
Lamb, roasts																					
Leg, bone in	.40	.42	.44	.46	.48	.50	.52	.54	.56	.58	.60	.62	.65	.67	.68	.71	.73	.75	.77	.80	.82
Shoulder, bone in	.43	.46	.48	.50	.53	.55	.57	.59	.62	.64	.66	.68	.71	.73	.75	.78	.80	.82	.85	.87	.89
Chops, loin	.43	.46	.48	.50	.53	.55	.57	.59	.62	.64	.66	.68	.71	.73	.75	.78	.80	.82	.85	.87	.89
Chops, rib	.52	.55	.58	.61	.64	.66	.69	.72	.75	.77	.80	.83	.86	.88	.91	.94	.97	.99	1.02	1.05	1.07

Kind & cut of meat	2.00	2.05	2.10	2.15	2.20	2.25	2.30	2.35	2.40	2.45	2.50	2.55	2.60	2.65	2.70	2.75	2.80	2.85	2.90	2.95	3.00
Beef, roasts																					
Brisket	1.03	1.07	1.09	1.12	1.14	1.17	1.20	1.22	1.25	1.28	1.30	1.33	1.35	1.38	1.41	1.43	1.46	1.48	1.51	1.53	1.55
Chuck, bone in	.90	.92	.94	.96	.99	1.01	1.03	1.05	1.07	1.10	1.12	1.14	1.16	1.19	1.21	1.23	1.25	1.28	1.30	1.32	1.35
Chuck, bone out	.70	.71	.73	.75	.77	.78	.80	.82	.84	.85	.87	.89	.91	.92	.94	.96	.97	1.00	1.02	1.04	1.06
Ribs—7th, bone in	.90	.92	.94	.96	.99	1.01	1.03	1.05	1.07	1.10	1.12	1.14	1.16	1.19	1.21	1.23	1.26	1.28	1.30	1.32	1.35
Round, bone in	.66	.68	.70	.71	.73	.75	.76	.78	.80	.81	.83	.85	.87	.88	.90	.92	.93	.94	.96	.98	1.00
Round, bone out	.62	.64	.65	.67	.69	.70	.72	.74	.76	.77	.78	.79	.81	.83	.84	.86	.87	.88	.90	.92	.93
Rump, bone in	.88	.90	.92	.94	.96	.99	1.01	1.03	1.05	1.07	1.10	1.12	1.14	1.16	1.18	1.20	1.23	1.25	1.27	1.29	1.32
Rump, bone out	.68	.70	.72	.73	.75	.77	.78	.80	.82	.83	.85	.87	.89	.90	.92	.94	.95	.97	.99	1.00	1.02
Beef, steaks																					
Chuck, bone in	.90	.92	.94	.96	.99	1.01	1.03	1.05	1.07	1.10	1.12	1.14	1.16	1.19	1.21	1.23	1.25	1.28	1.30	1.32	1.35
Chuck, bone out	.70	.71	.73	.75	.77	.78	.80	.82	.84	.85	.87	.89	.91	.92	.94	.96	.97	1.00	1.01	1.03	1.05
Club, bone in	1.14	1.17	1.19	1.22	1.25	1.28	1.31	1.34	1.37	1.39	1.42	1.45	1.48	1.51	1.54	1.56	1.59	1.62	1.65	1.68	1.71
Porterhouse, bone in	1.04	1.07	1.09	1.12	1.14	1.17	1.20	1.22	1.25	1.28	1.30	1.33	1.35	1.38	1.41	1.43	1.46	1.48	1.51	1.53	1.56
Round, bone in	.66	.68	.70	.71	.73	.75	.76	.78	.80	.81	.83	.85	.87	.88	.90	.92	.93	.95	.96	.98	.99
Round, bone out	.62	.64	.65	.67	.69	.70	.72	.73	.75	.76	.78	.79	.81	.83	.84	.86	.87	.89	.90	.92	.93
Sirloin, bone in	.86	.88	.90	.92	.94	.96	.98	1.00	1.03	1.05	1.07	1.00	1.11	1.13	1.15	1.17	1.20	1.22	1.24	1.26	1.29
Sirloin, bone out	.78	.80	.82	.84	.86	.88	.90	.92	.94	.96	.98	1.00	1.01	1.03	1.05	1.07	1.09	1.11	1.13	1.15	1.17
T-bone, bone in	1.10	1.13	1.16	1.19	1.21	1.24	1.27	1.30	1.32	1.35	1.38	1.41	1.43	1.46	1.49	1.52	1.54	1.57	1.60	1.62	1.65
Ground beef, lean	.52	.53	.55	.57	.58	.59	.60	.61	.62	.64	.65	.66	.67	.69	.70	.72	.73	.74	.75	.77	.78
Beef short ribs	1.16	1.19	1.22	1.25	1.28	1.31	1.34	1.37	1.40	1.43	1.46	1.49	1.52	1.54	1.57	1.60	1.63	1.66	1.69	1.72	1.74
Pork, fresh roasts																					
Loin, bone in	1.02	1.04	1.07	1.09	1.12	1.14	1.17	1.20	1.22	1.25	1.27	1.30	1.32	1.35	1.37	1.40	1.42	1.45	1.48	1.50	1.53
Loin, bone out	.69	.71	.73	.75	.77	.78	.80	.82	.84	.85	.87	.89	.91	.92	.94	.96	.98	1.00	1.01	1.02	1.04
Picnic, bone in	1.06	1.09	1.12	1.15	1.17	1.20	1.23	1.25	1.28	1.31	1.33	1.36	1.39	1.41	1.44	1.47	1.49	1.51	1.54	1.57	1.59
Chops, loin	.90	.92	.94	.96	.99	1.01	1.03	1.05	1.07	1.10	1.13	1.15	1.17	1.19	1.21	1.23	1.25	1.28	1.30	1.32	1.35
Chops, rib	1.02	1.04	1.07	1.09	1.11	1.14	1.17	1.20	1.22	1.25	1.27	1.30	1.32	1.35	1.37	1.40	1.42	1.45	1.48	1.50	1.53
Pork, cured roasts																					
Butt, bone in	.72	.74	.76	.78	.79	.81	.83	.85	.87	.88	.90	.92	.94	.96	.97	.99	1.01	1.02	1.04	1.06	1.08
Ham, bone in	.70	.71	.73	.75	.77	.78	.80	.82	.84	.85	.87	.89	.91	.92	.94	.96	.98	1.00	1.01	1.03	1.05
Ham, bone out	.52	.53	.55	.56	.57	.59	.60	.61	.62	.64	.65	.66	.68	.69	.70	.72	.73	.74	.75	.77	.78
Picnic, bone in	.92	.94	.96	.99	1.01	1.03	1.05	1.08	1.10	1.12	1.14	1.17	1.19	1.21	1.24	1.26	1.28	1.31	1.33	1.35	1.38
Picnic, bone out	.70	.72	.74	.76	.77	.79	.81	.83	.84	.86	.88	.90	.92	.93	.95	.98	.99	1.00	1.02	1.04	1.05
Ham slices	.62	.64	.65	.67	.69	.70	.72	.73	.75	.76	.78	.79	.81	.83	.84	.86	.87	.89	.90	.92	.93
Lamb, roasts																					
Leg, bone in	.84	.86	.88	.90	.92	.94	.96	.98	1.00	1.02	1.04	1.07	1.09	1.11	1.13	1.15	1.17	1.19	1.22	1.24	1.26
Shoulder, bone in	.92	.94	.96	.99	1.01	1.03	1.05	1.08	1.10	1.12	1.14	1.17	1.19	1.21	1.24	1.26	1.28	1.31	1.33	1.35	1.38
Chops, loin	.92	.94	.96	.99	1.01	1.03	1.05	1.08	1.10	1.12	1.14	1.17	1.19	1.21	1.24	1.26	1.28	1.31	1.33	1.35	1.38
Chops, rib	1.10	1.13	1.16	1.19	1.21	1.24	1.27	1.30	1.32	1.35	1.38	1.41	1.43	1.46	1.49	1.52	1.54	1.57	1.60	1.62	1.65

**TABLE 2B: Cost of 20 Grams of Protein from Selected
Meats and Meat Alternatives**

Food	Market Unit	Price per Market Unit	Part of Market Unit to Give 20 Grams of Protein(%)	Cost of 20 Grams of Protein
Dry beans	pound	$.29	$.24	$.07
Peanut butter	12 oz.	.78	.23	.18
Chicken, whole, ready-to-cook	pound	.56	.37	.21
Milk, whole fluid	½ gal.	.79	.29	.23
Eggs, large	dozen	.69	.26	.18
Hamburger	pound	.89	.24	.21
Turkey, ready-to-cook	pound	.59	.35	.21
Sardines, canned	3¾ oz.	.51	.94	.48
Tuna fish, canned	6½ oz.	.55	.44	.24
American process cheese	8 oz.	.67	.38	.25
Ham, whole	pound	1.19	.29	.35
Ocean perch, fillet, frozen	pound	.98	.36	.35
Liverwurst	pound	1.75	.60	1.05
Chuck roast of beef, bone-in	pound	.96	.35	.34
Frankfurters	pound	1.25	.36	.45
Salami	8 oz.	.95	.50	.48
Haddock, fillet, frozen	pound	1.20	.35	.42
Sirloin, beefsteak	pound	2.79	.28	.78
Bologna	8 oz.	.69	.73	.50
Pork sausage	pound	1.29	.52	.67

basic types: analogs and as textured vegetable protein (TVP). Analogs are cutlets, patties, and other forms of vegetable protein shaped and flavored to taste like their prototypes. But, they contain no meat. These meat substitutes are available already cooked in cans or in freeze-dried form, usually at health food stores. They are also quite expensive.

Textured vegetable protein (TVP) is available in supermarkets and health-food stores in a variety of flavors—beef, chicken, and ham being the most common. Adding TVP to ground beef in the ratio of 3 parts meat to 1 part reconstituted TVP (with water added to the dry material) not only produces more burgers, but the TVP absorbs the juices in the meat and reduces shrinkage. Some markets premix TVP with ground meat for patties or blends to reduce costs by about 20-25 percent. TVP is particularly useful in casseroles, meatloaves, and dishes where other flavors mask the bland or "nothing" taste of TVP. Flavored types of TVP are packaged for use without other meats, but the results seldom satisfy taste buds.

Check prices of different brands of TVP in supermarkets and health-food stores. TVP keeps for months, so buying in bulk will stretch dollars.

POULTRY

Chicken and turkey provide cheap, attractive protein along with many vitamins and minerals. Poultry of all kinds has increased in price at a much slower pace than the all-items cost-of-living index, and other meats.

Chickens, whether fried, broiled, barbecued, baked, or rotiseried, are a low-cost "company" meal. Check the women's magazines for more recipes than you can ever use. Whole chickens are frequently as much as 4 to 7¢ less per pound than cut-up chickens. If you buy favorite pieces, you pay even more—so much more that you can frequently pay the same for whole chickens, cut off the parts you want, and have the remainder as a free bonus. The less desirable parts, backs, necks, gizzard, and wings, make excellent soup and, with cut-up leftovers, make another main dish. Supplies of various parts affect chicken prices. Table 2C prices different parts relative to the cost of whole fryers. For example, if whole fryers are selling at 51 cents/pound, breasts are an equally good buy at 72 cents/ pound, but wings would have to cost 41 cents/pound or less to provide an equal amount of lean meat at the same cost/serving.

Poultry of all kinds, particularly chicken and turkey, provide a better meat-bone ratio in the bigger sizes (Table 2D). That is, the bigger the bird, the more meat and less bone you get proportionately. Often, the big birds

---

20% Savings Ideas

Since meat slices a big chunk of your food dollar, consider shortcuts like these:

1. Use a variety of low-cost meats, fish, and poultry. Enough deep-fried red snapper, for example, for a family of six costs about $1.29. With one big pack of French fried potatoes, you have fish and chips for six at 30¢ per serving—and the kids love it.

2. Don't try to upgrade children's appetites too early in life. They won't appreciate your efforts and it costs you money. If you like to splurge on steak, buy a hamburger pattie for each of the kids and broil it right along with the steak.

3. Cut down the quantity of the meat in a stew, casserole, or mixed meat dish.

4. Use canned fish, such as tuna or salmon, as the main ingredient in casseroles or other culinary concoctions. When a canned fish is to be chopped or flaked into a casserole, buy chunks, not the solid pack.

TABLE 2C: Cost of Chicken—Whole and Parts

Chicken parts are equally good buy if price/pound is:

Whole fryers ready to cook cents	Breast half cents	Drumstick and thigh cents	Drumstick cents	Thigh cents	Wing cents
39	55	50	48	52	31
41	58	53	50	55	33
43	61	55	53	57	34
45	63	58	55	60	36
47	66	60	58	63	37
49	69	63	60	65	39
51	72	65	63	68	41
53	75	68	65	71	42
55	78	71	68	73	44
57	81	73	70	76	45
59	84	76	73	79	47
61	86	78	75	81	49
63	89	81	77	84	50
65	92	83	80	87	52
77	95	86	82	89	53
69	98	88	85	92	55
71	1.01	91	87	95	57
73	1.04	94	90	97	58
75	1.06	96	92	1.00	60

TABLE 2D: Meat-to-Bone Ratio—Turkeys

Ready-to-cook weight (pounds)	Number of servings	Cost per serving* (cents)	Lbs./serving
4	4	.69	1.0
8	10	.55	.8
12	20	.41	.6
16	32	.35	.5
20	41	.34	.49
24	50	.33	.48

*Dressed turkey priced at 69¢ per pound.

cost less per pound than the more popular middle sizes. So, you save two ways on big birds—less cost and more meat per pound.

Poultry prices are hard to compare with other meats because of the many bones. As a general rule, frying chickens supply the same protein as fairly lean ground beef when the chicken costs three-quarters as much as beef per pound. In other words, frying chicken at 60¢ per pound supplies as much protein as ground beef at 80¢ per pound, in spite of the chicken's many bones.

EGGS

Not all eggs are alike—they differ in two important ways—size and quality. Almost all eggs you buy in a store are graded in accordance with standards set up by the USDA.

Size—Six sizes are marketed. Size is determined by the weight of a dozen eggs as detailed in Table 2E.

Quality—Although four grades of eggs are marketed, AA, A, B, and C, only AA and A grades are usually sold in supermarkets. Quality of

TABLE 2E: Egg Sizes and Equivalent Prices (For Same Grades)

Size	Min. Weight per Dozen (Ounces)	Weight of Each Egg (Ounces)
Jumbo	30	2½
Extra-large	27	2¼
Large	24	2
Medium	21	1¾
Small	18	1½
Peewee	15	1¼

Large eggs (2 ounces each) are most popular. Compare prices of other size eggs with large.

Small Eggs Are Good Buy At	Medium Eggs Are Good Buy At	If Large Eggs Are Priced At	Extra Large Eggs Are Equally Good Buy At	Jumbo Eggs Are Good Buy At
.45	.53	.60	.67	.75
.48	.56	.64	.72	.80
.51	.60	.68	.76	.85
.54	.63	.72	.81	.90
.57	.66	.76	.86	.95
.63	.73	.84	.95	1.05
.66	.77	.88	.99	1.10
.69	.81	.92	1.04	1.15
.72	.84	.96	1.08	1.20
.75	.88	1.00	1.13	1.25
.78	.91	1.04	1.17	1.30
.81	.95	1.08	1.22	1.35
.84	.98	1.12	1.26	1.40
.87	1.02	1.16	1.31	1.45
.90	1.05	1.20	1.35	1.50

Except for rounding half-cent increments to the higher figure, these columns allow comparison in either direction. For example, if large eggs are priced at 64¢ per dozen, extra-large eggs are equally priced at 72¢ per dozen. If extra-large eggs are priced at 71¢ per dozen or less, they are a better buy for weight. Obviously, if you use two extra-large eggs instead of two large or medium eggs in a recipe, the dish will cost more. For cooking, use medium-size, Grade B eggs. Often, for frying whole, poaching, or boiling, one jumbo or extra-large egg is enough for one serving instead of two medium or two medium or two small eggs.

eggs varies according to the appearance of the white and yolk when broken out, fried, or poached.

Check too for any price difference between white or brown eggs. Buy the lower-priced color, as they are the same once the shells are broken. Many markets will sell "checks" (or chex) eggs. These are eggs that would otherwise be graded AA, A, or B, except for thin spots or small cracks in the shell. For this slightly off-grade shell, a price reduction of 10¢ to 20¢ per dozen or more is common. Use "checks" eggs only when cooked before serving.

MILK

For any family with children, the milk bill typically runs from 10 to 20% of all food purchases. Whole, fresh milk runs around 39¢ to 59¢ a quart, give or take a few pennies. There are ways to shave the cost of whole milk, but bigger savings are possible by using dry skim milk, commonly referred to as nonfat dry milk. In stores, you buy nonfat dry milk as a powder, marked according to how many quarts it will make when reconstituted with water.

Many diet-conscious weight watchers are already drinking skim milk. But, when you buy skim milk delivered to your door in cartons or bottles, you are buying mostly water. For example, skim milk from your dairy may cost about 31¢ to 41¢ per quart. Reconstituted dry milk costs from 19¢ to 23¢ per quart—about half.

Reconstituted nonfat dry milk is not just for weight watchers, however. Depending on the size of your family, you can cut from a third to a half off your milk bill by using nonfat dry milk in cooking and substituting it for some of the whole, fresh milk your family drinks. Make sure the brand of nonfat dry milk you buy includes added Vitamins A and D and carries the label "instant." Look for a note on the box, "Fortified with Vitamins A and D," to assure good nutrition. Try mixing reconstituted nonfat dry milk with regular milk half-and-half. Most people can't tell the difference in taste. Others in your family can quickly learn to like 100% nonfat dry milk when it is mixed 50% stronger. The nonfat protein is often called the "lean" of milk.

Use nonfat dry milk for cooking, in making cream soups, in baking or recipes calling for milk, when making cream sauce or gravy, and in puddings, cooked cereals, and custards. For some recipes, you may find it necessary to increase the amount of shortening (butter, vegetable oil, etc.) by 1½ ounces to make up for the loss of butterfat in 1 quart of milk.

How Much Can You Save? How you buy the powder is a big factor—some dairies sell nonfat dry milk in 50-pound bags (that's the equivalent of 250 quarts of reconstituted milk) at about 16 to 18¢ per quart. On special, a 20-quart package is often priced at $3.59, or just under 18¢ a quart. Table 2F compares the projected savings for a family of four and a family of six.

Not all milk costs the same. Home-delivered milk, for example, usually costs from 2 to 7¢ more per quart than milk in a supermarket. At a differential of 5¢, that's an increase of about 10%.

TABLE 2F: Cost of Fresh Milk vs. Nonfat Dry Milk

	4 in Family	*6 in Family*
No. of quarts for drinking per year (1 pint for adults, 1 quart for children per day)	1095	1825
Milk for cooking (estimate)	183	183
Quarts used per year	1278	2008
Cost—Whole, fresh milk only*	$511.20	$803.20
Nonfat dry milk only* *	$242.82	$381.52
Half fresh + half nonfat dry for drinking—all nonfat dry for cooking	350.66	573.15
So, if you use nonfat dry milk only (no fresh milk), you save	$268.38	$421.68
Using half fresh + half nonfat dry for drinking, all nonfat dry for cooking, you save	$152.54	$230.05

*Whole, fresh milk priced at 40¢ per quart
* *Nonfat dry milk priced at 19¢ per quart.

Evaporated canned milk is another money saver when cooking. The tall can contains 13 ounces which, when mixed with an equal quantity of water, makes a "fifth" of milk; that is, about four-fifths of a quart. At about 25¢ a can, this is the equivalent of about 31¢ per quart for fresh, whole milk.

Cheese—So many different sizes, shapes, qualities, and flavors of cheese are available that comparisons are difficult. Whenever possible, compare the price per pound. The little glasses of cheese spreads, for example, may cost 61¢ for a 5-ounce glass. That's the equivalent of $1.95 per pound. Prepackaged packets of nationally advertised cheeses tend to cost more than bulk cheese cut and priced at each store. Watch differences in sharpness, as aging adds to the price. Special or loss-leader sales will sometimes upset this pattern, and the prepackaged chunks have changed from the even half-pound chunks to 6-⅔-ounce packets or similar odd sizes to make price comparisons difficult. So, use your computer (see page 54).

Ice cream—Most states set a minimum limit for butterfat in any frozen milk product labeled as ice cream. At least two qualities of ice cream are available in most freezer cases, one product for price competition, the other a deluxe, more expensive, and richer ice cream. Competitive ice creams will contain the minimum allowable butterfat and will be available in fewer flavors.

Another frozen product available almost everywhere is variously labeled as "ice milk" or "frozen dessert." It looks like ice cream, tastes like ice cream, but sells for less than ice cream. It can't be called ice cream because it doesn't meet state requirements for butterfat.

BREAKFAST CEREALS

Breakfast continues to be one of the most neglected meals of the day. After 8 to 14 hours of rest since the last meal, your system needs a substantial meal. Unfortunately, breakfast comes at the beginning of the day—when time is short and many persons are still operating in low gear. As a result, the do-it-yourself or pick-up breakfast of cold cereal has become popular for many families. By themselves, packaged cold cereals are poor substitutes for a stick-to-the ribs meal in the morning. While dry packaged cereals are highly profitable to the manufacturer, they are less beneficial for you, as noted by the USDA's Yearbook of Agriculture for 1959, *Food*. Here is a quote—

"A growing proportion of cereals reaches the consumer as ready-to-serve breakfast foods—flaked, shredded, granular, puffed, and toasted cereals. Some have sugar coating. The consumer usually pays more for the prepared cereals than for equal nutrients obtained from cereals she cooks herself."

But cooking cereal every morning can tire even the most conscientious housewife. So, how about letting the children serve themselves on a weekend day when family members are likely to be eating at different times. During the week when every member of the family needs a good stick-to-the-ribs breakfast, serve a cooked cereal.

40% Savings Idea

How much more? Packaged dry cereals cost about 6 to 8¢ per serving without a sugar coating and about 9 to 14¢ per serving when sugared. Cooked cereals cost about 2 to 5¢ per serving. For a family of five, a serving of dry cereal for each member of the family would cost about $3.50 each week. Cooked cereal, on the other hand, would cost about $1.15 to $1.50 per week. Savings: about $2-$2.25 week.

SHOPPING THE SPECIALS

Pick up the newspaper for Wednesday or Thursday, and you'll find it crammed with full-page ads for weekend specials. Sometimes the items listed in big, bold type are good buys; sometimes they are the store's regular prices. Knowing the regular price for popular items will steer you away from phony bargains.

Another way to spot a bargain is the limited quantity sign. Say a big supermarket chain advertises a well-known brand of tomato soup at 14¢ a can. A normal price might be 18¢. But in the store you're likely to find a

---

25% Savings Idea

Mildred Eberle reduced the food bill for her family of five by more than $500—just by shopping the specials. For part of one week's grocery needs, Mildred priced 36 items she planned to buy at one supermarket—not the most expensive or the cheapest, but a typical one. Cost for the 36 items—$37.01. She found that by shopping three stores and taking advantage of the advertised specials, she could buy the same 36 items for $32.63 for a dollar saving of $4.38. That amounts to an 11.8% saving. Quality, even brand names, were either identical or comparable.

However, by substituting certain items for others in the original list, Mildred saved even more. Some substitutions switched from national brands to house brands, and she switched from rib steaks to a roast of halibut which was plentiful that week. But, by shopping three stores and substituting special-sale items for regular-price items, she paid $27.37 for the 36 items. Mildred's dollar savings totaled $9.64 for a 26% saving compared to the original list of 36 items bought in one store.

When Mildred explained her technique to her friends, they countered that the extra time and extra driving wiped out any savings. "Not worth the time and trouble," they scoffed. But, Mildred explained this way—"Suppose you allow 18 minutes for shopping and checking out in two additional stores. Driving may take an extra 12 minutes; 6 minutes each for the second and third stores. Total—an extra 30 minutes. Around here certainly, and in most urban areas probably, three or more markets will be located within 2 miles of one another. Allowing 10¢ per mile for out-of-pocket driving costs, that's 20¢. Total dollar savings, $9.44. Over a year's time $10 per week amounts to $520. I figure that I'm earning almost $19 an hour for my time. Where can you earn or, more accurately, avoid spending that much cash per hour?"

sign limiting purchases to five cans—or even two cans. Such a bargain is a true loss leader.

Here's how you can follow Mildred's lead to cut your food spending by $500 per year or more.

When the weekend specials appear in the newspaper, plan your shopping for the next week. First, make a list of the staple items you must replace, such as flour, sugar, spices, shortening, cereals, etc. You'll be surprised at the special prices on flour and sugar, for example. A popular biscuit mix is a frequent special. List the items you need under two or three of your favorite supermarkets with the advertised price.

Second, when you have listed the items you want, you may find they are in three, four, or even five different stores. Ordinarily, that's too many. Consolidate the list to the items at two or three stores. Your shopping area will determine how many stores you can profitably visit.

For items you need that are not advertised as a special, select a large chain store that packs many staple items under its own brand. Or, you may be able to divide up the items in a way that permits you to check out at an express lane to save time. Sometimes a special will justify going to one store just for that one item. The key point is a plan—one you can stick to and one that will limit impulse buying.

When specials are offered on staples or foods that keep for long periods, stock up. Buy half a dozen 1½ quart bottles of a popular salad oil when it is on sale at $1.15 vs. the regular price of $1.39. The 24¢ saving on each bottle amounts to a 17% reduction. By buying six bottles, you save $1.44.

Buying in large quantities helps to pay off a freezer (see "Does a Freezer Pay?" page 54). Take frozen orange juice concentrate, for example. During normal times, the price fluctuates rather wildly. One week, the price may be two 6-oz. cans for 89¢. The next week, the price may be five cans for $1.79. And every once in a while, a really good buy will come along, such as five cans for $1.39. For a family that may use one or two cans of juice every day, buying a case at the low sale price really pays off. As an example, for ten cans at two for 89¢, the price is $4.45. But ten cans at the five for $1.39 price is only $2.78—a saving of $1.67 or 38%.

One other thing on sales—many supermarkets make a point of meeting any competition. If you are shopping in Supermarket A and Supermarket B is advertising a bargain on a standard food item, such as branded dry cereal, ask the manager of Supermarket A if he will meet the price. If he does, you have saved yourself a trip as well as the money.

If the one or two really hot specials are not in stock when you shop, don't simply walk out and give up your projected saving. Ask one of the stock clerks to replenish the supply. If the store's stock is completely gone, ask the clerk or check-out cashier for an "out-of-stock" slip or "rain check."

Keep an eye out too for extra-special promotions of food items at drug, department, and specialty stores. Canned tuna fish, peanuts, jam, and soft drinks are favorites. Many times you can profit from these promotions because they tend to be goods that store easily for long periods.

One extensive study[1] over an eight-week period near San Francisco turned up the not-so-astonishing fact that advertised specials cost only 78.6% as much as the same items' regular price. And this list contained 225 different items, more than a complete grocery list for most housewives.

Some specials are advertised almost every week. In the survey, 55 of the 225 items appeared two or more times in ads during the eight-week period. The average reduction on these 55 items was 26.3%. Certain food items appear to be "specials bait," and to make them extra appealing, they are cut more than one-quarter below their regular price.

Be alert for the competition between nationally advertised and "house" brands. Such nationally advertised brands as *Del Monte, Libby, Gold Medal*, are typically 1 to 5¢ higher than similar sizes of "house" brands. "House" or "private" brands are those owned by supermarket chains or certain wholesalers. *Town House, Kitchen-Kraft*, and *Ann Page* are typical house brands you'll find in Safeway and A&P stores. When too many people begin switching to the house brands, the national manufacturer retaliates by offering specials on his staple items—canned goods, for example. At these relatively infrequent specials, you can stock up for several months on soups, canned juices, applesauce, and canned vegetables and fruits.

New products are frequently advertised as specials. If you're not sure of the items, buy one as soon as the ad appears on Wednesday or Thursday. Try it the same day. If it is a good buy, return to the store and stock up at a substantial saving.

Summarizing the facts you can use from the Gray and Anderson study—

[1]*Advertised Specials and Local Competition Among Supermarkets*, Roger M. Gray and Roice Anderson, Food Research Institute, Stanford University, Stanford, California.

1. You can save more than 20% on the cost of advertised specials in all categories.

2. Pick the store and what you buy in the store carefully. Where the specials are extra low-priced, buy only the specials and few or none of the nonspecials.

3. Buy both specials and nonspecials in a store or combination of stores that trade heavily in their own house brands. But get to know which of the house brands are equivalent to the nationally advertised brands of similar merchandise.

MARK-IT-YOURSELF STORES

Minimum service stores operate in many communities. Often located in huge, barn-like warehouses in low-rent or out-of-the-way locations, the big pitch is low overhead, case-lot, or bulk sales of packaged foods. Most of these bulk stores ask customers to find the price on shelves and mark individual packages with a grease pencil provided when you walk in the door—hence the name, "mark-it" stores. Don't expect prices at mark-it stores to be consistently under those in other markets. Generally, you'll find advertised specials at supermarkets will be priced lower than the regular prices at mark-it stores. You can benefit from shopping in a mark-it store by following these tips:

● Avoid those stores that require a membership fee monthly unless no open mark-it stores operate in your community.

● Buy staples that are seldom if ever advertised as specials but only after checking prices at a supermarket that offers many of its own house brands.

● Buy in case lots if you gain a lower price and if you can store the goods easily and use the case within a reasonable time.

● Check prices on beer, wine, and mixes, as mark-it stores often break the established price lines for these products in other stores.

● Buy large packages if you can use them, such as No. 10 cans or restaurant-size containers.

● Nonfood items such as light bulbs, paper products, and sundries may be priced sharply under similar goods at supermarkets.

Large cities will have one or more "freight damaged" stores selling goods involved in a wreck or other damage. If you find a freight-damaged outlet, you may need to mark prices on the goods as in a mark-it store. You will find the stock quite variable and incomplete, but prices on goods available will likely be 15 to 25 percent less than similar or identical goods in supermarkets. When you find something in a freight damaged store you use regularly, such as canned soup, breakfast cereal, paper products, and items that will store for long periods, buy a bunch.

CONVENIENCE FOODS

Lumped among those foods which are fully or partially cooked and ready to serve are many cost-cutting items you can use to pare your food bill and save you time. The costs of these foods with "built-in maid service" were compared with those you prepare from scratch in a study by the U.S. Dept. of Agriculture. You'd expect to pay more for foods ready or almost ready to eat. And, of the 158 convenience foods priced, 116 *were* more expensive than their home-prepared counterparts. But, some of the most frequently used convenience foods cost less—enough less that the total bill, weighted on the basis of average purchases, was actually less by nearly 8% compared to home-prepared foods.

One of the biggest savings results from using frozen orange juice, rather than buying oranges and squeezing the juice yourself. Another big saving is the use of instant coffee. One dollar out of every $100 spent by the average shopper went for instant coffee. To get the same number of perked or drip cups of coffee from roasted and ground beans would cost 96% more.

Other convenience foods that cost less than their fresh or home-prepared equivalents include such items as canned peas, lima beans, and beets. Frozen peas, lima beans, and corn were also less expensive than fresh products. Cake and frosting mixes, complete waffle and biscuit mixes, sliced cheese, pudding mixes, frozen breaded shrimp, and canned salmon were also good buys.

Foods more expensive in their convenience form and ones to be wary of when keeping the food budget down include most of the ready-to-eat bakery products, such as cakes, pies, and muffins. Precooked and frozen (TV) dinners, the kind you merely warm up in the oven, cost considerably more than the home-prepared dinner. A frozen meatloaf dinner, for example, was checked at more than double the cost of one prepared at home.

COUPONS, "CENTS OFF" LABELS, TRADING STAMPS, AND PREMIUMS

Retailers, often in combination with manufacturers, attempt to increase sales by "gimmicks." If all shoppers were prudent and logical, a reduction in price would accomplish the same result. But, salesmen have found that too few people are prudent and logical to make a simple price reduction work. So—we have gimmicks! Let's examine each in turn to see how you, as a prudent, logical shopper, can benefit.

Trading Stamps—Trading stamps come in all colors and their merits or drawbacks are not up for debate. The fact is—they're here, but fading. Their cost is built into the prices you pay. If you don't keep stamps and redeem them, you lose their value. Sticking the pesky things in books is a nuisance, of course, so why not use the stamps to redeem articles you want and need in the same way you spend money?

Stamps supposedly develop store loyalty because shoppers prefer to keep only a few kinds of stamps. If you shop mainly at one or two stores for the stamps, you can miss out on specials offered by other stores. The money you save buying the specials will likely mean more to you than the pesky stamps. So—don't fall into the stamp trap. Buy the specials wherever they are and save all the stamps. If you get three or four kinds of stamps, redeem your stamps the way you budget for long-term purchases. Hold back on small items that require only one to three books until you have enough of the stamps you collect slowly. These could be the stamps you collect from a store that you shop at only occasionally or one that features exceptional specials and higher regular prices.

Save "fast stamps," those that accumulate in large numbers, for big items that require four or more books. Remember to buy from the retailer who gives your favorite kind of stamps only when other conditions—price, quality, service, are equal.

Take advantage of "double stamp" days. Supermarkets are not likely to give double stamps often, but may give double stamps on special items. Gasoline service stations, however, often give twice the normal number of stamps (double stamps) for gasoline purchases on a specific day "Tuesday is double-stamp day!" for example.

Spend the stamp books like money. Redemption stores, like other merchandisers, run specials on items that are shop-worn, out of season, last-year's model, or not moving for some reason.

Coupons—Nearly every newspaper's food shopper section includes some advertisements with a coupon. Or coupons may arrive in the mail. Other coupons spring out on cardboard inserts from your favorite magazines. Store coupons are those that you exchange in the store and for the face amount when you buy the promoted product. A 7¢-off coupon on a popular brand of corn flakes means you pay the marked price—less 7¢. When you can use the coupon product, it provides a real saving. Store coupons worth $2 to $4 in total appear regularly in newspapers.

Unfortunately, the abuse of store coupons has led many manufacturers to switch to mail-in coupons.

Mail-in coupons are usually worth more than store coupons. The higher value partly compensates for the cost of the stamp, envelope, and time required to put the coupon in the mail. If you are selective, mail-in coupons can mean a real cash saving. One example—a popular pancake flour maker offered 75¢ back on a purchase of 2 pounds of flour—with a special coupon. The pancake flour actually cost only 59¢ on a special. So, we got more than our money back—plus the 2 pounds of flour.

Getting into "couponing" in a big way can yield $100 to $200 per month, according to Carole Kratz & Albert Lee, authors of *The Coupon Way to Lower Food Prices*, a paperback that sold originally for $1.95 and was published by Workman Publishing Company of New York. Bulletins and exchange clubs foster the swapping of proofs-of-purchase, boxtops, and coupons. Couponing takes considerable time, but the rewards in refunds and merchandise can be substantial—and are tax-free.

"Cents Off" Labels—Bold markings on some packages say "blank ¢ off." New rules require that the label state the regular price, the "cents off," and the actual sale price. Compare the actual price marked with competing brands.

Premiums—Generally, premiums offered with certain products are seldom good buys. Except for a very few "in the box" premiums, these inducements are usually self-liquidating. That is, the $1.50 you send along with the special coupon pays for the full cost of the premium—including the cost of handling the order, packaging, and postage. So, there's little left to purchase the premium itself. The pictures on the boxes invariably promise more than the premium turns out to be. This is particularly true of toys, games, and gimmicks on breakfast cereals. Compare the price of the same product in a discount store before shelling out very much money. The "$3.50 Value" placed on a premium is probably inflated. The actual retail price is probably close to the $1.50 to be sent in with a coupon.

SHOPPING TACTICS

Outdated Bakery Goods—Smart shoppers will take advantage of the outdated bakery goods rack at the supermarket. "Thrift" stores operated by the bakeries themselves also dispose of day-old bread, rolls, cakes, and pastries at significant savings. Even 3-day-old bread makes excellent toast. Most bakeries now package bread in vapor-tight polyethylene bags to keep it fresh. When at a thrift store, buy a couple weeks' supply and freeze all but one or two loaves. When frozen, bread will keep for up to a year. If you freeze day-old bread and thaw it later, it seems fresher.

Outdated sweet rolls or pastries can be freshened by heating them briefly just before eating. Cakes, and particularly pies, should be inspected closely if they are outdated because they will not keep their freshness and flavor as long as bread or breakfast rolls.

New Food Promotions—When manufacturers introduce foods or new brands, they often cut the price or promote a coupon deal for advertising. Why not try a new brand of coffee, for example, that is 30¢ less than the brand you've been buying? Variety keeps your palate tuned to new tastes. And besides you may find something you like better than the brand you've been using.

Complete vs. Incomplete Mixes—Check the ingredients you need to add when buying cake, pancake, or biscuit mixes. Some mixes include everything you need. All you add is water. Other mixes require eggs, shortening, and/or milk. The difference in cost per serving can be considerable. For example, a popular pancake mix calls for one egg (7¢), 1½ cups of milk (15¢), and 3 tablespoons of shortening (5¢) to make 15 to 18 pancakes, enough for four persons. With the pancake mix costing about 24¢ (four servings), the egg, shortening, and milk, at 27 cents, more than doubles the cost. On this basis, pancakes cost about 10¢ per person, compared to about 6¢ per serving for a complete mix (you add water only).

Reusable Containers—Small quantities of honey are packaged in a squeeze-type plastic container shaped like a bear, pixie, or other figure. The plastic container is ideal for spreading honey with a minimum of waste and mess. But the container often costs more than the honey it contains. Save money here by buying honey in a 4- or 5-pound can to refill the plastic squeeze dispenser. In 4-pound cans, honey costs about 89¢ per pound. Honey in a bear-shape squeeze package costs 89¢ for 12 ounces or $1.19 per pound. So, save the bear and refill it yourself.

Reuse plastic-capped coffee cans by buying fresh grind-it-yourself coffee that is packaged in a paper bag. At home, transfer it immediately to the can and cap it with the plastic seal. You not only keep freshly ground coffee fresh, but save from 20 to 25¢ per pound.

Drinks—All kinds of drinks are available at your supermarket, whether it's *Coke* for the kids or something stronger for dad. Most of the soft drinks in cans or bottles are imitation flavors. If you buy noncarbonated, imitation "fruit" drinks in cans or bottles, you're paying mostly for water and the container.

Compare the cost of true fruit drinks, such as frozen lemonade or orange juice, to imitation soft drinks. Lemonade, for example, costs about 29¢ per quart compared to 22¢ for a 10-ounce bottle of pop. Lemonade also supplies a portion of your child's Vitamin C.

Canned and "no return, no deposit" bottles are the most expensive way to buy pop or mixers. Also, on a price-per-ounce basis, the small bottles are more expensive. If you're buying pop or mixers for a group, plan on using big bottles, 24 ounces or quarts, to supply the big demand—then fill out with "king size" or smaller individual sizes.

Buy beer in quarts for a party or when more than one person will be drinking. For example, an 11-ounce stubby may cost 26¢ each or 2.36¢ per ounce. Quarts of the same brand of beer may be selling for 65¢ or 1.94¢ per ounce. On this basis, beer in stubbies costs you 22% more than the same amount of the same brand in quarts.

Hotcake and Waffle Syrup—Buying imitation maple-flavored pancake syrup is another example of carting home water in a fancy glass or metal container. The real thing, boiled down from hard maple sap in the Vermont and Maine woods, long ago fell short of the demand. Real maple syrup is so expensive imitation syrups now supply most of the market. You can make your own easier than you can cart home a heavy glass container. Here's how—Simply add 1 cup of white and 1 cup of brown sugar to a cup of boiling water and stir until sugar dissolves. Add ½ teaspoon of concentrated maple flavoring. Result, nearly a pint of warm, flavorful syrup. If you like your syrup thicker, boil the mixture for a couple of minutes or add a couple of tablespoons of corn syrup. Your cost for a pint of syrup—about 18¢, as compared to 50¢ to 65¢ for the "store bought" kind.

CHECK-STAND ALERT

Make sure you get home with your bargains by checking the checker. If you trade at a store often enough, you'll see longer lines at certain check stands than others. A longer line indicates an expert checker, usually a woman. Expert checkers are fast, friendly, honest, and anxious to help you—real gems in the trade. Pick a checker whose primary job is at the check stand—not an assistant manager who helps out at peak periods or an extra stock boy pressed into service to divide lines. Regular checkers know special prices, even when they are not stamped on packages.

But, you can help keep your bargains intact by grouping similar buys together. If a fourth bar of soap costs only a penny, make sure all four bars are together. Even when items are priced in bunches, such as three for 19¢ or five for 79¢, arrange them together on the checker's belt or turntable. Otherwise, even the most conscientious checker may charge you the single price. Concentrate on the prices as the checker rings up each item or runs the bar code over the reader to make sure she charges you the correct price. Most checkers are honest, but they can easily make mistakes among the thousands of items they ring up every day. Know prices, particularly on the specials from your list. To jog your memory, particularly on fresh fruit or vegetable prices, keep a felt marking pen handy as you shop and mark the sack. If you pick items off the day-old bakery shelf, make sure the checker charges the reduced price rather than the full price of fresh goods.

PRICE COMPARISON COMPUTERS

Deliberately confusing packages make it difficult to tell whether a "giant" size is a better buy than a "regular" size. How can you tell, for example, whether cereal at 69¢ for 12⅞ ounces is a better buy than the same cereal at 39¢ for 7⅜ ounces? At these prices, the cost per ounce is practically identical. You may actually pay more per ounce in the large packages than in the small packages. Also, a special sale may offer a cut price on only one size. Of course, you can guess which size is the better buy. But a better way is to compare unit prices posted in small print along shelf edges from a computer if your state or city requires unit pricing. If not, carry one of the small electronic computers to calculate unit prices. The money you save will soon pay for the computer.

DOES A FREEZER PAY?

When all of the costs of operating a freezer are totaled, you have to work hard to make one pay in dollars and cents only. But a freezer pays off in other ways—being able to freeze meals ahead, always having a variety of food on hand, and being able to store homegrown produce at the height of the season. Table 2G details one look at the cost of operating a 15-cubic-foot freezer.

Immediately evident from the table is the lower cost per pound of food stored as the weight increases. On an average, 1 cubic foot of space will store between 25 and 35 pounds. If food is turned over four times

TABLE 2G: Home Freezer Costs

Cost Item	400 lbs.	800 lbs.	1200 lbs.	1600 lbs.
Depreciation[1]	$ 33.33	$ 33.33	$ 33.33	$ 33.33
Interest on investment (6½%)	13.00	13.00	13.00	13.00
Repairs	12.80	12.80	12.80	12.80
Electricity[2]				
Freezing costs[3]	1.40	2.80	4.20	5.60
Maintaining[4]	38.33	38.33	38.33	38.33
Packaging[5]	12.00	24.00	36.00	48.00
Total cost	$110.86	$124.26	$137.66	$151.06
Cost per pound (cents)	27.72	15.53	11.47	9.44

[1]Straight-line basis, 12 years, 0 residual 15-cu. ft. box
[2]Kilowatt-hour (kw-hr.) @ 3.5¢
[3]0.1 kw-hr. per lb.
[4]0.2 kw-hr. per cu.ft. per 24 hrs. @ 3.5¢
[5]6¢ per lb. (half to be wrapped)

during the year, storage costs for 1600 pounds average only about 9½¢ pound. For a freezer to pay its way, you must use it intensively. This means *using* frozen food—not *storing* it.

Here are several ideas for making your freezer pay its way—

1. Buy sale-priced steaks at the opening of a new supermarket. Typically you're likely to find extra-low prices and, even more important, better steaks. Practice the same economy of buying stocks of frozen food on extra-special sales of frozen orange juice, lemonade, chickens, or convenience foods.

2. Stock up on frozen fruits and vegetables just before a new season hits. Strawberries, for example, are often priced far below special-sale price to unload any remaining stock in warehouses to make space for a new crop.

3. Day-old bread is not always available when you need it. So, buy plenty and freeze it when you have the opportunity. If you are driving near one of the "thrift" stores for outdated bakery goods, stock up with 20 or 30 loaves of bread, rolls, doughnuts, or other pastries. Freeze them immediately upon getting home.

4. Jams, fresh fruit, applesauce, and fruit juices can be processed for storage much more easily by freezing than by old-fashioned canning methods—and freezing preserves the fresh taste. Store berry juice in large containers during the season. Later, thaw the juice and make smaller batches of fresh-tasting jams or jellies with a minimum of cooking. Or freeze berries, such as blueberries, whole for later use in pies.

5. Cook several meals at a time, particularly spaghetti sauce, stews, and other meals that normally require a long cooking time. You not only

save on time, but you save on cooking fuel and reduce the total number of dirtied pans. Later, just warm up the meals when time is short. Take turkey, for example. Since big birds are less expensive than small ones (see Table 2D), cook a really big bird (20 pounds or more), serve it right out of the oven at the Thanksgiving feast, then make up a half-dozen or so batches of turkey a-la-king for the freezer, or freeze slices in broth to keep them from drying out.

6. Coffee is often a good buy in 3-pound cans but is too much to use ordinarily before it gets stale. However, with a freezer, immediately after opening the can, repackage the ground coffee in half-pound containers and stash it in the freezer—the flavor stays fresh for months at 0°F.

7. Buying a side or quarter of beef, hog, or lamb generally will not pay off in lower meat prices. Avoid, particularly, those outlets that advertise in the TV program sections of your newspaper and offer gifts or unbelievably low prices. Such "locker beef" outlets have a dismal record with local consumer protection agencies. You may find, for example, a bait-and-switch game in play where a salesman attempts to upgrade your choice from the advertised special to a more expensive piece of beef, pork, or lamb. You may find your order is shorted or extra charges not mentioned are tacked onto your bill. Even under the best conditions, you can figure on losing 25 percent of the hanging weight of a side or quarter of beef in bone and waste. Also, you end up with many cuts of bony, less desirable pieces along with steaks and ground beef or sausage. Unless you have access to a farmer or feed lot owner you know who can sell you bulk meat at a known price under the usual market, you can stock your freezer at less cost by buying many packages of advertised specials at your supermarket meat counter. Studies have indicated overall savings of about 6 to 8 percent by buying specials compared to buying sides or quarters of beef. You cannot compare prices of bulk beef, for example, without considering the value of different cuts and knowing the yield grade of the animal. For a method of comparing prices of bulk beef with the equivalent prices of retail cuts in a supermarket, order a copy of a USDA folder, "How to Buy Meat for Your Freezer," available from the Superintendent of Documents, U.S. Government Printing Office, Washington, D.C. 20452. The price will be less than $1.00.

Consider the alternative use of a freezer locker if there is one near you. These locker plants lease below-zero storage space at a cost less than you pay for electricity alone. For example, a 12-cubic-foot locker rents for $28.50 per year in one area. The electricity for maintaining a 12-foot home freezer at 0°F. for a year costs about $34.00. So, use locker space for long storage and buy a smaller freezer for home. A small freezer costs less to buy and operate. A trip to the locker every two to three weeks loads up the freezer at home. Or, in the opposite direction, freeze fresh or cooked foods at home, plop them quickly into the freezer while flavors are at their peak, and then, later on, transfer them in larger loads to the locker.

CO-OPS

Two forms of cooperative buying can significantly reduce your food costs. One is the co-op store that operates with voluntary labor and sells regular or natural foods at a minimum markup over wholesale price. Low-income members of the co-op may buy food at only 1 percent above prices paid to wholesalers if they work a minimum number of hours weekly—typically 4 to 8 hours. Memberships in the co-op may cost only $5 at the beginning with a continued membership fee of $5/week until $50 to $100 has been paid in. Persons unable to contribute in cash may contribute extra time to the store. Generally, co-op storefront operations are one-third to half the size of a supermarket and may offer only a limited range of foodstuffs. Only by operating with volunteers can the co-op maintain their low prices. Nonmembers may be permitted to shop in storefront co-ops, but they will pay higher prices, possibly 15 to 20 percent markup over wholesale. Even at these higher prices, you may find costs of some foods, particularly organic or natural foods, lower priced than in area supermarkets. Since these storefront co-ops do not advertise, you may have to look for them.

A second form of cooperative buying involves groups whose members pool their money and combine orders to buy wholesale. Typically, a group of six or a dozen families organize an informal co-op to buy boxes of produce and fruit, cheese, organically grown foods, and boxed groceries from a wholesaler who is willing to sell to a group.

One 12-family co-op operates like this: Once a week, two of the families work together for the whole group. The two persons on duty for that week assemble orders from all 12 families for fruits and vegetables. The group operates with a rolling treasury to buy the crates or cartons of onions, lettuce, carrots, melons, or whatever is desired by the group in quantity. The two call in their order to a produce dealer the day before and pick up the crates in a station wagon or small truck. They pay for their purchases in cash. Back at one of their homes, the two divide the bulk quantities of fruits and vegetables into 12 bunches. The other 10 families send a representative to pick up their shares and pay for the amounts purchased. Prices for fresh fruits and vegetables purchased in wholesale quantities typically run 40 percent less than the retail prices in neighboring supermarkets. By sharing the duty, one family is responsible for the activity of picking up, dividing, and packaging the produce only once every six weeks.

For more information on the benefits of co-op buying groups, how to organize and run your own co-op, and how to recognize the problems, look into one of these helpful books: *Food Co-Ops for Small Groups* by Tony Vellela, published by Workman Publishing Co., 221 East 51st St., New York, NY 10022. Price at first printing was $2.95 plus possible handling and shipping. *The Food Co-Op Handbook* by The Co-Op Handbook Collective is a more extensive book published by Houghton Mifflin Co of Boston at $4.95. Food Co-op Project, 64 E. Lake St., Chicago, IL 60611 offers a co-op directory and publishes a co-op newsletter "Food Co-op Nooz." Self-Help Action Center, 11013 S. Indiana Ave., Chicago, IL 60628 can supply forms and aids for setting up your own food co-op.

BUY NUTRITION—NOT JUST FOOD

We all need adequate nutrition to stay healthy. But there are various ways to get good nutrition—and at a great difference in cost. First, there is a varied diet of natural foods, and second, there is a diet of readily available, low-cost foods supplemented by low-cost essential nutrients. The first route may cost twice, even three times, as much as the second route to good nutrition.

When you hear your neighbor or a friend talk about a "good" food, what does she mean? Generally, a reasonable serving of good food will supply a large measure of all the different essential nutrients that we need. The same quantity of a poor food will not.

No single food will supply the varied nutrition we need, even when eaten in reasonable quantities three times a day. One answer, of course, is to eat a variety of foods. If one food is deficient in one important element, some other food will supply it in quantity. Plan I is based on this precept—that you get all of the food elements you need from a varied diet.

PLAN I—Varied and Complete Diet

Nutritionists from the U.S. Department of Agriculture (USDA) and the National Academy of Science recommend a balanced diet from four basic food groups as follows:

Meat group—2 or more servings daily. One serving is 2 to 3 ounces of lean cooked meat, poultry, or fish. Or, one egg, ½ cup cooked dry beans or peas, or 2 tablespoons of peanut butter may replace ½ serving of meat.

Milk group—2 to 4 servings daily (2 for small children, 4 for teen-agers, 3 for children over 9 and adults). One serving is one 8-ounce cup of fluid milk. As alternatives, 1-inch cube cheddar-type cheese or ¾ cup cottage cheese, ice milk, or ice cream may replace ½ cup of fluid milk.

Vegetable-Fruit group—4 or more servings daily from a variety of citrus and other fruits, leafy green vegetables, and root vegetables.

Bread-Cereal group—4 or more servings daily. One serving is one slice of whole-grain bread, one ounce ready-to-eat cereal, ½ to ¾ cup cooked cereal, cornmeal, grits, spaghetti, macaroni, noodles, or rice.

Other foods needed to flavor or round out meals include sugar, vegetable fat, and condiments.

The USDA publishes several booklets to aid meal planning for good nutrition. Among them are: "Family Fare—A Guide to Good Nutrition," "Food and Your Weight," and "Nutrition—Food at Work for You." These booklets may be available at your Cooperative Extension Office, or you can order them from the Consumer Product Information Distribution Center, Washington, D.C. 20407.

USDA economists have worked out a series of food plans—call them food-value budgets, if you want—that provide a balanced diet at low, medium, and high cost. The differences between these plans reflect differences in tase and food preferences. Cost varies according to family size, ages of children, and the area of the country you live in. Table 2H details the cost of low-cost, moderate-cost, and liberal food plans for families and individuals.

PLAN II—Basic Food Plus Supplements

A somewhat drastic (by U.S. standards) method is available to achieve nutrition at a whopping reduction in cost. With this plan, you obtain the food energy and protein you need from low-cost sources and add the essential elements you need from pills or supplements.

Consider Vitamin C or ascorbic acid, for example. You need a new supply of Vitamin C every day because the body does not store it. English sailors were called "limeys" because they carried limes to ward off the scurvy that resulted from a lack of Vitamin C. Today, we get Vitamin C from fresh oranges, grapefruit, tomatoes, and other fresh fruits. But ascorbic acid in white pill form is a much cheaper source. Are they the

TABLE 2H: Cost of Food at Home for a Week (October 1978)

	Thrifty plan	Low-cost plan	Moderate-cost plan	Liberal plan
FAMILIES				
Young couple......................	$26.20	$34.10	$42.80	$51.30
Elderly couple	23.40	30.40	37.60	44.90
Family of 4 with				
preschool children	36.90	47.50	59.30	71.00
Family of 4 with elementary				
school children...................	44.40	57.30	71.80	86.10
INDIVIDUALS*				
Women				
20-54 years......................	10.70	13.90	17.30	20.60
55 years and over.................	9.70	12.50	15.40	18.30
Men				
20-54 years......................	13.10	17.10	21.60	26.00
55 years and over.................	11.60	15.10	18.80	22.50
Children				
1-2 years........................	5.90	7.50	9.30	11.00
3-5 years........................	7.20	9.00	11.10	13.40
6-8 years........................	9.10	11.70	14.60	17.50
9-11 years.......................	11.50	14.60	18.30	22.00
Girls 12-19 years	10.90	13.90	17.30	20.60
Boys 12-14 years...................	12.20	15.50	19.50	23.30
15-19 years...................	13.50	17.20	21.60	25.90

*Cost of food at home for any family can be figured by totaling costs shown for individuals of sex and age of various members of the family as follows:

—*For those eating all meals at home* (or carrying some meals from home), use amounts shown.

—*For those eating some meals out*, deduct 5 percent from amount in table for each meal not eaten at home. Thus, for a person eating lunch out 5 days a week, subtract 25 percent or one-fourth the cost shown.

—*For guests*, include for each meal eaten, 5 percent of amount shown in table for the proper age group.

Next, adjust the total figure if more or fewer than four people generally eat at the family table. Costs shown are for individuals in 4-person families. Adjustment is necessary because larger families tend to buy and use foods more economically than smaller ones. Thus, for a 1-person family, add 20 percent; 2 persons, add 10 percent; 3, add 5 percent; 4, use as is; 5 or 6, subtract 5 percent; 7 or more, subtract 10 percent.

"Family Food Budgeting for Good Meals and Good Nutrition," Home and Garden Bulletin No. 94, describes USDA's thrifty food plan and the three more costly plans, on which these costs are based.

same? The USDA's yearbook, *Food*, states, "Some vitamins exist in several forms, but Vitamin C occurs naturally in only one. Vitamin C is the same chemical compound whether it is isolated from foods or is synthesized and sold as pills or capsules."

Recommended allowances for Vitamin C call for 75 milligrams (mg.) for most adults, from 80 to 100 mg. for teenagers, and from 30 to 75 mg. for other children. To get all the Vitamin C you, as an adult, need each day from fresh food sources will cost from 5 to 50¢, depending on whether you eat a fresh orange or enough apples to provide the 75 mg. required. But Vitamin C or ascorbic acid pills are so cheap, you can get your 75 mg. for as little as ½¢ per day.

A good multivitamin pill for everyday use costs about one penny.

Calories are essential to a diet for energy. You need calories even on a reducing diet. How many? Only you can tell because caloric intake depends on your activity level. If you gain weight, you are eating too many calories. If you continue to lose weight, you are eating too few. Older people, particularly, eat more than they need. Most people over 30 could do with less than 2500 calories per day—possible less than 2000. Climb on your bathroom scale every morning before breakfast; your scale will keep you honest.

Protein for building and rebuilding the body is more difficult and more costly to obtain than the other nutritional elements.

A high-protein food called *Meals for Millions* is distributed in many countries of the world where nutrition is deficient. More than 100 million of these "1¢ meals" have gone to 129 countries. Basically, *Meals for Millions* is a powdered food that can be eaten alone or added to other foods to increase their protein. Only 2 ounces of it eaten three times a day supplies an adult's full requirements for protein, and all of the vitamins and most of the minerals for which there is a known nutritional need.

Multi-Purpose Food (MPF), similar to the *Meals for Millions*, is also available in the United States from General Mills Chemicals, Inc., 4620 W. 77th St., Minneapolis, Minn. 55435. *MPF* is sold by mail; request information and shipping costs.

Adults attempting to lose weight on one of the liquid diets that come neatly packaged in cans could get the same nutritional and low-calorie meals by adding 2 ounces of *MPF* to 1 quart of reconstituted dry milk mixed 50% stronger for a total of 50¢ per day. This way, you save money

---

50% Savings Idea

William Winover had been spending 45¢ per can for one of the canned diet foods for lunch. His routine was to cool the diet food in the refrigerator overnight and carry it to work in a vacuum bottle. He substituted *MPF* in lemonade for the canned diet drink and carried the mixture to work in the same vacuum bottle. Results: a reduction in his lunch cost from $112.50 to $56.20 per year; reduction in calories from 300 to 160 per lunch; assurance that he was cutting calories and not important nutrition with his new lunch routine.

while slipping off those pounds. Make your own low-calorie soups, add *MPF* powder to cookies, or add flavors to the milk to get away from the monotony of a single flavor.

A large family can use *MPF* to assure plenty of protein in diets for youngsters and still use low-cost, high-energy foods, hot cereals for breakfast, plenty of potatoes, noodle casseroles, and stretched meat or meat-substitute loaves. With *MPF* you need very little milk, vegetables, or fruits—all costly when out-of-season. The old saw, "Fill 'em up on bread," applies here too. Enriched wheat bread offers an excellent source of nutrition. Combined with jam or jelly for energy, bread and jam sandwiches make an ideal addition to meals built around the balanced protein, vitamin, and mineral content of *MPF*

One last bit of advice. Lunch eaten downtown or at the factory can be a large drain when trying to save big money on food. The costs cited in Table 2H cover only the cost of food eaten at home. You might consider "brown bagging" it—taking your lunch in a brown paper big—or attache case. If cold sandwiches are not appealing, add *MPF* to hot soup in a wide-mouth vacuum bottle.

SUMMING UP

Save money on food two ways: (1) buy less (most families eat too much anyway), and (2) pay less for what you buy. In this chapter, you learned that saving money on food purchases calls for—

- Spending less of the food budget on meat and other "big dollar" items.

- Substituting low-cost poultry for high-cost red meat in menus that encourage you to practice creative cookery.

- Using a variety of milk products—not just fresh, whole milk for all purposes.

- Cooking hot cereals for breakfast instead of pouring high-cost, sugared dry cereals out of a box.

- Planning meals from advertised specials.

- Saving money and time with certain convenience foods.

- Taking full advantage of marketing gimmicks—coupons, "cents off" labels, trading stamps, and premiums.

- Learning the shopping tactics used by smart thrifty housewives when buying in supermarkets.

- Making your freezer (if you own one or are thinking of buying one) pay off on a dollar-and-cents basis.

- Buying balanced nutrition—not just food—for your family.

3

HOW TO SAVE CASH WHEN YOU BUY
AND OPERATE A NEW OR USED CAR

Probably the biggest money drain from your family's pocketbook is
the one, two, or more cars you own and operate. To cut these
costs, learn the money-saving secrets of—

- When to buy a new or used car.
- How to get the lowest possible price when you buy.
- How to avoid being "taken" when you deal with an auto dealer.
- How to finance a car purchase and pay the least interest.
- How to buy insurance protection for the lowest cost.
- How to find the right gasoline for your car at the lowest price.
- How to learn which oil is best for your car's engine plus when
  and how often to change it.
- How to analyze tire expense on a cost-per-mile basis.
- How to select the right battery for your kind of driving and
  location.
- How to compromise between "cream puff" maintenance and
  benign neglect.
- How to shop for the best buy/coverage on insurance.

America's long-standing love affair with the motor car has chilled of
late. Gasoline prices, taxes, and occasional unavailability have taken their
toll of enthusiasm. More and more owners are thinking of their cars as
transportation—a means of getting from point A to point B. Emphasis on
public transportation, van pooling—even bicycling for commuting is
cutting the number of two-car families.

With costs escalating on every front, the dollar-conscious family or
individual needs to look at transportation expenses for today—and
tomorrow. For, the car you may buy today can affect your spending

significantly next year. So—before you buy your next car, analyze your situation and the potential costs involved.

Buying and operating one or more cars are, after food and housing, the biggest items in your budget. And car expense is growing, both in total dollars and as a percentage of your spending. In 1950, the average urban family spent $443 per year to buy and operate a car. In the 1975-76 period, the figure had increased to $1409.

HOW MUCH DOES A CAR *REALLY* COST?

Many car owners deliberately delude themselves about how much it costs to operate their car(s). They know a car costs a lot, but as long as they don't know how much, they tend to rest easy. Car expenses are, in fact, a major money leak in many family budgets.

Standing (Fixed) Costs—These are the costs that go on and on whether you drive your car 1000 or 50,000 miles per year—within certain limitations. As noted in Table 3A, these costs break down into the following elements—

● Depreciation. Mileage and how well a car is kept up affect depreciation, but time is the biggest factor. While you don't actually pay out money every week or month, depreciation represents the biggest cost of operating most cars. The bite comes when you trade in or sell your old car.

Ask your friendly banker for a peek at his blue, red, or black book that lists used-car market values. If your car is in exceptionally good condition, it will probably bring more than the "book" price. Do not use the trade-in value allowed you by a new car dealer to figure depreciation. The difference between your car's present value and the price you paid for it originally is depreciation. Any way you figure it, a new car loses about half of its value during the first three years. At the end of 10 years, most cars are worth only their junk or rebuild value, about $35 - $80.

● License and Taxes. Most states levy two kinds of taxes on the value of your car. One is a license fee. The other is a personal property or excise tax.

● Insurance. These costs are detailed in a later section. The costs noted in Table 3A are for a reasonably average example only.

Running or Variable Costs—These costs are the out-of-pocket charges that vary as you drive. Take gasoline, for example. The more you drive, obviously, the more gasoline you burn, and costs vary directly with use. The variation in miles per gallon affects yearly gasoline costs more

TABLE 3A: Annual Cost for Operating a Full-Size Car Over 10-Year Period

Year Annual Miles	Total 100,000	1 14,500	2 13,000	3 11,500	4 10,000	5 9,900	6 9,900	7 9,500	8 8,500	9 7,500	10 5,700
Item											
Fixed Costs											
Depreciation	$4,864.00	$1,215.00	$748.00	$637.00	$446.00	$340.00	$306.00	$292.00	$292.00	$291.00	$277.00
License & title	495.76	225.70	30.00	30.00	30.00	30.00	30.00	30.00	30.00	30.00	30.00
Insurance	1,678.00	214.00	200.00	200.00	182.00	182.00	140.00	140.00	140.00	140.00	140.00
Garage & parking + tolls	2,208.80	250.98	240.94	230.91	220.88	220.21	220.21	217.54	210.85	204.16	192.12
Subtotal	9,246.56	1,905.74	1,218.94	1,097.91	898.88	772.21	696.21	679.54	672.85	665.16	639.12
Variable Costs											
Gasoline	4,060.00	588.70	527.80	466.90	406.00	401.94	401.94	385.70	345.10	304.50	231.42
Repairs & maintenance	3,664.13	157.05	199.95	414.67	548.03	406.54	471.46	704.82	280.80	431.20	49.63
Tires & accessories	561.34	40.83	36.88	32.91	32.33	67.48	79.15	70.75	68.31	66.86	65.83
Oil	172.00	15.05	13.98	15.05	13.97	19.35	19.35	21.50	19.35	20.43	13.97
Sales tax	174.93	8.45	9.97	18.45	23.72	19.61	22.66	31.76	14.62	20.63	5.06
Subtotal	8,632.40	810.08	788.58	947.98	1,024.05	914.90	994.56	1,214.53	728.18	843.62	365.91
TOTAL	$17,878.96	$2,715.82	$2,007.52	$2,045.89	$1,992.93	$1,687.11	$1,690.77	$1,894.07	$1,401.03	$1,508.78	$1,005.03
Cost/mile	17.88¢	18.73¢	15.44¢	17.79¢	19.23¢	17.04¢	17.08¢	19.94¢	16.48¢	20.12¢	17.63¢

Costs are taken from "Cost of Owning and Operating an Automobile 1976," issued by the U.S. Dept. of Transportation. The full-size car with a V-8 engine is fully equipped—purchase price, $4,899. Repairs and maintenance include routine tune-ups, brake linings plus major repairs, such as "valve job" when required. Gasoline is figured at 15 miles/gallon and a price of 60.9 cents/gallon. Insurance includes $50,000 combined public liability and $5,000 property damage. $2,500 personal injury, uninsured motorist coverage, and full comprehensive. Collision insurance with $100 deductible was figured for first 5 years only. Garaging includes $12/month allowance for owner's garage or carport. Financing cost is not included. On a usual 36-month contract with one-third down, financing would add about 1½ cents/mile. *Note:* Cost per mile appears to be unrealistic due to assumption that many more miles will be driven while car is new. If an average of 10,000 miles/year were to be assumed, cost/mile would be much higher in first few years and less in later years due to influence of depreciation. Using the same analysis, average costs/mile over 10 years and 100,000 miles for a compact are 14.6 cents for a compact car and 12.6 cents for a subcompact.

than small changes in the price of gasoline. For example, at 80¢ per gallon, a car that averages 36 miles per gallon costs $222 for 10,000 miles of driving. A car that averages only 14 miles per gallon costs $571—or $349 more for the year. At 15 miles per gallon, the gasoline price would have to decline from 80 to 28¢ per gallon to effect a similar $349 per-year saving.

Table 3A represents only a sample set of car-operating expenses. You should estimate yearly car expenses, then keep track of actual expenses for a year to substantiate estimates.

WHICH CAR FOR YOU

You may analyze your car situation. You know how much it costs to operate a car. And you need a car. Which kind?

The confusing maze of models, makes, sizes, and optional equipment requires study. And study begins at home. One of the first decisions is whether to buy a new or used car. Should you buy a compact, intermediate, full-size, or foreign car? Which series? Sedan, two-door, or station wagon? Four, six- or eight-cylinder engine, automatic transmission, power options, or custom trim?

Every fall, shortly after new-car announcement time, a number of magazines publish the suggested list prices of the new cars along with

---

20% Savings Idea

Walter Blake had always bought a new car every other year. "I like new cars. I like the new look—to smell the new fabric and rubber and leather in a new car. I figure the warranty protection I get saves me money on repairs. But, most of all, I like the feeling I get when I drive down the street in a new car!" But, Walter did not receive his expected year-end bonus. Also, his boy was entering college—at new-car introduction time. When he looked at his bank account and the new sticker price, the cash wasn't there. His 2-year old car was still not paid for—another year to run. He had to draw down his savings to pay Mike's tuition. A close look at the cost of driving his present car one more year vs. trading it in showed a cost avoidance of close to $600—give or take a little. So—reluctantly, at first, but more willingly later when he realized that not buying a new car would make available the money he needed, he kept his car. "With the money I save, I might even drive it 'till the wheels fall off.' "

tables of wheel base, engine horsepower, curb weight, etc. You won't want to buy at the suggested list price, but use it as a guide for study.

BUYING A USED CAR

Many dollar-conscious owners buy used cars to save money. From Table 3A you see how you can save $755 by driving a car during its third and fourth years instead of its first and second years. That's about $1.05 a day. Many families find more satisfying uses for their disposable income than watching $31 disappear as they tear off every month of the calendar.

Develop a Shopping Plan—Unless you are well prepared with facts, know-how, figures, and, most of all, a plan, you'll only last a few seconds of the first round in the used-car buying ring. Salesmen on used-car lots are real pros at closing a sale—many times completely honest but frequently a bit shady.

• What Kind of Car? The trend is to fuel-efficient small cars. Full-size cars may be priced lower as a percent of their original new price, but operating costs could make up the difference quickly. Some makes of cars depreciate faster than others. A station wagon only one or two years old may have been used commercially as a light truck.

• Which Dealer? Normally, you do better buying a used car from a new-car dealer who operates his own used-car department. A new-car dealer who maintains a reliable and reputable service shop and stands behind both his new and used cars can be a good choice. Avoid particularly the used-car dealer who uses bait advertisements.

• Research the Car You Want. Before you start to shop seriously, research the facts on the cars that interest you. In the library, check original prices from back issues of one of the mechanical magazines (*Popular Mechanics,* etc.), *Consumer Reports,* or *Changing Times.* Then, check *Blue Book* or *Red Book* prices of the cars at your bank. Note both wholesale and normal expected retail prices. Fill in both prices on your Buying Plan (Fig. 3-2). Determine how much you can pay and pick models within your limit.

• Arrange Your Own Financing. Before starting to bargain, be prepared to offer cash. Arrange your own loan from your bank, credit union, or other source.

• Buy Your Own Insurance. Like financing, buy insurance on your terms, not the dealer's.

• Evaluate Your Trade-In Car. If you plan to trade an older car in on a used car, find out yourself what it's really worth.

Selecting Your Used Car—You've finished your research, you have your financing and insurance arranged for, you have a pretty fair idea of the range of cars you can afford, have picked a representative make and model, and you have tabulated Buying Plan (Fig. 3-2). Now you're ready to select a car you can buy—and then drive for the next 2, 4, or possibly 10 years. Use the Checklist (Figure 3-1) to help you evaluate the cars that interest you objectively. Remember, no reputable dealer will object to a detailed examination or road test.

● Three-Step Screening. Expert appraisers use a progressive system of screening and evaluating cars. First, the walk-around look both from far away and close up. Second, the inside examination, both under the hood and inside the passenger compartment. Third, the road test. A car may flunk out at any of these progressively stiffer checkpoints. Unless you are an expert, you may wish to take a fourth step. When you have selected what you believe to be a good buy, take the car to your friendly mechanic for his detailed examination. If you have developed a rapport with an individual mechanic, you will get his honest opinion of the car you have selected. Since you expect to pay him for his time, take only the one or two cars you have picked from your three-step screening. Taking a candidate car through a diagnostic center accomplishes the same check if you do not know a friendly mechanic.

Selecting Your New Car—If you elect to buy a new car to gain the latest technology for control emissions and to get better fuel mileage, follow somewhat the same procedure. That is, do your homework before venturing into the dealer's showroom. So much information, drivers' reports, test data, and government releases are available on new cars, you can gain a good impression of various makes and models before driving possible candidates. Buying a new car has one big advantage over buying a used car—you are covered with a warranty and you can expect the car of your choice to perform reasonably consistent with the test reports you may have read. Whether you buy a new or used car, timing and bargaining tactics can be similar.

SAVE MONEY WHEN YOU BUY

Once you have decided to buy, don't let a wave of enthusiasm black out your logical plan for getting exactly the car you want at the best possible price. Any time you sense car fever engulfing you in a showroom, simply say, "No!" and walk out.

FIGURE 3-1: Used Car Shopping Plan—Checklist

	Starting choice	Other possibilities		
		1	2	3
Manufacturer				
Year				
Model				
Equipment				
Heater				
Radio				
Automatic transmission				
Power steering				
Power brakes				
Air conditioning				
Dealer (seller)				
Guarantee				
Wholesale price*				
Retail price*				
Checkpoints				
(1) Exterior walk-around				
Level and in line				
Body and paint				
Chrome, rust				
Glass				
Tires				
Shocks, suspension				
(2) Inside look				
Door & window operation				
Upholstery				
Switches & handles				
Wear points				
Brake pedal				
Engine compartment				
Oil & water leaks				
Fan belt				
Oil dipstick				
Starting				
Noises				
(3) Road test				
Noises				
Brake operation				
Transmission				
Clutch				
Steering				
Tracking				
Drive-by check				
Lugging check				
Smoke				
(4) Mechanic's appraisal				
Engine condition				
Gear boxes				
Brakes				
Vacuum gauge check				
Noises				
Generator				
Sale Price				
Repair list (For each car note repairs needed and estimated cost.)				
Total Price				

*Determine from one of the used-car pricing guides at your bank.

FIGURE 3-2: New and Used Car Buying Chart

	Dealer's cost	List Price		
		Dealer #1	Dealer #2	Dealer #3
Manufacturer				
Model (4-door, station wagon, etc.)				
Series				
Equipment (standard)[1]				
Heater				
Engine				
Transmission				
Interior items				
Exterior items				
Base price				
Equipment (extra)[2]				
Radio				
Engine option				
Power options				
Steering				
Brakes				
Windows				
Automatic transmission				
Air conditioning				
Freight and make-ready cost				
Local taxes				
Gross price				
Gross trade-in allowance				
Net difference (actual cost)				
Cash price (without trade-in)				
Dealer (name and address)				
Salesman				

[1] Different series include a varied list of equipment as "standard" in price.
[2] Optional equipment listed and priced separately.

Find the Dealer's Cost—*Consumers Digest, Car Prices*, and other books list purported dealer costs of new automobiles and accessories. Another system is to figure the dealer cost in two steps: (1) Multiply the base sticker price without options, dealer prep, freight, or local taxes by a dealer percentage that varies according to the size of the car and the manufacturer. For subcompacts and compacts, the dealer percentage ranges from .83 to .88 with Volkswagen costing the dealer 91 percent of the base sticker price. Full-size cars carry a higher markup and cost the dealer about 78 percent of the base sticker price. Apply a dealer percentage of .77 for options separately from the car itself. Add freight and local taxes to arrive at the cost of the car to the dealer.

Another way to buy a car for $125 over the dealer's cost is through Car/Puter, 1603 Bushwick Ave., Brooklyn, NY 11207. For $10 Car/Puter prices the exact make and model of the car you want plus the optional equipment you have decided to buy. Armed with the cost, you can bargain with a local dealer. If that doesn't work, Car/Puter arranges for you to buy the car of your choice for invoice plus $125. Prices were current when this was written. Write for more information and an application to start the Car/Puter process.

If you plan to trade in a car, evaluate its trade-in potential separately. Any additional trade-in amount allowed over your car's market value amounts to a discount on the new car.

Pick the Best Time to Buy—Look for a time when the dealer is in a mood to "deal." One of the best times is from 85 to 120 days after the official announcement date for new models. The hoopla accompanying new car showings moves many cars at close to list prices. Also, rental agencies and car leasing firms take early cars off the assembly lines. A dealer may actually be limited on the number of new cars he can deliver—so he sells at his price—not yours. But after about 3 months, winter hits many areas, and buyers would just as soon wait until spring. So, the doldrums set in. Sales begin slowing down, losing headway. Meanwhile, back at the factory, cars are popping off the assembly line at nearly the same rate. They begin to stack up in the dealer's parking lot. Conditions are ripe for discounting, and you can benefit.

Another good time to shop is in a blizzard or after a spell of icy, snowy, or rainy weather that keeps shoppers out of new car showrooms. Often a salesman will offer huge discounts to get a lift from a sale. Another good time is on the last selling day of the month, particularly during sales contest months, such as "Summer Sellathon" or "Circus Days." Cars sold during a special promotion rate an extra $100—even $200 profit from the manufacturer. If your timing is right, you pick up part of the bonus as an extra discount.

Is buying a car just before the new models are announced a good idea? Sometimes. It depends primarily on how you plan to drive it. If you keep cars for 6, 8, or 10 years, then the year's depreciation you lose when the new models appear washes out over that time span. Ordinarily, however, the $100 to $200 extra discount the average dealer allows to clear out his old stock isn't enough to compensate for driving last year's model a few weeks later. So, if you trade often, you need to get at least 25% off list for a year-end model to be a good buy.

Buying and "Dealing" Tactics—Trading tactics reminiscent of the old horse trader, David Harum, are the rule at car dealers these days. You don't expect to pay "list price." The dealer doesn't expect to sell for "list price."

● Bait Advertising. Beware of such high-pressure advertising as "Lowest Prices in Town," "Buy Below Dealer's Cost," "Discounts Galore," printed business cards stuck under your windshield wiper that state, "Would you take $2,000 for your 1974 Chevrolet?" and "No Down Payments" or "Take 4 Years to Pay." These eye-catching ads include one or both of two basic appeals—low cost and lots of credit.

● Fast Financing. Unusual financing is another trick used by fast-shuffling new- and used-car dealers. Many buyers are so interested in the monthly payment charge that they forget to ask how much the total will be. There are only two ways to keep monthly payments low. One is to stretch out the financing period for 2, 3, 4—even 5 years. The other is to cut the interest rate. See "Save Money on Financing," page 75.

● Trade-In Tactics. In addition to the "bait and switch" tactic, watch out for the "highball," "lowball," and the verbal offer that must be authorized by the sales manager. These tactics are so old, you'd think everyone would know them by now. Not so! Every year, unwary car buyers are hooked into paying more than they should. The "highball" tactic is aimed at shoppers. The salesman offers so much more than you expect for your car in trade that other dealers don't come even close. The high trade-in value for your car won't stand up—the salesman will often wait until the unwary shopper has pen in hand before realizing his "mistake." The salesman then quotes a more competitive figure. The "lowball" is primarily for buyers with no cars to trade. But, again at the last minute, the unusually low offer is snatched away on some pretense. "Unauthorized" verbal offers usually go hand-in-hand with "highball" and "lowball" strategy. The salesman may pencil in a high trade-in value for your car and comment that he will have to get the manager's O.K.— but "that's only a formality." Later, when you've ironed out details, the salesman goes away, then comes back with a long face. It seems the manager won't go along with the trade-in value; the highest he will go is X dollars. If you go ahead with the sale, you've been had!

High-pressure tactics depend on breaking down your psychological defenses. While you're talking with one salesman after he has made a pie-in-the-sky offer for your trade-in, your wife decides on the color you want. You then haggle over accessories and options. During the whole time, your mind is adjusting to the idea of buying *that* car. Your sales resistance drops as car fever mounts. You picture yourself driving away in *that* car. Suddenly, almost as innocuously as a comment on the weather, the salesman tells you the trade-in value is a mistake. Your old car is suddenly worth $300 less. That's $300 more you are going to have to pay. You may find it easier to go ahead with the sale rather than begin shopping all over again. Practical psychology has won again!

Buying at the Best Price—Mentally condition yourself for bargaining before you venture forth. As part of this research you may have visited a few showrooms, kicked a few tires, and sat behind a few wheels. But, don't begin dealing until *you are ready*. Make yourself a Buying Chart like the one in Figure 3-2, then use it. Here's how.

You have already picked the best time to buy. After you have talked about the model and accessories you want, simply ask the salesman for his best discount. If you plan to trade in a car, you'll probably start with the list price. The salesman will discount the price by increasing the trade-in allowance above its actual "wholesale" value. Since you have already researched the value of your trade-in, you know how much he is discounting the new car price. At this point, ask for a straight cash price with no trade-in. This ploy affects dealers differently. Some dealers actively sell their own used cars. A straight no-trade-in deal will not appeal to this dealer if you have a clean, relatively late model trade-in. Other dealers wholesale out their used cars. Handling these trade-ins costs them money, so they are frequently ready to offer a better no-trade-in price.

Does it pay to shop around? Absolutely. One business school study turned up some surprising facts on the art and science of haggling and shopping for a new car. The study confirmed that dealers not only are willing to sell at a discount but also actively suggest reductions of several hundred dollars. As a final ploy, an experienced car buyer will bargain by saying something like— "Your price is too high. I'll pay you _____ dollars." The offered price is deliberately too low and is rejected. His next tactic is to say, "Well, how low can you go?" or "How close can you come to my figure?" This simple bargaining tactic can lower a previously discounted price by $50 or more. It's your money you're bargaining for, so what have you got to lose?

All the while, you're compiling figures on your Buying Chart (Fig. 3-1). Compare financing and insurance charges you get elsewhere. To take advantage of the dealer's end-of-month propensity to deal, do this shopping and analysis before the last day. Then, with a solid background of data you can deal decisively—and know it is the best deal.

A few cautions on closing the deal—

● Don't sign a blank contract; fill in all dollar amounts and conditions.

● Read the sales agreement and make sure it agrees with your deal.

● Don't leave the trade-in value to be determined later when your car is delivered.

● Account for any and all extras, such as make-ready charges, "service" charges, etc.

SELL YOUR OWN CAR?

When you're ready to buy either a new car or a younger used car, you may do better selling your old car yourself instead of trading it in. Market value may be as much as 20-25% more than your car's wholesale value as a trade-in. Also, you can frequently make a sharper "clean" deal for a new car with no "old dog" to trade in. So, consider advertising and selling your used car yourself.

SAVE MONEY ON FINANCING

Only about 35% of the car buyers in the U.S. plunk down cash for their cars. So, if you buy on credit, shop for a loan with the same audacity as you shop for a car. Depending on how you arrange financing, you may save up to $200-$500 on the purchase of a new car.

Cost of Financing—Money is a commodity that reacts to the law of supply and demand the same as other goods. Suppose you select a car that costs $5,200 and your trade-in is valued at $1,400. You still have to pay $3,800. Suppose further that you elect to pay the $3,800 in regular monthly installments over a 3-year period, the most common time and repayment interval. Also you get a 12% annual percentage rate (APR) on the loan. According to tables issued by the Federal Reserve System to assure compliance with Truth-In-Lending, monthly payments for financing only would be $126.21. The dollar cost of financing over 3 years would be $743.66. On the basis of 10,000 miles per year, the finance charge adds almost 2½ cents per mile to your driving costs for the 3-year period.

TABLE 3B: Monthly Payment Chart

12 months

Annual Percentage Rate / Total Dollars Borrowed	9½% Finance Charges	9½% To Be Repaid	9½% Monthly payments	10¾% Finance Charges	10¾% To Be Repaid	10¾% Monthly Payments	12% Finance Charges	12% To Be Repaid	12% Monthly Payments	14% Finance Charges	14% To Be Repaid	14% Monthly Payments	16% Finance Charges	16% To Be Repaid	16% Monthly Payments
$1,200	$ 62.64	$1,263	$105.22	$71.04	$1,271	$105.92	$ 79.44	$1,279	$106.62	$ 92.88	$1,293	$107.74	$106.56	$1,307	$108.88
1,600	83.52	1,684	140.29	94.72	1,695	141.23	105.92	1,706	142.16	123.84	1,724	143.65	142.08	1,742	145.17
2,000	104.40	2,104	175.37	118.40	2,118	176.53	132.40	2,132	177.70	154.80	2,155	179.57	177.60	2,178	181.47
2,400	125.28	2,525	210.44	142.08	2,542	211.84	158.88	2,559	213.24	185.76	2,586	215.48	213.12	2,613	217.76
2,800	146.16	2,946	245.51	165.76	2,966	247.15	185.36	2,985	248.78	216.72	3,017	251.39	248.64	3,049	254.05
3,200	167.04	3,367	280.67	189.44	3,389	282.45	211.84	3,412	284.32	247.68	3,448	287.31	284.16	3,484	290.35
3,600	187.92	3,788	315.67	213.12	3,813	317.76	238.32	3,838	319.86	278.64	3,679	323.22	319.68	3,920	326.64
4,000	208.80	4,209	350.73	236.80	4,237	353.07	264.80	4,265	355.40	309.60	4,310	359.13	355.20	4,355	362.93
4,400	229.68	4,630	385.81	260.48	4,660	388.37	291.28	4,691	390.94	340.56	4,741	395.05	390.72	4,791	399.23
4,800	250.56	5,051	420.88	284.16	5,084	423.68	317.76	5,118	426.50	371.52	5,172	430.96	426.24	5,226	435.52

24 months

Annual Percentage Rate / Total Dollars Borrowed	9½% Finance Charges	9½% To Be Repaid	9½% Monthly payments	10¾% Finance Charges	10¾% To Be Repaid	10¾% Monthly Payments	12% Finance Charges	12% To Be Repaid	12% Monthly Payments	14% Finance Charges	14% To Be Repaid	14% Monthly Payments	16% Finance Charges	16% To Be Repaid	16% Monthly Payments
1,200	122.28	1,322	55.10	138.96	1,339	55.79	155.76	1,356	56.49	182.76	1,383	57.62	210.12	1,410	58.76
1,600	163.04	1,763	73.46	185.28	1,785	74.39	207.60	1,808	75.32	243.68	1,844	76.82	280.16	1,880	78.34
2,000	203.80	2,204	91.83	231.60	2,232	92.98	259.60	2,260	94.15	304.60	2,305	96.03	350.20	2,350	97.93
2,400	244.56	2,645	110.19	277.92	2,678	111.58	311.52	2,712	112.98	365.52	2,766	115.23	420.24	2,820	117.51
2,800	285.32	3,085	128.56	324.24	3,124	130.18	363.44	3,163	131.81	426.44	3,226	134.44	490.28	3,290	137.10
3,200	326.08	3,526	146.92	370.56	3,571	148.77	415.36	3,615	150.64	487.36	3,687	153.64	560.32	3,760	156.68
3,600	366.84	3,967	165.29	416.88	4,017	167.37	467.28	4,067	169.47	548.28	4,148	172.85	630.36	4,230	176.27
4,000	407.50	4,408	183.65	463.20	4,463	185.97	519.20	4,519	188.30	609.20	4,609	192.05	700.40	4,700	195.85
4,400	448.36	4,848	202.02	509.52	4,910	204.56	571.12	4,971	207.13	670.12	5,070	211.26	770.44	5,170	215.44
4,800	489.12	5,289	220.38	555.84	5,356	223.16	623.04	5,423	225.96	731.04	5,531	230.46	840.48	5,640	235.02

36 months

1,200	183.84	1.384	38.44	209.16	1.409	39.14	234.84	1.435	39.86	276.48	1.476	41.01	318.84	1.519	42.19
1,600	245.12	1.845	51.25	278.88	1.879	52.19	313.12	1.913	53.14	368.64	1.969	54.68	425.12	2.025	56.25
2,000	306.40	2.306	64.07	348.60	2.349	65.24	391.40	2.391	66.43	460.80	2.461	68.36	531.40	2.531	70.32
2,400	367.68	2.768	76.88	418.32	2.818	78.29	469.68	2.870	79.71	552.96	2.953	82.03	637.68	3.038	84.38
2,800	428.96	3.229	89.69	488.04	3.288	91.33	547.96	3.348	93.00	645.12	3.445	95.70	743.96	3.544	98.44
3,200	490.24	3.690	102.51	557.76	3.758	104.38	626.24	3.826	106.28	737.28	3.937	109.37	850.24	4.050	112.51
3,600	551.52	4.153	115.32	627.48	4.227	117.43	704.52	4.305	119.57	829.44	4.429	123.04	956.52	4.557	126.57
4,000	612.80	4.613	128.13	697.20	4.697	130.48	782.80	4.783	132.86	921.60	4.922	136.71	1,062.80	5.036	140.63
4,400	674.08	5.074	140.95	766.92	5.167	143.53	861.08	5.261	146.14	1,013.76	5.414	150.38	1,169.08	5.569	154.70
4,800	735.36	5.535	153.76	836.64	5.637	156.57	939.36	5.739	159.43	1,105.92	5.906	164.05	1,275.36	6.075	168.76

48 months

1,200	247.08	1.447	30.15	281.76	1.482	30.87	316.80	1.517	31.60	374.04	1.574	32.79	432.35	1.632	34.01
1,600	329.44	1.929	40.20	375.68	1.976	41.16	422.40	2.022	42.13	498.72	2.099	43.72	576.48	2.176	45.34
2,000	411.80	2.412	50.25	469.60	2.470	51.45	528.00	2.528	52.67	623.40	2.623	54.65	720.60	2.721	56.68
2,400	494.16	2.894	60.30	563.52	2.964	61.74	633.60	3.034	63.20	748.08	3.148	65.59	864.72	3.265	68.02
2,800	576.52	3.377	70.34	657.44	3.457	72.03	739.20	3.539	73.73	872.76	3.673	76.51	1,008.84	3.809	79.35
3,200	658.88	3.859	80.39	751.36	3.951	82.32	844.80	4.045	84.27	997.44	4.197	87.45	1,152.96	4.353	90.69
3,600	741.24	4.341	90.44	845.28	4.445	92.61	950.40	4.550	94.80	1,122.12	4.722	98.38	1,297.08	4.897	102.02
4,000	823.60	4.824	100.49	939.20	4.939	102.90	1,056.00	5.056	105.33	1,248.80	5.249	109.35	1,441.20	5.441	113.36
4,400	905.96	5.306	110.54	1,033.12	5.433	113.19	1,161.60	5.562	115.87	1,371.48	5.771	120.24	1,585.32	5.985	124.69
4,800	988.32	5.788	120.59	1,127.04	5.927	123.48	1,267.20	6.067	126.40	1,496.16	6.296	131.17	1,729.44	6.529	136.03

Reduce Financing Costs—Follow these ideas for whittling bucks off financing costs—

● Make as big a down payment as you can. Paying cash, of course, eliminates all of the financing costs. Using the previous example, if you paid $2,800 down, instead of only $1,400, finance charges over the 3-year period would be only $469.68 (instead of $743.66). Also, monthly payments would have been only $79.71 (instead of $126.21). By financing $3,800 of the purchase over 3 years, your car actually cost $5,943.66—not the $5,200 bargained-for price. By paying $2,800 down, the same car costs $5,669.66.

● Pay off the loan quickly. Instead of paying off the $2,400 over 3 years, shorten the time to 18 months or, better still, one year. Using the same example, borrowing $2,400 for one year at 12% means you pay $158.88 financing charges (instead of $469.68) and monthly payments would be $213.24. Your new car then costs $5,358.88

● Bargain for your interest. Depending on your credit rating, you might be able to finance your car as low as 9½% APR. Figuring a 9½%

FIGURE 3-3: Financing Cost Chart

	Bank (name)	Bank (name)	Credit Union	Dealer	Other
Interest rate and time					
Cost of car (include all extras)					
Trade-in					
Subtotal					
Cash down payment					
Remaining balance					
Monthly payment					
Total payments (payments number)					
Credit investigation					
Other charges					
Total contract					
Principal (total financed)					
Finance charges					
Insurance coverage					
Insurance cost Financed					
Cash					
Finance cost for insurance					

loan shows finance charges are only $25.28 and monthly payments over one year would be $125.28 for the $2,400 example loan.

● Look out for hidden charges. Not all of the difference between the car's sale price and your total payments is interest. You may also be charged for a credit investigation, credit life insurance, a "finder's fee," legal fee, or other "extras." These extra costs should be included in the Finance Charge. An extra charge for credit life insurance may be added but only if you agree to it in writing. Use your Financing Cost Chart (Fig. 3-3) to get a clear, itemized statement of exactly what you are paying for.

Shopping for a Loan—Fewer than 5 out of 100 car buyers actually compare loan costs. Before you begin shopping for your car, check financing costs at—

● Local banks. Ask for the consumer credit manager at your own bank.

● Credit union. CU car finance plans are likely to be quite competitive with bank rates and are often less costly.

● Car dealer. Dealer financing is likely to be considerably more expensive than a similar loan from your bank.

● Consumer credit companies. Most expensive of the credit sources is likely to be a small loan or credit company organized exclusively to extend installment credit.

20% Savings on Interest

Money trades like any other product, and the price goes up and down. Tom Hane discovered that when he was about to finance his used car. He had spent weeks looking for just the right car. Finally, he found a real cream puff in a suburban new-car dealer's lot. Tom was about to sign a contract to finance the car with the dealer when his wife, Edith, motioned for him to step out of the "closing booth." "Don't we belong to the credit union?" she asked. Tom nodded. "Then, let's see what they can do." Tom hated to leave such a good car, and the salesman wouldn't reserve it for them. But, the credit union offered them a loan at 9½ APR instead of 12%—and the fee included credit life insurance on the loan at no additional cost. Extra charges Tom hadn't noticed on the dealer's loan slip didn't show up on the credit union loan either. Overall, Tom saved $176.80—and the car was still there. Shopping for financing before shopping for a car would have permitted Tom to sew up the deal on his cream puff without waiting.

GASOLINE SAVINGS

Almost $2 billion is wasted by motorists each year because they buy better gasoline than they need or their car can use. Gas stations offer a bewildering assortment of gasolines. One brand is an all-purpose gasoline. Another station offers as many as three gasolines. Most common is the selection between "regular" and "premium." Octane number is the key difference among these many fuels and represents a gasoline's anti-knock rating.

How can you pick the right gasoline for your car? First, look at your owner's manual. If it recommends using regular gasoline, don't burn premium or unleaded. Keep these dollar savings in mind.

Gasoline—

● Regular gasoline is the choice of truckers (except diesels) and commercial drivers.

● Not all gasolines are alike. When a company markets one all-purpose grade of gasoline, check its octane rating. It will probably carry an octane number between the regular and premium grades marketed by a two-grade station. Likewise, the regular sold at a two-grade station is likely to be better than the regular sold by a company that markets three grades of gasoline.

● Additives are important in gasoline. Various additives help to reduce spark-plug fouling. A detergent prevents gum and varnish from clogging the small fuel passages in your carburetor. Anti-icing additives may prevent frozen gas lines and carburetor icing. Up to 10 different additives may be found in today's gasoline.

● On cross-country trips, remember that prices vary widely from city to city and in between.

Your own driving habits can make as much as 4 or 5 miles per gallon difference in mileage. Some of the tricks professional drivers use to get every last inch out of a gallon of gas are—

● Use high gear as soon and as much as possible. At 20 mph your car will use about 50% more gas in low gear than in high gear over the same distance. With a stick shift in normal driving, shift from low to second at 5 to 8 mph, from second to high around 18 to 20. With an automatic, accelerate easily and let up slightly on the pedal at around 15 to 18 mph to allow the transmission to shift automatically into high gear.

● Avoid rapid "jack rabbit" starts. Rapid acceleration is fun—but the gas fairly sluices through the carburetor during wide-open throttle pickups.

11% Savings on Gasoline

James Watson always burned premium gasoline in his car because "it's the best." After reading the first edition of this book, James wrote that he made two switches. Since his car was 3 years old, he switched to regular gas—at a cost saving of 5¢ gallon. The engine knocked occasionally, but a change in ignition timing corrected that immediately. He reported an almost indiscernible change in "pep," but he admits it was probably his imagination. Further, he found a service station that knocked off an additional 3¢ gallon when he brought his car in for regular lubes and oil changes. The 8¢ difference cut his gasoline bill an even 11%, as he had been paying an average of 69.9¢ gallon for premium.

● Drive at even speeds and change speeds gradually.

● Look and plan ahead to minimize stops. Using the brake costs you two ways—added brake and tire wear plus additional gasoline to get going again.

● Climb hills briskly with an automatic transmission to reduce slippage.

ENGINE OIL SAVINGS

Engine Oil—Few factors affecting car operation start as many arguments as motor oils and how often they should be changed. What kind of driving is toughest on engines and oils? Any one or a combination of the following—

● Extremely cold weather and short trips where the engine never really warms up.

● Slow-speed or idle operation.

● Sandy or heavy dust conditions.

● Long, sustained, high-speed driving common on Interstate highways.

How do you know which oil is best for your car? And how do you know which oil includes which desirable additives? You don't, for sure, but oil compounders have agreed, along with the American Petroleum Institute (API), the Society of Automotive Engineers (SAE), and the American Society for Testing Materials (ASTM), on designations that divide oil into the following categories—

● SE for Service Extreme replaces extended service oils and is required in all new cars manufactured from 1972 on to protect warranties.

Additives to protect oils from high temperatures during continuous high-speed driving and the extra heat generated to keep air conditioning and other power options working are included in these oils—plus the additives common in lower-grade oils. The new additives prevent oxidation and deterioration of oils under extreme engine heat.

- SD for Service Deluxe replaces the former MS (Motor Severe) designation. Additives in SD oils provide protection against low-temperature sludging and rust. They also offer multiviscosity ranges, 20-30 and others, and detergent dispersants to keep engines clean.
- SC for Service Common.
- SB for Service Brief replaces the old MM (Motor Medium) and is generally devoid of all but a few additives.
- SA for Service Austere replaces the old ML (Motor Light).

SB or SA motor oils are intended mainly for lawn mowers or other nonautomotive engines. SA oils may be mixed with gasoline for use in two-stroke cycle engines, such as outboards or some lawn mowers.

You will find these and other designations on the top of engine oil cans at your service stations. You may also find some other designations that apply to diesel engines, but you can ignore them. "Meets Manufacturers' Sequence Tests" may also show up on oil cans—but the important letters are SE, SD, and SC. These letters indicate that the oils contain alkaline substances, detergent dispersants, and antiwear additives to prevent acid wear, sludging, and other ills of engine oil. The SE oils also contain additives to help the oils resist high temperatures.

These suggestions will help you select a good engine oil—

- Follow the recommendations in your car owner's manual for oil according to the year it was made. As long as the warranty is in effect, use of any other oil could void your protection. All of the oils recommended for new cars will be multigrade oils. But, don't buy a better oil than you need. After the warranty period expires, select an oil consistent with your driving habits. SE oils cost 15¢ to 20¢ more per quart than SD oil, for example.
- Oils manufacured by companies that sell only oil represent a branded product that is consistent all over the country.

How often should you change oil? Your owner's manual offers one recommendation. Your type of driving and how long you expect to drive your car affects how often you should change oil. But remember *do change it!* Unless you change oil occasionally, the crankcase becomes a cesspool of dust, acid, abrasive particles, and metallic bits. Filters will not remove many of the harmful chemicals, including acids, that build up from blow-by gases and water.

On older cars if you get as much as 2000 miles before the oil level is down a quart, this is a good time to change. If oil level is down a quart after 1000 miles, it makes sense to add a quart and change when oil level is again down a quart. If your owner's manual recommends a change at 4000 or 6000 miles, use the extended service oils and follow the recommendations.

Basically, you're better off to change oil at least every 2000-2500 miles, unless your owner's manual specifically recommends a longer period. Ordinarily, filters should be changed every 5000-6000 miles to remove accumulated dirt. Otherwise, the filter gets plugged, the bypass valve opens, and oil flows around the filter—unfiltered.

During winter change oil more often, even though mileage is low. Every 30-45 days isn't too often. In dusty areas, change oil and filters and service the air cleaner frequently. Under ideal driving conditions, as on a long vacation trip, you can extend drain periods safely.

Money-Saving Tips on Gasoline and Oil—

● Don't waste your money on "top oil" additives for gasoline.

● Oil additives are likewise costly and unnecessary. Rather than spending money on "mouse milks" at $1.95 per half-pint, buy a good SE multigrade or extended service oil that already includes useful additives.

● Don't idle for long period on cold mornings. As soon as oil pressure is up, move out and drive normally. Idling to warm up induces sludging.

● Check spark plugs at least every 10,000 miles; clean points or replace them when required. Plugs that misfire waste power (as gas) and allow unburned gasoline to dilute crankcase oil, which, in turn, reduces oil mileage.

● Check the automatic choke for proper operation at every grease period. Use the hand choke sparingly in winter, almost never in summer.

● Keep heat-riser valve operating smoothly. If it is stuck open, you'll use more gas for warm-up every time you start up. If it's stuck closed, added heat to the intake air will increase the tendency to knock and reduce mileage.

TIRES

Tires cost more than twice as much per mile as engine oil. And this is the way to analyze tire costs—on a per-mile basis. Consider safety too when you buy tires. To help you buy replacement tires effectively, let's lay some facts on the table—

Tire Cords—Nylon, rayon, polyester, steel wire, arimid, and glass fibers are used singly or in combination to reinforce the carcass of tires. Nylon is strong, stretchy, and tough, but it develops flat spots in contact with cold ground or concrete while parked. For a few miles after starting, flat spots thump and cause vibrations. Auto manufacturers for years installed rayon cord tires to eliminate the thumps. Now, polyester cord offers strength without the thumps and may be furnished as original equipment. If you drive over rough road for long distances at high speeds or carry heavier than normal loads in your car or station wagon, nylon offers a good combination of strength and heat resistance. Rayon tires may save you as much as $1 or $2 per tire compared to nylon.

Construction—Bias-ply construction is the oldest and most common type. Layers of reinforcing fabrics criss-cross at an angle, usually 30-40 degrees to the tire centerline. Bias-ply construction provides easy riding qualities, but the tread surface squirms in contact with the road, and the tire runs hotter than either belted-bias or radial tires. Belted-bias construction combines a carcass of two or four plies laid on a bias with two plies (belts) of fabric directly under the tread. Treads in the belts criss-cross at an angle. Belt fabrics may be steel wire, glass fibers, or rayon in combination with carcass cords of nylon, polyester, arimid, or rayon. Belted-bias tires squirm less than bias-ply tires, run cooler, and give more mileage. Radial tires are built with cords running perpendicular to the centerline. A belt of up to four plies is added under the tread. Radial tires carry an "R" in the number to designate radial construction. Radial tires combine flexible sidewalls with great strength and stiffness in the tread areas. Radial tires run cool and provide longer wear than either the bias or belted-bias tires but may produce a stiff ride.

Tire Grades—After several false starts, litigation in courts, and several years of delay, the National Highway Traffic Safety Administration (NHTSA) as part of the Department of Transportation (DOT) issued uniform tire quality grading standards in July, 1978, with a series of effective dates. By March, 1980, the grade must be molded into the tire sidewall. Three grading standards are included in the DOT regulations for treadwear, traction, and temperature resistance.

Treadwear grades are probably the most important for motorists as quality indicators. Treadwear grades do not specify the actual number of miles the buyer can expect the tire to last. Instead, the treadwear grades express a relative tread life compared to other types or brands of tires. The relative ratings are based upon actual performance over a test course established by NHTSA at San Angelo, Texas. Treadwear grades are expressed numerically as 80, 90, 100, 110, 120, 130, 140, 150, 160, etc. You can expect the tire with the highest number to wear the longest when driven under the same conditions. A tire graded at 150, for example, would be expected to wear one and a half times as well on the government test track as a tire graded 100. Generally, you can expect to get 50 percent more miles from a tire graded 150 compared to one graded 100—providing you drive under the same conditions, with proper inflation, balancing, and wheel alignment. In actual service treadwear performance is likely to vary widely due to different driving habits, service practices, road characteristics, and climate.

Traction grades are marked simply as A, B, and C. A tire graded A would offer the best traction.

Temperature resistance grades are also important, as excessive high temperatures from high speeds, high loads, hot temperatures, or various combinations of those three effects could cause the tire to degenerate and reduce tire life or lead to sudden failure. Temperature resistance levels are also graded as A, B, or C with the A-grade representing the highest temperature resistance.

Guarantee periods or tread wear mileage also offer a useful clue to quality. Most tire manufacturers warrant a tire against defects and road hazards until the tread wears to about 1/16th inch. Replacement or adjustment is on a basis proportionate with wear, although the price for an adjustment may be the posted list price rather than the reduced price you may have paid. Warranties for tread wear are more meaningful. Tire companies may warrant a tire for 12 to 40 months, 12,000 to 40,000 miles. If the tire is worn to less than 1/16th-inch tread in less than the stated time or mileage, the company adjusts the price for a new tire. Companies use either time or mileage, but not both. Since average passenger cars travel about 12,000 miles a year, figure 1000 miles per month when comparing grades according to guaranteed mileage. You can expect a better tire to be guaranteed to wear a longer time than a cheap tire. Belted tires will wear and be guaranteed for longer periods than bias-ply tires. Radial tires wear longer than either of the other two types. Radial tires also cost more. One way to choose between tires is to figure the cost per 1000 miles of guaranteed wear, as detailed in Table 3C.

Retreads are common for trucks and commercial airplanes. Retread tires are also practical for your car unless you drive long distances at high speeds. A good quality retread, particularly if the carcass is a belted-bias or radial type, will likely serve you better than an inexpensive second- or third-line new tire.

TABLE 3C: Cost of Tires

Grade	Wear-Out[1] Period (Months)	Total Miles[2]	Cost[3]	Cost (Cents/mile)
Premium				
120 Level	40	42,000	$82.30	.20
110 Level	40	40,000	76.45	.19
First Line				
100 Level	36	36,000	68.70	.19
Second Line				
90 Level	24	24,000	55.80	.23
Thrid Line				
75 Level	18	20,000	34.60	.17
Retread	18	12,000	20.20	.17

[1]Wear-out period as guaranteed; assume tire worn at end of period.
[2]Assume average of 1000 miles/month.
[3]Cost includes Federal Excise Tax and mounting; does not include local tax or balancing. Prices compared for F78-14 or equivalent size—blackwall.

Balancing and Alignment—Both of these factors affect tire life significantly. If you notice cupped or irregular wear patterns developing or if you feel your tires thumping or shimmying, see a serviceman about balance right away. Improper inflation pressure also wears tires more rapidly than is necessary.

Money-Saving Tire Tips—

● Maintain tire pressure at about 2 pounds more than is called for in your owner's manual to reduce wear.

● When you're in the market for tires, buy in pairs, even in fours, to get a price reduction. Also, keep a lookout for tire sales, particularly around Memorial Day, 4th of July, and Labor Day holidays and inventory reduction sales in January. When comparing prices, make sure total price includes Federal excise tax, delivery, mounting, and balancing.

● Don't buy used tires or regrooves. The mileage you may get isn't worth the chances you take.

● Check your driving habits. Rapid accelerations and sliding stops eat tires away quickly. Hot-rodders refer to rapid starts as "spreading a patch," with the "patch" a black line of rubber ground from the tire. Brake evenly at stops. High speeds shorten tire life as much as 50%.

● Consider buying a larger tire. Most rims will accommodate at least one size larger tire.

29% Savings Idea

Buying tires had always been a problem for Evelyn Green, a widow with two children. She usually bought tires at the service station where she traded. When the station manager said the tires were worn, she instructed him to install new ones. A friend told her about the first edition of this book. She wasn't aware that tires sold by discount stores under their own trade names were usually made by one of the "big four" tire manufacturers. The next time she needed tires she watched the ads. Instead of paying $59.95 per tire at the gas station, she bought tires guaranteed for 3 years at only $42.50—a savings of more than 29%. And the tires were mounted free.

BATTERIES

Another part of your car used up regularly, though not often, is the battery. On a new car you can expect from 2 to 3 years of service before the battery quits. When you buy a replacement battery, you're interested in starting ability, life, and cost. As detailed in Table 3D, cost per month is the important figure.

TABLE 3D: Comparative Cost of Batteries (12 Volts)

Relative Quality	No. of Plates	Cold Cranking Power²	Ampere Hours	Guarantee Period (Months)	Price¹	Cost/ Month (Cents)
1	78	500	81	60	$47.00	78.3
2	66	410	67	48	40.00	83.3
3	66	385	62	42	35.00	83.3
4	54	300	53	36	30.00	83.3
5	42	210	38	24	21.00	87.5
6	42	180	33	18	18.00	100.00

¹Price does not include sales tax, installation, or trade-in value of old battery.
²Amps. for 20 sec. at 0° F.

MAINTENANCE

Every mechanical device requires service and repairs at some time in its useful life. Automobiles are no exception, although manufacturers have designed a remarkable degree of reliability into today's cars. Maintenance of your car, then, falls into two classes, preventive and corrective maintenance. Preventive maintenance includes such things as regular lubrication, washing and waxing, tightening bands and changing

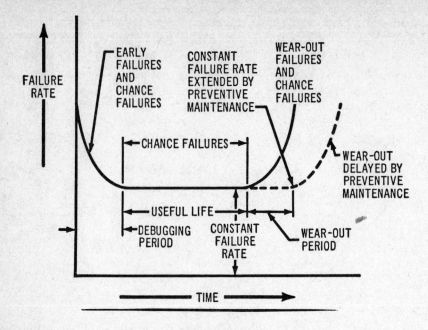

FIGURE 3-4:

Reliability "bathtub chart" diagrams expected occurrence of failures whether a car, airplane, or some other mechanical system. Early-period failures are usually due to some bug in design or an undiscovered fault during manufacture. Warranties usually cover repairs of these early failures. After the debugging period, a long useful life occurs with only an occasional chance failure. After the normal life, failure rate increases as parts and assemblies wear out. Useful life can be extended and wearout failures delayed by good preventive maintenance.

automatic transmission oil, and checking tire pressure. Corrective maintenance includes such jobs as tune-ups, relining the brakes, aligning the front end, and replacing any part or assembly that fails, such as bearings or grease seals. How you practice preventive maintenance determines, in some degree, how much corrective maintenance is required (Figure 3-4).

Big, thick books are available to describe how to repair every car built. If you have a yen for tinkering, do-it-yourself maintenance pays off. Otherwise, your best investment is to locate a reliable and trustworthy mechanic who knows your car. There are still some around—those individuals who still take pride in their work, who may have a small one- or two-man shop off the main street, and who do a good part of the work themselves. Ask around your area for a lead to one of these modern-day saints. Often you'll find one in a service station that specializes in repairs. And, when you find one, cultivate him like the rare specimen he is, because individualized, mother-hen attention to your car by a knowing mechanic will save you many dollars over the life of your car.

Lubrication—Consult your owner's manual. Lubrication schedules tend to be conservative, and unless you live in a sandy, dusty area, you can probably extend mileage by at least a half. That is, if your owner's manual calls for a chassis lubrication every 1000 miles, you can probably get by with a lube every 1500 miles.

Brakes—Different driver, hilly terrain, traffic vs. open-road driving—all affect the rate of brake wear. Ask your friendly mechanic to check lining wear by pulling a front wheel at least every 15,000 miles—and to lubricate front wheel bearings at the same time. As linings wear thin, check more often to make sure brake shoes or rivets don't begin gouging the smooth surface of the drum. Otherwise, you'll be stuck for turning drums—at about $4-$5 per wheel.

When it comes time to reline brakes, don't bite on a "bargain brake" job. There are no bargains. Since a chunk of the cost for a brake relining job is labor, long-life lining is a better buy, even if the lining material itself costs 50% more. A good lining will outwear a cheap lining at least 2:1.

Tune-Up—Defining a tune-up runs something like this: "To make fine adjustments to an engine as necessary for it to operate in top condition." These fine adjustments affect spark plugs, breaker points, and carburetor at least. Tune-ups are basically corrective action. You need a tune-up when your engine exhibits such symptoms as—

- Hard starting.
- Noticeably poorer gasoline mileage than normal.
- Rough engine operation, particularly at low speeds.
- Engine missing at any speed, but most often on the open highway.
- Noticeable lack of "pep" on hills or when passing another car on the highway.

Minor tune-ups may use no parts and involve only adjustments, such as retiming ignition, cleaning and regapping spark plugs, and smoothing the idle adjustment on the carburetor.

Major tune-ups usually call for the installation of new plugs and breaker points. Also, your mechanic should service the air cleaner, possibly install a new dry-type filter, clean the oil filler cap and fuel-pump filter bowl, and service the PCV and pollution control system. If your mechanic suspects other troubles, he may check compression on

50% Doing-It-Yourself Savings

Labor at $16-$22 per hour runs up the cost of tune-ups and other "light" maintenance, as Winston Hollis discovered. When his plant schedule switched to four 10-hour days, he resolved to learn about tune-ups himself—to put some of that new free time to good use. He had been watching the ads for spark plugs at 79¢ each vs. the $1.35 he was charged the last time he took his car in. Also, a new condenser and points cost $3.25. Win enrolled in an evening course in auto mechanics. As part of his investment, he bought a socket-and-wrench set plus a timing light—about $60 total. On his first tune-up, Win figured he saved $30—half the cost of his tools. When his second car needed a tune-up a few months later, he did the whole job on a Saturday morning. So, he saved the cost of his tools doing one tune-up on each of his two cars.

cylinders, generator brushes, and voltage regulator setting. A major tune-up, if done right, also includes tightening cylinder head bolts and checking water and heater hose connections, fan belt tension and condition, manifold heat control (heat riser valve), and fuel pump vacuum.

Replacement Maintenance—Keep an eye on dash instruments and listen attentively to engine and chassis noises. If water temperature begins to run over the normal range consistently, ask your mechanic to check for the cause. Unusual squeals, thumps, click-clicks that correlate with either engine speed or wheel rotation, whistles, clonks, and whines may be the first clue to trouble that, if corrected in time, can save you a major expense. Ask your friendly mechanic for his professional advice when you suspect trouble.

SAVE MONEY ON INSURANCE

Car insurance is a fixed or standing cost. Considerable ferment and tumult have resulted from the rapidly spiraling cost of car insurance, the number of policies cancelled by private insurance companies, and the introduction of "no fault" insurance. Some states require insurance as a preliminary to being granted a driver's license. Department of Transportation studies indicate that as many as 35% United States passenger cars are not covered with liability insurance in some states. During one year, automobile liability insurance reportedly repaid only a fifth of the $11.5 billion losses. As a result, auto insurance concepts and practices are under attack at state and Federal levels.

"No fault" insurance systems compensate injured parties promptly without waiting for a determination of whose fault the accident might have been. Hence, the "no fault" name. The tort system, as more widely used, puts responsibility on the negligent driver. The victim seeks compensation from the negligent driver's insurance company. Often such procedures wind up in court with delays of 2 years or more. Briefly, four kinds of insurance are most often bought—

● Collision—Repairs damage to your car whether damage was due to your fault or not.

● Liability—Covers damage to persons or property not in your own car up to the limits of your policy. This is the policy that protects you against lawsuits in case you accidentally injure or kill some person or damage someone's property. *Don't drive without liability coverage*—not even around the block. If an accident is proved to be your fault, liability coverage pays for fixing the other fellow's car. Coverage is usually spelled out by limits—maximum coverage for bodily injury to one person, total bodily injury per accident, and property damage limit. Thus, 10/20/5 liability coverage limits the insurance company's liability to $10,000 for injuries to one person, $20,000 maximum for two or more persons injured in one accident, and $5000 for property damage.

● Comprehensive—Losses of many kinds, such as fire, theft, windstorm damage, vandalism, etc. Glass breakage normally falls under comprehensive coverage, but may be paid for separately.

● Uninsured Driver—Pays for damage to your car and costs of medical care if another driver is at fault but is not insured. With so many uninsured drivers on the road, this coverage is becoming more important.

Other options cover medical payments to a passenger in your car or to yourself, accidental death while in a car, and provisions for towing and road service in case your car breaks down.

Shopping for Insurance—Auto insurance is expensive, but no two companies charge the same even for identical coverage. You can probably save money by shopping around for a policy that fits you best. Here's why—Auto insurance companies set their rates according to risks. For example, a driver who covers 15,000 miles in a year exposes himself to greater accident risks than a driver who covers only 5000 miles. So, the 15,000-mile driver pays a higher premium. This system of rating risks varies all over the map, literally. Companies have found that big-city driving produces more accidents per mile than rural- or suburban-area driving. So, where you live affects premium costs. But not all companies separate city from suburb along the same lines. If one company places you in a suburb and another says your address falls within the city, the first company's premium will probably be less for exactly the same coverage.

Driving use is another rating category. If all you do is drive your car around town and on trips for pleasure, you will pay less than the salesman who uses his car every day on business.

Age of the drivers in a family is a major difference. A male driver under 25 years of age who drives the family car frequently or owns his own car pays up to five times the basic premium for liability coverage—if he can get it at all.

When comparing costs, use the Insurance Cost Comparator (Table 3E). Often an agent will quote a total price for a package of coverages. Unless you know what's in the package, you can't tell whether the total price is actually less or you're just getting less coverage. Note particularly the limits of liability, the deductible amounts, and the different items covered in a total quotation price.

When you buy a new or used car, shop separately for insurance. A dealer or finance company will insist on collision and sometimes liability coverage. But an acceptable policy with first claim by the financing company will satisfy most dealers.

Liability Insurance—You can cut the cost of buying liability coverage in most cases by doing one or more of the following—

● Shop around to find a company whose risk rating plan fits you best.

● Qualify for a compact car discount. Most companies cut premiums by as much as 10% for compact cars.

● Earn a multiple-car discount. Make sure your company allows a discount for a second car. Some companies allow up to a 20% discount on both cars.

● Qualify for a limited-use premium for young drivers.

● Qualify for a driver-training discount for the young driver in your family, up to 10%.

● Check for a "good student" discount. If your son and/or daughter qualifies (in upper one-fifth of class, on dean's or honor list—rules vary among companies), your cost may be 20% less. Ordinarily, you may qualify for a driver-training or good-student discount for young drivers, but not both.

● Select and stick with a company that offers merit policies. Companies differ in their policies for cutting premiums for good driving records. One company discounts a renewal by 5% after a full year of claim-free driving. Another 5% is knocked off after a second claim-free year and a third 5% after the third year.

TABLE 3-E: Insurance Cost Comparator

	Company #1	Company #2	Company #3	Company #4
Agent's name Address Telephone no.				
Liability 10/20/10				
25/50/10				
50/100/25				
Collision $250 deductible				
$100 deductible				
$50 deductible				
Sliding scale				
Comprehensive Full coverage				
$50 deductible				
Medical payments $500 (each)				
Miscellaneous Uninsured driver				
Towing and road service				
Total (checked items)				

Rating facts

    One car (popular make)
    15,000 yearly mileage
    No under-25 drivers
    Drive 12 miles one way to work
    No business driving
    Suburban address

Collision Insurance—Like liability coverage, you can tailor collision insurance to cover your needs at minimum costs by doing one or more of the following—

● Assume part of the risk yourself. Policies may include $50, $100, $250, and sliding-scale deductions. Deductible policies are written to cut off the smaller, nit-picking claims that often cost more to process than the damage is worth. If you select a $100 deductible, you will pay about 20% less than the premium for $50 deductible. A $250 deductible cuts the cost by about 40%.

● Drive an old car to work and assume all collision risks. (But *do* carry liability.)

• Assume all collision risks. Even with no specific collision coverage, you may have at least two kinds of protection: (1) damage from an accident caused by the other driver will usually be repaired under the other driver's liability policy; (2) an uninsured loss in an accident, even if it is your own fault, can be included as a casualty loss on your income tax return, except for the first $100.

Comprehensive—This catch-all policy is subject to more variations than the other two combined. For example, full-coverage comprehensive costs about $53 at one company. But, if you include a $50-deductible clause, the same coverage drops to $36. Buying full coverage puts you in the position of paying $17 for $50 worth of protection. Another variation offers fire and theft coverage only for $11. Some companies offer comprehensive policies without coverage for glass breakage. So, check coverages and compare costs.

Other Coverages—Towing and road service policies pay for the cost of emergency service (up to a limit, usually $25). Depending on your location and car, this coverage is usually a good buy. Uninsured motorist is also a good buy. Medical payments for your family and others, accidental life policy, and other similar coverages should be considered as a part of your over-all insurance program.

Package Policies—Sometimes called "special policies," a group of coverages under one policy may be offered for a single price. The idea is similar to homeowner or tenant packages for home insurance (see Chapter 5). Package policies typically state one liability limit, rather than three (10/20/5, for example). In using the Insurance Cost Comparator, Table 3E, enter prices for single coverage equal to either the maximum for one accident or the total of maximums for one accident plus the property damage portion. For example, if the single limit is $25,000 on the package policy, compare it to 10/20/5 or 10/25/10.

Group automobile insurance is becoming more available. Group coverage cuts administration costs and saves up to 15% compared to buying individual policies. Check with your employer or labor union for group auto insurance coverage.

Substandard Policies—Along with stiff increases in repair costs, higher jury awards in injury cases, and increased medical costs, insurance companies are increasingly vigilant in weeding out high risk drivers. As a result, many drivers no longer qualify for normal or standard auto insurance policies. If you should be turned down for insurance, you have two choices—buy a substandard policy or enter the assigned risk pool. Substandard policies are written by different companies or subsidiaries of the major auto insurers. Because they consider the risks higher, premiums are distinctly higher—up to three or more times the cost of standard policies. Shopping around is even more important if you must buy substandard policy coverage. Assigned-risk policies are written by major insurers on the basis of their volume of business in a state, and the limits are restricted. You may find that a substandard policy will cost less than an assigned-risk policy; sometimes the reverse is true. You can find out the differences only by shopping aggressively. Apply for an assigned-risk policy through your normal insurance agent. Look in the classified section of your telephone directory for substandard insurers. If you can find one, pick a subsidiary of one of the major companies, such as Allstate, State Farm, Aetna, or one of the other biggies, as some substandard insurance companies have gone bankrupt, leaving their policyholders uninsured.

TAX-DEDUCTIBLE CAR EXPENSE

Facts and figures in this chapter point out where the dollars for car expense go. Some of these dollars can be deducted from your Federal income tax. Specific tax-saving pointers you should remember about cars are—

● Interest on car payments. All of the interest paid on your car loan is deductible for the year in which it is paid.

● Licenses, state and local. Formerly, all license fees were deductible. Now, only the excise portion of licenses can be deducted. See your license bill for a breakout of the excise tax portion.

● Charitable driving. If you drive for charity, such as soliciting contributions for a children's hospital, you can deduct the running expense (but not depreciation, etc.). List out-of-pocket driving costs

---

20% Savings Idea

One major insurance company offers a 20% reduction on a package insurance policy if you don't smoke, worth $40/car on an average, in one state. The package policy includes rate reductions on bodily injury, property damage, medical, and collision coverages. So, if you don't smoke, look into the 20% savings possible on car insurance. And, if you do smoke, consider this savings potential as an additional price you pay for smoking—not for driving your car.

under "Contributions." Out-of-pocket per-mile costs are specified by the IRS—currently 7 cents/mile.

● Medical driving. Miles driven to visit a doctor's office or a hospital are deductible. List out-of-pocket costs only under "Medical."

● Car damage or loss. Any loss you may have suffered because your car was damaged in a collision or fire or was stolen becomes a casualty loss in the amount not covered by your insurance. Check the fine print of the tax regulations. Casualty losses, such as collision, are deductible only after the first $100.

● Business driving. Running and standing expenses for cars used in business can be deducted in proportion to the amount of business use. If you drive less than 15,000 miles per year on business, you can deduct 17¢/mile, at this writing. For more than 15,000 the per mile allowance is 10¢ per mile. But, check current allowances. You may charge off actual costs as an option instead of the mileage allowance by using Form 2106.

To qualify for and substantiate car-expense deductions, keep a detailed logbook of charity, medical, and business mileage. Note the mileage at the beginning of each year and the mileage when you turn in a car on a new one. Keep a detailed expense book and use a credit card for all gas and oil purchases. These receipts are good evidence of money spent for gas, oil, tires, and some repairs.

SUMMING UP

The money spent for cars is one of the most manageable expenses common to most individuals and families. This chapter covered the many varieties of information you need to buy the car of your choice that serves your needs at a minimum cost and ideas for keeping operating costs to a rock-bottom level. Among the topics covered in detail were—

● Reasons for buying a new or used car according to income available and needs—whether cars are a necessity or fun.

● How much a car really costs. A cold, logical look at total car costs can be a jolt.

● How to learn the shopping and bargaining skills necessary to get the car you want for the least cash.

● How to pay less interest and financing costs when buying a car on time.

- Selecting from among the many grades, brands, and prices of gasoline.

- Matching the engine oil grade, viscosity, and change schedule to your car and your kind of driving.

- How to pick tires for your car and driving conditions.

- How to divide maintenance costs into two categories—preventive and corrective maintenance—and knowing that good preventive maintenance pays off in lower corrective maintenance costs and longer car life.

- How to shop for insurance and choose the protection levels you need.

- Taking income tax deductions for certain car operating expenses as one way to cut your actual out-of-pocket costs.

4

ENERGY SAVINGS MEAN MORE
SPENDABLE DOLLARS IN YOUR POCKET

You CAN do something about those heating and electrical power bills whether you are buying cuddly warmth in winter or refreshing "coolth" in summer. Home heating and cooling are spending musts, but you gain little satisfaction from paying more than necessary. Cost cutting ideas you'll find here include:

- Investing in insulation to restrict the flow of heat out of your home in winter and into your house in summer.

- Picking the right fuel—and matching it to your heating system.

- Using new technology to reduce heating and cooling costs.

- Balancing your heating system to stop wasting heat.

- Adjusting your furnace to extract all possible usable heat in fuel.

- Heat-saving tactics.

- Electrical power reducing tactics that cost little or nothing.

- Ideas for saving electrical energy to reduce costs.

Energy sources—home heating oil, natural gas, and electrical power—are reacting to the law of supply and demand like any other commodity. As energy supplies dwindle and demands increase, prices go up. Thus, saving energy affords a double thrust—you aid our country's economy by reducing the need for foreign oil and you spend less hard cash every day, month, and year. Saving gasoline helps too, and tips for spending less cash to run your car are noted in Chapter Three.

Look ahead. Inflation and limited supplies of fossil fuels will combine to drive up the cost of heating and cooling your house and powering your electrical appliances. Anything you can do now to reduce the consumption of oil, gas, or electrical energy will pay increasing dividends as time goes on. Saving cash on utilities involves more than simply reducing consumption. You may need to invest money now in order to save cash later. In many cases an investment in more or better insulation for your house will earn (through savings in fuel costs) several times the yield rate you could expect from deposits in a bank savings account or dividends on stock you may hold.

One chapter cannot hope to provide you with all of the ideas for saving money on fuel and electricity. A listing of useful books and pamphlets is included later in this chapter. Rather than depend on other resources, you should understand the concepts of how savings are possible and use your own initiative in finding ways to conserve energy which translates into saving cash.

CONTROLLING SPACE

The walls and roof of your house enclose a volume of space that is warmer in winter than all outdoors and cooler in summer. Heat tends to seek its own level, just as water seeks its own level. Heat escapes from inside a warm house to the outside. Nothing you can do can prevent heat from passing through walls, roof, and foundation. The best you can hope for is to retard or restrict the flow of heat from warm space to cool space. In summer, flows are reversed with warm outside air seeking to level with cool air trapped inside either from low-temperature night air or from air conditioning.

All the good things you read about insulation, calking, double windows, and storm doors and windows boil down to one basic idea— how to slow the flow of heat from warm space to cool space. Heat flow is similar to water flow in another way too. The steeper the slope (gradient) the faster the flow. You have seen water in a steep mountain stream rushing downhill. A similar quantity of water may move slowly when the change of elevation is less. The same holds for heat. More heat passes through walls and roof when the temperature is zero outside than when the temperature is only 45. As the difference in temperatures between inside and outside (gradient) increases, the heat escapes faster.

Look at heat flow another way—suppose you hold a tipped pan of water under a running faucet and adjust its flow until the water running out of the low side of the pan exactly balances the flow of water from the faucet. As you move the pan toward a more level position, less water from the faucet is needed to maintain the level. So it is with insulation. The more insulation (and double windows, storm doors, and caulking) in your house, the less heat flows out. And, with less heat flowing out, you must burn less fuel to maintain comfort levels inside. The less fuel you burn, the less cash you spend. It's that simple.

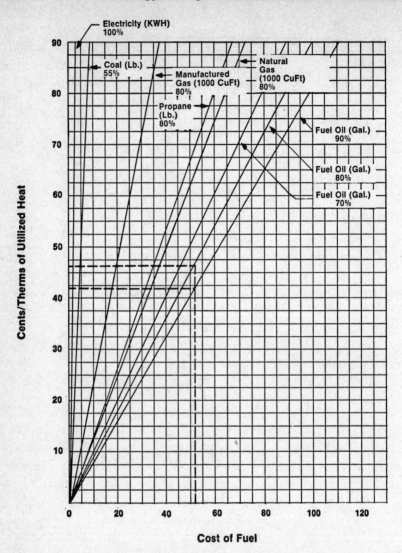

FIGURE 4-1: Cost of Fuel (cents/unit)

Relative fuel costs for providing one therm (100,000 BTU) of heat to a house interior. Cost of utilized heat depends on the cost of fuel and the efficiency of extracting the fuel's latent heat. Example line for fuel oil at 52 cents/gallon provides one therm of heat to house at about 41½ cents if burned at 90 percent efficiency, but cost increases to 46½ cents/therm if burned at 80 percent efficiency. Comparisons of various fuels at different prices are simple with this chart.

Fuel, electrical power, and water are necessities—important and indispensable. But, nobody gets an emotional kick out of spending cash for fuel oil. So—here is one area where you can cut back on spending for essentials in order to retain more cash for spending on fun activities. Here's how—

PICK YOUR FUEL

Dislocations in the availability and prices of fuel in the past few years may make changing your heating system economically desirable. Depend on it—natural gas will continue climbing in price, or its availability will become too unreliable for use as a home heating fuel. Politics cannot change the amount of gas available. Oil will follow gas into a shortage position later. Solar energy and electricity will eventually supply most homes with heat in winter and energy for keeping cool in summer. The chart in Figure 4-1 can help you sort out the best energy source for your home on a basis of competitive cost.

Approach your objective of using less energy (and, thus, spending less cash for fuel) from two directions. First, reduce the heat flow out of your house in winter and into your house in summer by every means possible. Second, resolve to use every bit of the energy you pay for to the best advantage; that is, to use it most efficiently.

REDUCING HEAT FLOW

Insulation ranks high on any list of options for reducing heat flow. Insulation is more than thick batts of spun glass fiber or other bulky material. Insulation also includes double or triple glazing, storm doors, a vestibule, and all kinds of weatherstripping and caulking (Figure 4-2). But not all insulation is equally effective. Since heat rises, 4 inches of ceiling insulation prevent more heat from leaving a house than 4 inches of sidewall insulation. Today's standards call for at least 6 inches of loose-fill or batt insulation in ceilings. As an example of the difference insulation can make, consider an inside temperature of 75° F and outside of 0° F. Each 1,000 square feet of uninsulated ceiling area will lose 23,000 Btu per hour. By installing 6 inches of mineral wool insulation, the heat loss drops to only 2,900 Btu each hour. That's a reduction of 87 percent. Ceiling insulation also raises the surface temperature to help you feel warmer even with the same air temperature. With 6 inches of insulation, the ceiling temp will be around 73 degrees—12 degrees warmer than without insulation when outside temperatures are at zero.

Installing 3½-inch (thickness of 2x4 studs) in sidewalls reduces heat flow by three-fourths with a 75-degree difference in temperature (75°

FIGURE 4-2

Effectiveness of various forms of insulation and resulting heat losses through walls. Note differences in wall and ceiling temperatures with various thicknesses of insulation.

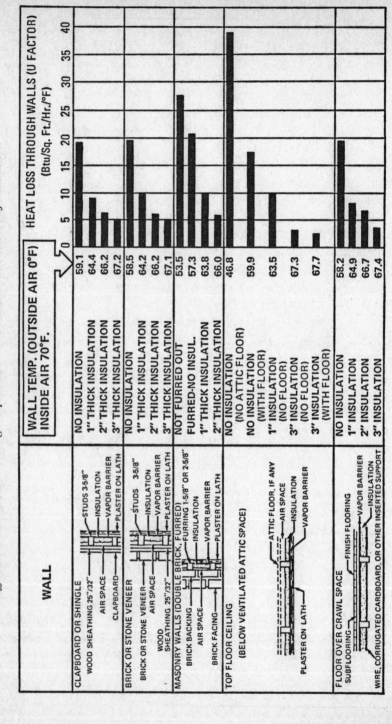

inside; zero outside). If sidewalls are not insulated, a professional can blow in loose fill wool or fill the space with a foam-in-place insulation. If 2-inch batts are already installed in walls, additional wool or foam cannot be added, and the cost of removing a wall to install more insulation is more than heat savings could justify over a reasonable period.

How much insulation you can effectively use depends on your location—see Figure 4-3. The R-values noted indicate the resistance to heat flow for insulations with those ratings.

Storm windows and storm doors are installed to insulate these areas of heavy heat loss. Two layers of glass trap air between them to retard heat flow, as air is a poor conductor of heat. Even better are hermetically-sealed double windows that prevent any airflow in or out of the space between the glass panes. Double windows or storm windows outside of single pane windows as part of the house were formerly considered adequate. But, with more insulation in ceilings and walls, a third layer of glass, usually inside, reduces heat losses further.

Air flows into and out of houses in large volumes, particularly when a wind is blowing. Houses with insulation properly installed tend to leak air less than older houses. However, the heat loss due to air infiltration and air moving out can be considerable. On a cold day with a good wind blowing, notice the difference in air temperature between rooms on the windward side and rooms on the leeward side of your house. Wind can actually blow heat inside the house to the far corner—and then out.

To reduce heat losses from air infiltration caulk around windows, corners, and joints of all kinds. Older caulks made from oil-base materials tend to harden as solvents evaporate. When caulks harden, they lose their ability to flex as materials expand and contract. So, the cracks open again and the wind blows through. Rubber-base caulks cost more but retain their elasticity for years to keep joints air tight. Of course, there is little point in sealing cracks and joints to prevent air infiltration and then leaving the damper of a fireplace chimney open to allow cold air to flow down the chimney and spill into the room.

Reducing inside temperatures slows heat loss by reducing the gradient between inside and outside temperatures. Keeping a thermostat at 68° F instead of 72 can cut heating bills by about 12 percent: that's a saving of one gallon of oil in eight. Reducing the night-time temperature to 60°—possibly even 55°—can cut heating costs another 8 to 10 percent. A thermostat keyed to a clock automatically reduces temperatures in late evening and turns up the heat again in the morning to avoid getting up in a cold house.

FIGURE 4-3

Heating zones for planning insulation. Increased insulation pays off as degree-days increase in northern states.

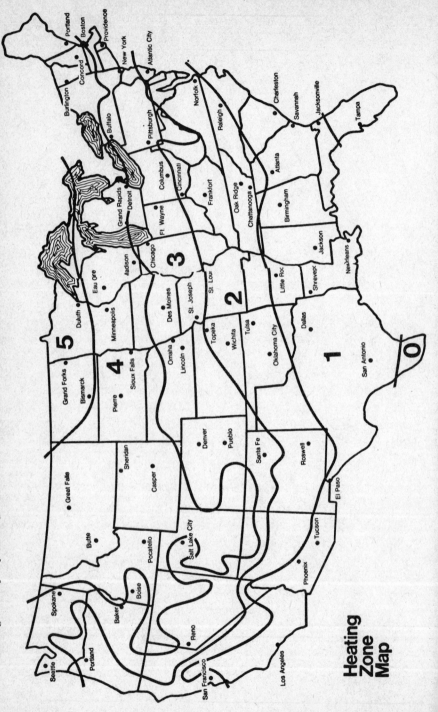

FIGURE 4-3 (Continued)
HEATING ZONE MAP

Heating Zone	Recommended for	
	Ceiling	*Floor*
0,1	R-26	R-11
2	R-26	R-13
3	R-30	R-19
4	R-33	R-22
5	R-38	R-22

R-Values	Batts or Blankets		Loose Fill (Poured In)		
	glass fiber	*rock wool*	*glass fiber*	*rock wool*	*cellulosic fiber*
R-11	3½"-4"	3"	5"	4"	3"
R-13	4"	4½"	6"	4½"	3½"
R-19	6"-6-1/2"	5¼"	8"-9"	6"-7"	5"
R-22	6½"	6"	10"	7"-8"	6"
R-26	8"	8½"	12"	9"	7"-7-1/2"
R-30	9½"-10½"	9"	13"-14"	10"-11"	8"
R-33	11"	10"	15"	11"-12"	9"
R-38	12"-13"	10½"	17"-18"	13"-14"	10"-11"

Many of the same tactics apply to keeping the inside of a house cool in summer. Turn the thermostat up to reduce the difference between outside and inside air temperatures.

GAINING MORE HEAT

Gaining the maximum usable heat from any fuel calls for using improved technology wherever possible. If you have not installed a new oil burner or furnace in your house within the past five years, you could be missing out on significant savings.

Two new systems for burning home heating oil more efficiently are now available. One system, "flame retention," derives its name from the burner's characteristics of burning oil just beyond the end of the burner head. The flame is kept there by negative pressure. Thus, the flame is "retained" near the head. A second system, a blue-flame burner, operates in its own special furnace. A two-stage system mixes oil and air more effectively than in other systems to achieve more complete combustion—hence, the blue flame. At this writing, blue-flame burners are not available as replacements; you must buy the complete furnace. However, an all-new furnace could be a better option than merely replacing the burner if yours is more than 15 years old. Operating a furnace burner for 15 years is roughly equivalent to driving one car 500,000 miles. Even without the available new technology, replacement could be economical.

Replacing an existing burner in a hot-air furnace or boiler has achieved savings 20-36 percent. Translated into gallons of fuel oil, the 36 percent improvement reduced consumption by 479 gallons for a typical house in one area. At 53 cents/gallon, saving 479 gallons reduced home heating expense by $249.08. For that installation the cost of the burner replacement was recovered in just over one year.

Two efficiencies are important when comparing oil burners. One is peak efficiency—the relationship between the oil's heat content and heat released by a burner adjusted for best burning. Older furnaces operate in the 70-80 percent range. New flame retention burners deliver up to 90 percent of the oil's heat.

Average or seasonal efficiency is more difficult to measure. Over a full season older high-pressure oil burners may deliver only 50-55 percent of available heat if air-fuel mixtures get out of adjustment. Frequent ON-OFF cycling also wastes fuel. Older burners shoot a high-pressure stream of oil that mixes with air and burns in a firebox. Each time the burner starts, the flame must warm the cold firebox and bits of oil are not fully burned. Smoke in the chimney is a sign of unburned or partially burned fuel oil. New flame retention burners operate without a firebox and reach their optimum burning efficiency in a fraction of a second. Thus, new burners improve on both efficiencies.

As a first step ask a dealer to test the burner in your furnace for combustion efficiency and measure the stack temperatures. A test device draws off a sample of flue gas and records the carbon dioxide (CO_2) content of the sample. A 15-percent CO_2 reading would indicate practically perfect combustion. Older high-pressure burners typically test in the 6 to 8 percent range when properly adjusted. Flame retention burners regularly record 11-12 percent CO_2. Blue-flame burners equal the flame retention burners and sometimes do a little better.

Stack temperatures represent another key to furnace or boiler efficiency. When heat is being wasted in the stack, temperatures may run as high as 700-800° F. For top furnace efficiency stack temperatures should be closer to 300-325° F—high enough to keep water vapor from condensing and to assure venting.

Natural gas furnaces or boilers typically burn with high efficiency and require little maintenance because operating pressure comes from the pipeline. Gas is a simple hydrocarbon molecule that naturally burns cleanly.

Electricity has become a more competitive "fuel" since the tripling of heating oil prices and the rising controlled price of natural gas. In certain areas of the United States where electrical rates are low, as in the Pacific

Northwest and the Tennessee Valley, heating with electricity makes economic sense. Along the Sunbelt states where air conditioning and light heating are required, a heat pump does double duty.

Any use of electricity for heating gains efficiency from using a heat pump. Operating on the same cycle as a common household refrigerator, a heat pump extracts heat from outside air or a nearby water source, pumps up the temperature, and distributes the heat throughout the house. For air conditioning, a simple switch reverses the process and heat is abstracted from inside the house and exhausted outside.

Heat pumps lose their efficiency for heating when outside air temperatures drop below 30° F. Sometimes a heat pump is installed along with an oil or gas burner as backup to supply heat when the heat pump works inefficiently. Or, resistance units supply heat directly. Research is going ahead with a plan to combine solar collectors with a heat pump to increase efficiency.

Balancing Your Hot-Air Heating System—One centrally located thermostat controls the heating cycle in most homes. Only the air temperature in the one room will remain relatively constant unless you balance your heating system to supply just the right amount to heat each room. You may vary the temperatures in different rooms—warmer in bathrooms and cooler in bedrooms. But, you save most when you avoid imbalances. Don't send more heat to two or three rooms than is needed just to keep temperatures comfortable in living areas where the thermostat is typically located. You can balance a hot-air system yourself; here's how:

Take each of the following steps in turn. By adjusting air-flow dampers or room registers, you can vary the amount of heated air coming into each room. When you reduce the air flow to one room, the air automatically flows to another room. Balancing is a cut-and-try method; change dampers and registers gradually. You may need to recycle the balancing several times before all rooms receive the desired amount of heat.

1. Begin by picking a cold day with little wind outside.
2. Calibrate several thermometers by lining them up near the thermostat. After 15-20 minutes read and compare the temperatures indicated on each. Mark the difference between the thermostat thermometer and each of the individual thermometers directly on the case. Cheap thermometers may indicate an error, but the error will repeat itself quite accurately. So, if No. 1 thermometer registers 70° F when the thermostat thermometer registers 72° F, you know No. 1 reads two degrees low and you can allow for it.

3. Hang a calibrated thermometer near the center of each room at chair height-about 3-4 feet from the floor. Air must circulate freely around the room thermometers.

4. Adjust the central house thermostat to 68°.

5. Check room registers to make sure they are free from obstructions and that furniture does not interfere with hot air circulation.

6. After the system has operated for half an hour or so, read each of the room thermometers. If wide variations are noted between rooms, write down the readings, because several tries will be needed to balance heat flow throughout the house.

7. Work the hot rooms first. If ducts to each room are accessible in a basement or crawl space, check for a damper in each duct. A damper is simply a sheetmetal vane or flap that turns inside the duct. A handle and pointer indicate valve-flap position. Partly close the damper to restrict the flow of hot air to the register in the hot room. Or, you may find a damper in each room register. Some registers can be adjusted to a partly open position and still permit opening and closing for night cooling. After adjusting dampers allow the house to adjust to the new heat-flow pattern for at least an hour. Then read the room thermometers again. If necessary repeat the process.

8. Cool rooms require opposite treatment—more hot air. Check duct dampers and room registers for damper position. Open them gradually if they are partly closed.

9. After adjusting duct dampers and room registers, you may find that one or more rooms still won't reach a comfortable temperature without overheating other rooms. The cool room may be too far from the furnace, the duct may be too small, or the hot air may be cooled before it reaches the room. If the duct passes through a cold area, insulate the duct to prevent heat loss. If that doesn't work, you may need to add a small electric or gas heater to heat the cool room during really cold weather. Otherwise, you waste heat by keeping the other rooms too warm.

Adjusting Furnace Air Flow—Unless the fan or blower in a hot-air furnace is moving the right volume of air through the exchanger, you will be losing heat up the chimney (and increasing your costs), or your rooms may feel drafty. Any time you change the firing rate of your furnace or change a burner, you should check air circulation through the furnace as follows:

1. Open all ducts and registers to full open. If you have previously balanced the distribution system (as noted earlier), mark positions of

dampers or registers before opening, so you can move them to their balanced position again.

2. Pick a cold day. Adjust the room thermostat to a temperature high enough to keep the furnace operating continuously while you are checking the fan or blower.

3. Drill or punch a small hole in the main warm-air outlet duct and the return air duct near the furnace. With a cooking thermometer inserted into the hole measure the temperature of the cool inlet air first and the warm outlet air second. Check the limit control on the furnace to make sure it is set at the 200-degree safety limit. Wait 15 or 20 minutes for the system to stabilize. Read the temperature of the return air and the outlet air.

4. Note the difference in temperature between the return air and the warm air. If the difference is greater than 85 to 95 degrees, the blower should be adjusted to move more air through the furnace. If the difference in temperatures is less than 85 degrees, adjust the blower to move less air through the furnace.

5. Adjust the volume of air moved by the blower by changing the ratio of pulleys at motor and blower. To increase volume, use a larger pulley on the motor or a smaller pulley on the fan. Or if the fan pulley is adjustable, increase the fan speed by decreasing the pulley diameter. To decrease blower volume, do the reverse—that is, decrease pulley diameter at the fan or increase pulley diameter at the motor. Make these pulley adjustments only when the heating system is turned OFF. Several tries may be necessary before achieving the desired air flow. Close the holes punched in the ducts with short pan-headed sheetmetal screws.

Another heat-saving trick is to drive the blower with a two-speed motor. When the furnace burner is OFF, the blower operates at a low speed to keep air circulating inside the house. When the burner is ON and the plenum temperature reaches its cut-in temperature, the blower switches to high speed. Continually circulating air reduces stratification and some of the hot air that rises to the ceiling is recycled throughout room spaces. If you opt to install a new burner, include a two-speed fan motor at the same time.

Adjusting The Furnace—If you are mechanically inclined, check your library for one of the handbooks published by one of the mechanical magazines for instructions on tuning up your furnace burner and blower. You may need replacement parts for the flame igniter and the nozzle that controls oil flow and firing rate. Otherwise, servicing the furnace may involve only cleaning and adjusting the air-fuel ratio. Oil-burners, particularly, work themselves out of adjustment. If you don't service the burner yourself, hire a professional for the job—at least once every two years, preferably every year.

Between calls by a professional repairman, you can adjust your heating system to generate and circulate more heat for fewer dollars by some or all of these tactics:

1. Check the chimney for draft. It should be free of soot and not plugged with something that may have fallen or blown in. Open the draft damper; it will be in the smoke pipe between the furnace and chimney. Blow cigarette or candle smoke a foot or two from the opening. The smoke should be drawn into the damper opening and up the chimney. If not, some plugging is possible. If you find the chimney heavily sooted, hire a professional to clean it with proper tools. A heavily sooted chimney is a fire hazard, and it clues you to a problem in combustion. A flame burning efficiently will not generate enough soot to clog a chimney.

2. Keep air filters clean. In a hot-air system, return air is filtered on the inlet side of the furnace. Loosely packed glass fiber filters strain the biggest particles of dirt and lint from the air. A sticky film on the fibers attracts some of the fine particles. Filters clogged with a collection of dirt and lint slow air flow. With less air flowing, less heat is transferred from the firebox to room air and that allows more heat to escape up the chimney. Open the access door on the inlet side of the furnace and remove the filter packs. Vacuum the incoming air surface and then blow through the back side—someplace outside the house. At least once or twice during a heating season, replace the air filters, as the fine dust cannot be vacuumed from the sticky fibers.

3. Adjust fan controls on a hot-air system. The blower turns ON automatically in a hot-air furnace when the temperature in the plenum reaches a comfortable level. Sometimes a blower may be set to come ON between 130-150 degrees and to shut OFF again when plenum temperature drop to 115-120 degrees. These temperatures are unnecessarily high when room temperatures average 68-72° F. Adjust the blower to come on earlier, when plenum temperatures reach 110°F and to stay on longer, until the plenum temperatures fall to 90°F. A two-speed blower avoids the loss of heat escaping up the chimney when the blower is OFF, because with a two-speed motor, the blower is always ON. You'll find the blower ON-OFF switches in a control box near the firebox end of the furnace.

Balancing a Hot-Water System—Follow the same step-by-step procedure for balancing a hot-water system as for a hot-air system. Depending on the design, you may adjust valves in the piping systems to each room radiator. Or, dampers in enclosed radiators can be adjusted to increase or decrease the air flow from the bottom past the radiator and out the upper grills.

Steam systems can be adjusted at each radiator vent. Do not attempt to regulate heat at steam radiators by partly opening the main valve. This valve must be fully closed or fully open to allow water to flow back to the boiler. Hot-water and steam systems change temperatures much more slowly than hot-air systems. You may need to change valve or vent positions gradually over several days when balancing a steam or hot-water system.

HEAT-SAVING TACTICS

Regardless of the fuel burned or type of distribution system, you can cut fuel costs by practicing all or most of these heat-saving tips—

1. Close off rooms not used. Shut off the air duct or water line to an unused sunroom, unused bedrooms, and storage areas. In addition to closing off the heat source, pad the air gap at the bottom of the door and weatherstrip around edges to keep cold air from escaping into the rest of the house.

2. Close doors and windows. If you prefer to sleep in a cool bedroom, shut off the heat at the register or radiator, then open the window a crack. Train your children to close doors quickly and tightly. Weatherstrip cracks or openings to attic or unheated spaces.

3. Check room thermostat temperature. Sometimes a thermostat is in error and controls house temperature to a different degree setting than indicated. If you set the thermostat at 68° F. and find the temperature actually hovers around 72°F., you are using an additional twelve percent fuel.

4. Pull drapes across windows at night for insulation. In living areas with large windows, drapes also present a warm surface and prevent loss of body heat by radiation to cold window surfaces. You feel more confortable even though room air temperature remains constant.

5. Install reflective insulation between radiators and an outside wall. An aluminum foil layer over a one-inch thickness of insulation prevents as much as thirty five percent of the radiator heat from escaping through the wall. Reflective foil radiates the heat out into the room.

6. On bright sunny days, open drapes or curtains and turn on the blower to distribute solar heat that streams into south-facing rooms. As soon as the sun disappears, draw curtains or drapes to trap heat inside.

7. Install an outside air vent to the furnace if possible. About 2,000 cubic feet or air are consumed in burning one gallon of fuel oil. As this warm air is burned and exhausted up the chimney as smoke and carbon dioxide, an equal amount of replacement cold air must be drawn in from outside and heated. Burning unheated air drawn directly from outside through a separate duct reduces drafts, retains more heat in the house, and avoids the leat loss from exhausted air.

8. Add a radiant panel or heat lamp to the bathroom. Since we wear fewer clothes in a bathroom at times, temperatures must be higher to maintain comfort. But, instead of ducting extra heat to the bathroom 24 hours a day, turn on a heat lamp only when needed.

9. Keep air registers and radiators free of obstructions. Don't place furniture directly over ducts of in front of radiators and expect them to work effectively.

10. Turn the thermostat down to 55° F any time you will be away from the house for a full day or more.

The above tips are only a few of the many you can use. Check the books and publications listed at the end of this chapter for other ideas.

MORE COOLING FOR FEWER DOLLARS

Insulation, weather stripping, and caulking work even more effectively for air conditioning (A/C). The cost of keeping the inside of a house cooled to 75° F. when the outside temperature is 95° F is three to five times more expensive than keeping the same house warmed to 70° F. when the outside temperature is only 50° F. Air conditioning systems are complex, use electricity for power, and much of the energy is used for condensing water vapor out of the air to maintain comfort.

Basically, when you buy air conditioning, you buy comfort. How much comfort you choose to buy affects the cost of A/C. A window unit to keep a sleeping room comfortable obviously costs less than a central unit to cool the whole house. How many degrees lower than outside air temperatures you set the thermostat significantly affects costs; each degree lower than 80° F. when outside temperatures are 95° F. or higher increases costs by five to six percent depending on your A/C system.

Practice these tips for getting more cooling comfort at less cost—

1. Leave storm windows and doors from winter installed for summer to increase insulation. Keeping hot air out of the house in summer pays higher dividends than keeping cold air out in winter.

2. Apply a reflective aluminum coating to your roof. Millions of tiny aluminum plates reflect the sun's radiant energy. Temperatures inside a house can be ten degrees lower when the roof acts as a mirror instead of absorbing heat.

3. Install an attic fan to blow out hot air that builds up under the roof before it penetrates inside the house. On mildly hot days an attic fan may be all the cooling needed—a further saving.

4. Shade windows with trees, blinds, or screens to keep heat away from the house. Windows particularly need to be shaded to keep the sun's radiant energy from streaming in through the glass. Roll shades on the outside of windows are more effective than shades inside because once the sun's radiant energy gets inside the house, it must be removed with A/C equipment. Keeping the energy outside is cheaper than removing it.

5. Exhaust cooking heat and shower or dryer steam with a ceiling fan.

6. Schedule house cleaning chores that release lots of moisture in the air, such as floor mopping, early in the morning or postpone such tasks to cool days. Don't leave wet clothes to dry in a kitchen, laundry, or bathroom, as this moisture must be removed by the dehumidifying section of the A/C unit. Ironing clothes also releases moisture, particularly if you use a steam iron.

7. Begin air-conditioning early on days forecast to be hot.

8. Close hot-air registers in any room where a window A/C unit is operating to prevent cooled air from draining into the duct system; cool air is dense and collects near the floor.

9. Clean unit fans and radiators frequently to keep them free of dust and lint. Efficient heat transfer depends on air movement, so make sure the air passages and the filter are not plugged. Lint and dust act as insulators.

SAVING ELECTRICITY

Improving technology countered inflation and kept electrical rates low for years. Now, environmental concerns, quadrupling cost of oil, rising natural gas prices, a growing dissatisfaction with nuclear power, and few sites for hydroelectrical development are pushing up the cost of electricity. So—it makes uncommonly good sense to save it and cut your monthly cost of power. Here's how—

1. Use less hot water if your tank is heated electrically. Keep faucet washers in leak-tight condition. Hot water faucets drip more frequently than cold because washers deteriorate quicker at hot water temperatures. A

steady drip can waste hundreds of gallons each month. Insulate hot water pipes that run considerable distances from the heater. Install a flow-control valve at the nozzle in your shower to control flow. A quick shower uses only a quarter of the hot water used in a tub bath. Wash clothes in warm rather than hot water and rinse in cold. Water temperatures above 90 degrees do not improve washing action. Wash only full loads of clothes and dishes. If your automatic dishwasher includes a drying cycle, open the door and let the dishes air dry.

2. Keep appliances working efficiently. Lint in a clothes dryer, for example, impedes the free flow of air and forces the dryer to work harder and longer to dry the same batch of clothes. Clean the lint trap before each use. Vacuum or blow the dust and lint off the cooling coils under or in back of a refrigerator to maintain efficiency. Dust and lint act as insulators causing the motor and compressor to work longer maintaining an even temperature inside refrigerator or freezer.

3. Use lights sparingly. Even President Johnson created a stir when he cautioned White House staffers to turn off unused lights. Wherever possible substitute fluorescent lights for incandescent bulbs; fluorescents produce up to four times as much light for each watt of electricity as incandescents. Get in the habit of turning out lights when leaving a room and train children to turn OFF radios and T.V. when they are not actually listening or watching. Switch to low-power bulbs where light is needed only for general lighting and use point lamps for reading and close work.

FOR FURTHER READING

Since the energy crunch of 1974 and federal emphasis on energy conservation and alternative systems, a rush of books and pamphlets has appeared. Following are a few useful sources of information for further study if these few ideas have attracted your attention to the immense possibilities for reducing energy costs in your home:

"Home Heating"
"Firewood for Your Fireplace"
"How to Save Money by Insulating Your Home"
"In the Bank or Up the Chimney?"
"Save Energy, Save Money"
"Solar Hot Water and Your Home"
"Tips for Energy Savers"

The above publications are published by various agencies of the U.S. Government and are available from the Consumer Information Center,

Pueblo, Colorado 81009. Some are free; others cost a nominal sum that tends to increase each year. Write to the Center for a current catalog and price list.

How to Improve the Efficiency of Your Oil-Fired Furnace, LC 1085, U.S. Dept. of Commerce, 14th and Constitution Ave. N.W., Washington D.C. 20230.

350 Ways to Save Energy (and Money) in Your Home and Car by Henry R. Apies, Seichi Konzo, Jean Calvin, and Wayne Thoms, Crown Publishers, New York.

Energy in the Home—Changing Your Habits, HE 407, Cooperative Extension Service, Purdue University, West Lafayette, Indiana.

150 Ways to Save Energy and Money by Vi Bradley Felton, Pilot Books, 347 Fifth Avenue, New York, New York 10016.

"Fuel-Saving Devices for the Home," Consumer Reports, January 1977.

"101 Ways to Cut Home Energy Costs—Right Now!", Popular Mechanics, September, 1977.

SUMMING UP

Managing expenses for heating, cooling, and lighting falls into the category of controlling the many small but repetitive money leaks. A small saving of fuel or electricity repeated daily or weekly amounts to a really big sum over a year's time. Keeping your home comfy but spending 25-35 percent less than you might expect is reasonable and allows you to restructure your spending plan. The cost-cutting ideas detailed were—

- How to select the most cost-effective fuel when remodeling or building.

- Benefits from upgrading your furnace and heating system.

- Understanding the investment trade-offs and payouts.

- How to get the most heat from your furnace through system balancing.

- Tips and tactics for saving heat and keeping cool with air conditioning.

- How to save electrical power with minor changes in living habits.

5

SAVE MONEY ON HOUSING
WHETHER YOU'RE RENTING OR BUYING

To find the best answer for housing your family, analyze a number of factors, including—

- Exchange costs, the money you spend to first buy and then sell a house, trailer, or other housing unit.

- How much house can your family afford?

- Mortgage costs, repayment time, and interest.

- Operating costs. Surprising differences in the day-in, day-out costs of operating a house show up according to the way you manage these expenses.

- How to buy furnishings and home equipment that suits you best at the right price.

The place you hang your hat bulks first among most families' necessary expenses. Housing expense is infinitely more varied and, therefore, subject to greater management control than food. Family size, your wife's nesting instincts, and your income level—all affect your choice of housing and how much you spend.

WHICH SHELTER FOR YOU?

Selecting a house or other shelter is a long-term proposition. If you make a mistake, you may have to live with it for many years. So, consider—

- How often do you move? Does your company pack you off to some new location every 2 or 3 years?
- Is your family home-oriented? Does your wife like to stay home, sew clothes and curtains, work creatively in the kitchen, and generally consider the home the hub of her existence? Do you spend more of your time outside the home on fishing trips, etc.?
- How much money could you spend for housing?

● What is the *modus operandi* of your friends and associates? Do they live in houses, apartments, mobile homes, or boats?

Buy or Rent? In the United States, about one out of every five families will change locations this year. Many large corporations with widespread operations move their work force around like checkers on a country- or world-wide board. If your job requires you to move often, renting may very well cost less than buying—overall. The important figure is the cost per year. One way to determine whether you should rent or buy is to make a break-even analysis. When you buy, you may also have to sell. So, you must balance buying and selling expense (exchange costs) against the lower owning and operating cost and possible investment gain. Consider the example in Figure 5-1. Remember, this is only an example. You may

FIGURE 5-1: Housing Rent-or-Buy Analysis

Decision: Should you buy or rent a house?

Home prices at $50,000—10% down

Mortgage loan—$45,000 @ 9½% interest, 29-year loan period

Rental—Various prices

Buying and operating costs for the house:

Initial Buying Costs

Mortgage lender's fee (2½%)		$1,125	
Sales tax (1%)		500	
Stamps (0.1%)		50	
Title insurance ($4.50/$1,000)		203	
Inspection & appraisal fee		100	
Credit report		20	
Survey		100	
Legal opinion		50	
	Subtotal	$2,148	$2,148

Selling Costs

Real estate agent's commission (7%)		$3,500	
3 month's loss on unoccupied house		1,200	
Prepayment penalty		800	
Discount points (2)		1,000	
	Subtotal	$6,500	$ 6,500
	TOTAL EXCHANGE POINTS		$8,648

Annual Variable Operating Costs

Insurance		$250	
Taxes		900	
Maintenance (1½% of value)		750	
Interest loss on down payment (6½%)		325	
Mortgage interest + interest loss on accumulating equity		4,275	
	Subtotal	$6,500	
Less income tax saving from taxes and interest at 32%		1,568	
	Subtotal	$4,932	$ 4,932
	Average Monthly Cost	$411	
Cumulative Cost after 1 year			$13,580

be interested in a $35,000 house—or a $100,000 house. The analysis technique, however, remains the same.

Many families tend to overlook the big items in exchange costs. Take maintenance expense, for example. If you buy directly from a builder, the expense of maintaining a new house is usually small for several years. But, you'll probably want to plant a lawn and shrubs, build on a patio, add shelves in the garage, or install wall-to-wall carpeting. When you sell, some of these additions may increase either the sales price or its salability—sometimes. Few homeowners, however, will recoup full value of landscaping and interior finishing costs when they sell.

If you buy an older home, possibly one that has been around for 50 to 75 years, you can figure maintenance costs in excess of the annual 1½% of the house value allowed. Even houses 4 to 5 years begin to need regular repairs.

Two other items in the list of Annual Costs (Fig. 5-1) deserve comment: (1) Interest loss on your down payment. The $5,000 down payment could have been invested. At a conservative return of 6½%, the $325 per year loss of interest represents a cost to you of owning the house. (2) Gain from the income-tax saving on taxes and interest varies according to your tax bracket. At 32% in the example, the $1,568 represents your gain if you paid taxes and interest of $4,900 rather than spending the same amount for rent.

Table 5A compares the costs of renting vs. buying a typical home, as detailed in Figure 5-1.

TABLE 5A: Comparison of Owning vs. Renting Costs

| | BUY* | | | | | | | | RENT | | | |
| | | | | $400/Month | | $500/Month | | $600/Month | | $500/Month + 8% Annually | |
Year	Cumulative cost	Average cost/ year	Cost/ year	Cumulative cost	Cost/ year	Cumulative cost	Cost/ year	Cumulative cost	Cost/ year	Cumulative cost
1	$13,580	$13,580	$4,800	$4,800	$6,000	$6,000	$7,200	$7,200	$6,000	$6,000
2	18,512	9,255	4,800	9,600	6,000	12,000	7,200	14,400	6,480	12,480
3	23,444	7,815	4,800	14,400	6,000	18,000	7,200	21,600	6,998	19,478
4	28,376	7,094	4,800	19,200	6,000	24,000	7,200	28,800	7,558	27,036
5	33,308	6,662	4,800	24,000	6,000	30,000	7,200	36,000	8,163	35,199
6	38,240	6,373	4,800	28,800	6,000	36,000	7,200	43,200	8,816	44,015
7	43,172	6,167	4,800	33,600	6,000	42,000	7,200	50,400	9,521	53,536
8	48,104	6,013	4,800	38,400	6,000	48,000	7,200	57,600	10,283	63,819
9	53,036	5,893	4,800	43,200	6,000	54,000	7,200	64,800	11,106	74,925
10	57,968	5,797	4,800	48,000	6,000	60,000	7,200	72,000	11,994	86,919

*See Fig. 5-1 for analysis of exchange costs associated with buying and owning a house.

20%+ Savings Idea

Bob Symonds found himself on the musical-chair circuit with a big computer company. Every third year, as regular as clockwork, he packed up and moved across country to a new assignment. When he figured the costs of buying and selling a house, he decided to rent. He found a house he might have bought for lease at $250 per month because the owner couldn't sell in a down market. Compared to his last house, Bob figures to save at least $2100 over 3 years. Plus, he had no problems selling the house when the company uprooted him for his next move—or the expense of maintaining the leased house.

How about profiting from house appreciation over the years? For many families the equity in their personal residence has turned out to be the best investment they could have made. Investing in a house actually puts inflation to work in your favor. Here's how—Using the example in Figure 5-1, you have a $5,000 down payment invested plus $8,648 in exchange costs for a buy-and-sell round trip. Houses have been appreciating recently at a rate of 10 to 16% yearly. Conservatively assume the price of the house appreciates 12% yearly or 1% each month. After one year the house is worth $56,000. At 1%/month you can recover the exchange costs in a little over 17¼ months. After another 10 months your $5,000 down payment has grown to $10,000 in equity—even after paying exchange costs. Thus, in 27¼ months, the $5,000 originally invested has doubled. Minor quibbles can be raised at this simplistic example, but the pluses and minuses tend to cancel out. The central point is that the equity in your house protects some of your capital from being eroded by inflation. If you should sell your house and buy another one, the price of the new house will also have increased, but your down payment will have grown faster because inflation was working for you on the money you had borrowed from the mortgage lender.

Trading Off Commuting Costs for a Better House—Spend your money on a house or for commuting? It's your choice. Unless you lump car operation costs, train tickets, or bus fares along with mortgage loan payments, you may unbalance your spending plan. When you bundle commuting expense with mortgage loan payments, your options boil down to—(1) Buy a big, expensive house close in and spend less on commuting, or (2) Buy a smaller, less expensive house far out in the boonies and spend more of your income to commute.

High gasoline prices, 70-80 cents/gallon and rising, impact your housing decision if you drive to work. Buying in a location far from public transit or potential car poolers could lead to punishing car costs and, possibly, a white elephant of a house when you decide to sell.

Suppose you decide to buy a $50,000 house and borrow $40,000. With loan interest at 9½ percent over a 25-year period, your monthly payments would total $349.48. Taxes and hazard insurance are extra. Your dream house, however, is located 25 miles from your work and no public transportation is available. Commuting alone by car can be figured conservatively at 15 cents/mile or $7.50/day for a 50-mile round trip. Over a month's time you'd spend $150 on car expense (including depreciation). Further, you would probably need a second car mainly to drive back and forth to work. Monthly spending for a mortgage loan and car expense would total $499.48 plus taxes, insurance, and utilities.

Instead of owning and driving a second car, you could borrow $17,168 and cover the interest and loan amortization over 25 years for the same $150/month spent for commuting. To apply the full saving to a bigger house, you would have to live close enough to walk to work. A more reasonable option near public transportation might cut commuting cost by bus to $1.00/day. Or, you could trade rides in a car pool to limit expense to $5/week. Either alternative cuts commuting cost to $20/month. The difference between $150 and $20/month would service a mortgage loan of $14,879 at 9½ percent interest for 25 years. With a 20-percent down payment, you could finance a home costing $68,599 instead of $50,000 and spend the same number of dollars—$479.48/month.

Obviously, this concept of trading commuting expense for a bigger, better house would call for higher taxes, more maintenance, and higher hazard insurance premiums. These facets of the trade-off do not disturb the big question—should you spend your limited dollars for a bigger house or for commuting?

Two tables help you figure the trade-offs. Table 5B extends daily commuting costs to monthly and yearly totals.

Table 5C converts monthly commuting expense to equivalent mortgage loan servicing costs at interest rates from 8½ to 11 percent. If your monthly commuting costs $75/month, simply add the mortgage servicing costs for $15 and $60, for example.

Combining mortgage service costs and commuting expense opens a number of alternatives:

1. Using public transportation for commuting eliminates the need for a second car. Ordinarily, bus and train fares will cost less than commuting by car when you recognize full operating costs.

2. When public transportation is not available, joining a car pool may also eliminate the need for a second car.

TABLE 5B: Commuting Expense

Daily Cost	Monthly Cost*	Annual Cost**
$ .40	$ 8	$ 96
.50	10	120
.75	15	180
1.00	20	240
2.00	40	480
3.00	60	720
5.00	100	1,200
6.00	120	1,440
7.50	150	1,800
8.00	160	1,920
10.00	200	2,400

*20   commuting days average per month
**240 commuting days per year
    52 weeks x 5 = 260
    10 days vacation
    10 holidays &
       sick leave   20
               240 days

TABLE 5C: Mortgage Servicing Trade-off Against Commuting Expense

Interest & Amortization of Loan—25 Years—Monthly

Monthly Commuting Expense	8½% $8.052*	9% $8.392*	9½% $8.737	10% $9.087	10½% $9.442	11% $9.801
$8	$994	$953	$916	$883	$847	$816
10	1,242	1,192	1,145	1,100	1,059	1,020
15	1,863	1,787	1,716	1,651	1,589	1,530
20	2,484	2,383	2,289	2,201	2,118	2,041
40	4,968	4,766	4,578	4,402	4,236	4,081
60	7,452	7,150	6,867	6,603	6,355	6,122
100	12,419	11,916	11,446	11,005	10,591	10,203
120	14,903	14,299	13,735	13,206	12,709	12,244
150	18,629	17,874	17,168	16,507	15,886	15,305
160	19,871	19,066	18,313	17,608	16,946	16,325
200	24,839	23,832	23,895	22,099	21,182	20,406

*Monthly payment for interest and principal amortization for each $1,000 of original loan value.

3. Using a variety of commuting systems calls for more figuring, but the concept still applies. You may find that the cost of driving to a train, bus, or ferry terminal, riding that system, and then transferring to another bus or streetcar costs $2 to $4 daily. Convert daily commuter fares into a monthly total and compare those costs against a higher price for a close-in house, apartment, or condominium. In each case bundle commuting expense with mortgage loan and related housing costs.

4. Buying an older, close-in house could be a bargain when you pay for extensive remodeling with savings from commuting. Allocate your

savings on commuting to two parts: (1) Higher mortgage loan payments for a more desirable house. (2) Monthly payments on a separate remodeling loan.

Table 5C relates the difference in loan values you can finance at different interest rates. For example, $100 cut from monthly commuting expense would service a loan of $12,419 at 8½ percent interest. If you must pay 9½ percent interest, the same $100/month saving would service a loan of only $11,446. Table 5C considers only a loan repayment period of 25 years. Shorter repayment periods would reduce a loan—to $11,523 for a 20-year loan at 8½ percent at $100/month. Longer periods would enlarge a loan—to $13,005 for a 30-year loan at 8½ percent at $100/month. Your friendly banker can provide the figures for other periods and interest rates.

Finally—this concept of trading commuting dollars for housing loan dollars yields a long-term benefit—equity build-up. By spending dollars on your house, you save that portion credited as payment on the loan principal each month. No long-term savings accrue from the dollars you spend on commuting.

Remodel or Sell and Rebuy? Similar to the buy-or-rent decision is one faced by many families as income and/or family size expands. If you are thinking of selling your small, inadequate house in order to buy or build a larger house, you will face exchange costs similar to those detailed in Fig. 5-1. Consider, instead, adding on a new wing or finishing off existing space in your present house to gain the room you need. You may find that the exchange costs saved will pay for the added space you need. However, consider the following items as part of your trade-off analysis—

● Overbuilding on a small lot in a neighborhood that is definitely stabilized at a fixed price level may not be economical.

● Even a remodeled house will not achieve a more prestigious address—if this was one of your goals.

● Moving to a new, bigger house in a upgraded neighborhood may force you and your family to cut the friendly ties with neighbors, community, and school that you may have built up in your old location.

Much of the pain and strain from a decision to remodel or sell or rebuy can be avoided by looking ahead when you first buy. If your housing needs are due to expand, look for a house with space to add rooms on the second floor or in a basement. Or buy a larger house and omit the costly gimmicks available in a small house. The gimmicks can be added later, but in the meantime, you have the space you need.

Stretching your budget to buy a bigger house in a neighborhood that is likely to remain stable and suitable for the rising and growing family can also save the cost of selling and rebuying. Determine the dollars available for housing in your Spending Plan and ask a lending officer to help you decide how big a mortgage loan you can handle. (See pages 126 and 127.)

A young couple, getting started, could advantageously live in a small apartment and accumulate a down payment. But instead of using the down payment money to reduce interest costs, the couple could use it to buy a bigger, better house. A family needs more room as children arrive. Also, most young men just establishing a family can look forward to a rising income. Buying a larger house might pinch the budget for a few years, but the savings of exchange costs are likely to be substantial.

You may detect what appears to be a reversal of attitude on using credit. In any trade-off you are looking for the lowest cost for equivalent value. Housing credit costs least (except subsidized education loans)—so, it makes sense to borrow for housing and pay cash for other purchases.

Shopping for a House—For most families, buying a house is a major decision and warrants considerable study, as follows—

• Determine first how much you can spend for housing from your Spending Plan analysis in Chapter 8. Make sure your allocation accounts for everything from mortgage payments to light bulbs.

• Shop widely and intensively. If you are new to a city or area, find temporary housing first. Take time to search out neighborhoods, drive over alternate routes to your work, learn about school systems, pick up a feel for trends—which areas are headed for blight, which areas are building prestige, and where you will be convenient to the activities that interest your family. Remember, location is the most important element in a housing decision.

• Evaluate houses, builders, and local designs. Land use and house designs vary widely around the country. Look at as many houses as several Realtors will show you. Only after studying the market thoroughly will you begin to sense a pattern of values and prices.

• Don't depend entirely on Realtors. Drive around desirable neighborhoods on weekends. Look for owners who are selling houses themselves. Look on company bulletin boards, in plant newspapers, and Trading Posts for leads to houses that could be priced below the market. The "market" is a changeable thing that exists in the minds of Realtors and is determined only in part by actual purchases. Find out for yourself why different houses are priced differently.

$3800 Savings Idea

Harriet Belcher had spent days riding around in a Realtor's station wagon looking at houses she sensed were overpriced. She and her husband had just moved to a West Coast city where he had found a job in aircraft maintenance. They were still living with their three young children in a motel room when Ron brought home a copy of the company newspaper. It listed homes for sale among other entries. Harriet bundled up the kids and started finding her way around to the addresses noted. Most of the houses were for sale by their owner. It took some digging, but she found one that suited their needs to a T— and it was close to Ron's work. Harriet examined the house in detail and negotiated a sale with the owner herself. "Compared to the houses I saw in company with the Realtor, I figure Ron and I saved over $3800 on our $42,000 house."

Closing the Deal—No owner or Realtor expects to sell a house at the asking price. Such a price is simply a place to begin bargaining.

When closing the deal for the house you have selected, remember—

● A Realtor cannot refuse to transmit to the owner any bona fide offer accompanied by earnest money.

● A house that has been on the market for several months may be ripe for a cut-to-the-bone offer, but make sure you know why the house has not sold.

● The "ridiculous" offer sometimes buys the house. When you see many houses standing vacant in an area, only the bargain houses are selling. When you have selected the house you want, don't hesitate to make a "ridiculous" offer. A figure 20% below list may be accepted by a desperate owner—particularly one who has moved out of town. If you don't make the offer, you'll never know.

Mobile Homes, Co-ops, and Condominiums—Consider mobile homes if your job requires frequent moves. Mobile homes can be factory built and transported to small lots in an attractive park—both of these factors can save you money. Mobile homes, though fixed on blocks most of the time, can be moved. Professional towing fees for the largest roadable homes are still much less than the exchange costs for buying and selling a house.

Basically there are two disadvantages of mobile home living—

● Your family may feel like gypsies. However, if you move regularly, you will put down few deep roots in a community anyway.

● Buying a mobile home frequently requires more cash and higher monthly payments than buying a house. Terms for mobile homes may require 15 to 25% down with the remainder financed over periods no longer than 12-15 years.

Cooperative apartments are another combination form of owning and renting. Laws vary in different states, but you do not actually own your own co-op apartment; instead, you own a share in a corporation or trust which, in turn, owns the apartment house.

Condominium apartments are replacing most cooperatives. In a condominium, you actually own your own apartment under an exact definition of space, and you can sell it, rent it, lease it, or leave it empty without affecting the surrounding apartments, or the apartment house.

FINANCING YOUR HOME

Mortgage Costs—Nearly everyone buys a home with the aid of a mortgage; most families because they can't pay cash, others because they obtain low-cost financing and can use the deductions from taxes and interest.

Two major factors affect mortgage costs—repayment period and interest rates. Table 5D briefly sorts out these effects for a principal amount of $1000. These figures are for an amortized loan; that is, each monthly amount over the mortgage period includes a payment on the principal along with interest. At the end of the loan period, the principal plus all interest are paid in full.

Table 5D highlights two points: (1) Repayment time has a greater effect than the interest rate on monthly payments. (2) Repayment period greatly affects the dollars paid in interest over the mortgage period.

Shopping for Financing—A surprising variety of organizations loan money for home purchases. Sources of home loans include savings and loan associations, banks, particularly savings banks, fraternal organizations, credit unions, insurance companies, and individuals. Check them all before you sign up for differences in cost and interpretations of your ability to repay.

Conventional, Federal Housing Administration (FHA) insured, and Veterans Administration (VA) guaranteed mortgage loans also differ. Mortgage companies making conventional loans usually require higher down payments than either the FHA or VA because the loans are not backed by the U.S. Government. Interest costs are usually similar, but conventional mortgages can usually be obtained quicker than FHA and

TABLE 5D: Factors That Affect Mortgage Financing Costs

Effect of Interest Rates

Rate	Monthly payment required to repay $1,000 in 25 years	Total interest paid during 25 years for each $1,000
8%	$7.72	$1,315
8½	8.06	1,416
9	8.40	1,518
9½	8.74	1,621
10	9.09	1,726
10½	9.45	1,833
11	9.81	1,940
11½	10.17	2,049
12	10.54	2,160

Effect of Repayment Period (Per $1,000 Principal Amount)

Repayment period (years)	Monthly payment to repay principal and interest @ 9½%	Total interest paid during period @ 9½%
10	$12.94	$553
15	10.45	880
20	9.33	1,237
25	8.74	1,621
30	8.41	2,027
35	8.22	2,451
40	8.11	2,888

VA loans. FHA and VA loans extend over long repayment periods. VA loans are usually the most liberal, and new houses within prescribed dollar limits can be obtained with little or no down payment and only nominal closing costs.

To borrow under FHA, you and the house you intend to buy must meet a number of requirements. It is the review of these rules and how they apply to each transaction that eats up the time and tangles the red tape. Your best bet is to have a quiet chat with a savings and loan company officer of an organization authorized by the FHA to make insured loans.

When you begin to shop for a mortgage to buy a specific house, use a chart similar to the Mortgage Comparator in Fig. 5-2. Obtain the information you need for comparing costs without committing yourself to a signed loan application.

In addition to closing costs, ask about specific clauses—

● Prepayment Penalty. What will your costs be in case you pay off the mortgage ahead of the full period?

FIGURE 5-2: Mortgage Comparator

	Lender #1	Lender #2	Lender #3
Name of Potential Lender			
Address			
Person Contacted			
Down Payment Required			
Loan Amount			
Interest Rate			
Monthly Payment (Principal + Interest)			
Escrow Payments (?) (Taxes + Insurance)			
Type of Mortgage			
Total Mortgage Cost (Monthly Payments x No. of Months)			
Dollar Cost of Interest (Total Cost−Loan Amount)			
Appraisal Fee			
Survey Fee			
Title Search and Insurance			
Revenue Stamps			
Recording Fees			
Credit Check			
Mortgage Finder's Fee			
Mortgage Service Charges			
Other Costs			
Total Loan Costs			
Open-End Mortgage			
Prepayment Penalty			
Insurance Required			
Appliance Package			

● **Taxes and Insurance Escrow Account.** Will your mortgage agreement require you to deposit a monthly amount equal to 1/12 of the estimated taxes and insurance on the house you buy?

● **Insurance.** Are you required to purchase fire and extended damage insurance on the house and mortgage insurance on your own life from the mortgage company?

● **Mortgage Loan Insurance.** Does the quoted interest rate include loan insurance premium? Commercial companies offer loan insurance on conventional (non U.S. backed) loans similar to FHA insurance. The usual fee is ¼ percent plus a one-time charge of ½ to 1 point.

● **Interruption Provisions.** Some mortgages include automatic extension privileges in case you are hospitalized or unable to work for a short period.

● **Open-End Provisions.** Will the mortgage permit borrowing later to finance improvements without refinancing?

Financing Home Improvements—Want to finish off rooms in the basement, add another bathroom, rebuild a roof, or build on another room or two to accommodate a growing family? Before plunging into such a program, investigate the various possible sources of money. In terms of their potential cost, they might rank as follows—

● Open-End Mortgage. If your mortgage includes an open-end provision, interest rate will likely continue at the same rate.

● FHA Home Improvement Loan. Title I FHA home improvement loans are limited to $10,000 for repayment over periods as long as 12 years. Interest on the first $2500 is figured at 5.5% (not simple interest), and the amount from $2501 to $10,000 is figured at 4.5%.

● Bank or S&L Home Improvement Loan. Rather than depend on FHA backing, individual lenders develop their own programs with rates around 12-14%.

● Life Insurance Loan. Consider the cash values built up in your life insurance policies as collateral for borrowing (see Chapter 10).

● Collateral Loan. By pledging collateral, such as stocks, you can often borrow from a bank at rates 2 to 4% above the current prime rate.

● Second Mortgage. As risk increases, so do interest rates. Generally, you'll find a second mortgage costs from 12 to 20% interest.

● Credit Union or Other Organization. Don't overlook such semi-parental organizations as your company's credit union, your lodge, or some other source of funds for home improvements.

Housing Insurance—Regardless of where you live, you need insurance on your dwelling (if you own) and on your furnishings and possessions if you own or rent. You also need liability insurance for protection against possible lawsuits and theft insurance. You can buy each of these insurance policies separately, but you'll save money if you buy them in a package.

● Fire and Extended Coverage. Mortgage companies insist that the house be covered with this basic home policy at least up to the mortgage amount. You can buy your fire and extended coverage policy from the mortgage company, but you can usually do better elsewhere. The usual fire and extended coverage policy affords protection from fire, lightning, hail, windstorm, damage from falling aircraft and land vehicles other than your own (or a renter's), explosion, civil commotion, and smoke. Most companies also issue a "broad form" or "further extended coverage" policy that, in addition to the hazards listed for the fire and extended coverage policy, also protects you against glass breakage (either with or without a deductible), collapse due to ice or snow, reimbursement for living expenses while your home is being repaired, bursting of water or steam pipes, damage by vehicles driven by a member of the family, freezing of plumbing, and many other listed hazards. Broad form policies must specifically list a hazard; otherwise, it isn't covered. Another, even broader policy, variously called "all risk" or "all loss," covers everything except certain hazards, such as termite damage, wear and tear, water backing up through sewers, war, landslide, settling, and earthquake. In "all risk" policies, only listed hazards are excluded— everything else is covered.

● Family Liability. This protects you and your family when other persons are injured or their property is damaged on your premises. Liability policies also cover property damages by some member of your family away from your own house and lot. Suppose a delivery man trips over a crack in your sidewalk, falls, and breaks a leg. If he sues, your family liability policy protects you up to the limit of the policy and pays for defense of the suit. If your boy knocks a baseball through a neighbor's view window, your liability policy pays because the damage occurred off your own premises.

● Theft Insurance. This covers not only your losses in case of burglary, but damage by thieves, loss to a holdup man or pickpocket on the street, or loss of certain kinds of personal property away from home.

Home insurance costs vary mainly in accordance with the fire risk attached to your home by an independent rating bureau. Some rating factors, like the efficiency of your fire department, if any, or the distance your home may be from a fire hydrant and the fire house are beyond your control. Other factors, like the kind of roof you select, whether your home is masonry or wood, and the area you select for a building site, are subject to your decision and can have a major effect on premium costs.

Premium costs for separate coverages may run something like those listed in Table 5E. Contrasted with the total of the separate policies are prices for homeowner's package of insurance that provides the same protection. Note that Homeowner Package No. 1 corresponds roughly with the fire and extended coverage policy plus theft and family liability. Homeowner Package No. 2 covers all the items in the No. 1 package plus the "broad form" coverages noted under the separate fire policy. The No. 3 package also covers many of the hazards reserved for the "all risk" policy, such as damage accidentally inflicted on your house by a member of your family. The Homeowner Package No. 3 includes more coverages than the combination of separate policies and costs more. If you rent, consider a tenant package which includes protection for your furnishings, theft, and family liability coverages.

TABLE 5E: Typical Home Insurance Comparison

| | Yearly Premium Costs | | | | | |
| | Individual Policies | | | Homeowner Policies | | |
	Basic Dwelling	Broad Form	Special All-Risk	No. 1	No. 2	No. 3
House ($60,000)						
Frame dwelling	$ 70	$ 70	$ 70	$128	$170	$197
		30	30			
			42			
Personal Property	43	43	43	Incl.	Incl.	Incl.
		12	12			
			18			
Theft ($6,000)	1	1	1	Incl.	Incl.	Incl.
Family Liability						
($25,000)	23	23	23	Incl.	Incl.	Incl.
$500 Medical	Incl.	Incl.	Incl.			
TOTAL	$137	$179	$239	$128	$170	$197
Deductible	$ 50	$ 50	$ 50	$ 50	$ 50	$ 50

Pay for policies at least once a year rather than monthly or even on an easy-payment plan.

One point to remember—maintain fire and extended coverage equal to at least 80 percent of the replacement cost of your house to avoid partial loss payments. For example, suppose your house would cost $50,000 to replace. Your policy must be written for $40,000 (80%) or more to be fully covered. With less than 80% coverage of replacement cost, you lose on either a partial or full loss. Suppose a fire should damage one room and the roof. Rebuilding costs $12,000. Suppose further that instead of $40,000 coverage, as in the example above, you were carrying only $30,000. Instead of paying the full $12,000, your insurance would pay the larger of the actual cash value of the property (replacement less depreciation) or the proportion of the cost that your coverage is to 80% of full replacement cost—$9,000 in this example ($30,000 is ¾ of $40,000, so $9,000 is ¾ of $12,000). If the house had been a total loss, the full $30,000 would be paid, but you would lose $20,000.

Replacement cost is the key. Not all of the original or appreciated price you paid for the house needs to be included. Exclude the cost of the land, as it will not be destroyed in a fire. Also exclude the cost of lot grading, all of the underground facilities—water line, sewer, and all or part of the foundations. Because building prices are rising at 12 to 15% a year, estimate replacement costs regularly to be sure your homeowner or fire and extended coverage policy is not lagging.

OPERATING COSTS

Landscaping and Yard Maintenance—If you buy a new home, you'll quickly discover the high cost of putting in a lawn and adding shrubs. Follow these ideas to keep planting and grounds maintenance costs low—

● Grow your own topsoil before you start a lawn. Instead of hauling so-called black dirt in at $5 to $7.50 per cubic yard and laying a 2- to 3-inch thick cover over the clay and sand the builder left, develop a deep seed bed like the farmers do. Good growing soil contains about equal portions of clay, humus, and sand, "Black dirt" is simply soil rich in humus, so why add more dirt to your lawn? Instead, after grading, add humus and fertilizer and grow one or two crops of rye, turning each under as "green manure." Plant your final lawn in the fall after another grading and smoothing.

● Native shrubs, plants, and trees not only cost less but require less care than exotic hybrids. Buy the plants you need from a supermarket or discount house nursery. They will be root pruned in cans and may be small. But planting relatively small plants pays off in two ways: (1) Plants can be transplanted easily with little chance of loss. (2) Small plants cost considerably less. Once in place, shrubs grow rapidly and you'll soon be pruning them back to manageable sizes.

● Save on water for shrubs by mulching around their base with ground bark, sawdust, leaves, or grass clippings. Lawn areas can survive weeks without rain if they have a deep seed bed. Don't worry about a

---

95% Doing-It-Yourself Savings Idea

As an example of what a scrounger can do, take the example of Betty Mariner. Friends marveled at the shrubs and plantings around her attractive Northwest home. When she moved to the area, she had joined a garden club. They studied the plants, flowers, and ground covers most adaptable to the soil and climate. She picked extra plants started from roots or by layering from her garden club friends—starts they would have discarded. She also dug native plants from forest areas (after obtaining a permit). As part of her long-term plan, she started other plants from slips cut from the shrubs in the gardens of club members. Over a 3-year period, she filled out her landscaping plan with absolutely no outlay of cash. One of her garden club friends estimated the landscaping must have cost her at least $2000. Actually, her out-of-pocket costs were less than $100 for planting soil, ground bark, and fertilizer.

slight browning of the lawn; grass will start growing again after the first rain.

● Shop for fertilizer in a farmer's or professional grower's market. You pay handsomely for small, gaily printed sacks of fertilizer at local hardware stores. Instead, buy fertilizer by analysis at a source that supplies fertilizer to farmers by the ton. All fertilizer is marketed with numbers, such as 10-10-10, indicating their contents. In order, the numbers specify the percentage amounts of nitrogen, phosphorus, and potassium. Basically, you need high nitrogen fertilizers for lawn and high phosphate-potash fertilizers for blooming flowers and shrubs.

Repairing and Maintaining Household Equipment—Servicing the many appliances and labor-saving equipment in a modern house can be costly and annoying. But, first make sure you need service. By actual count, 43 service calls out of 100 result from an appliance not being plugged in, a fuse blown, a circuit breaker tripped, or a loose wire in a socket or plug.

The next biggest reason for service calls, according to manufacturers' service departments, is user ignorance. Manufacturers spend thousands of dollars on instruction books to tell the housewife in words and pictures how to operate her electrical servants. But, housewives happily ignore these sources of information. Result! Service calls that become expensive instruction courses.

● Read the instruction book to make sure you understand which switch or which handle is to be used to obtain which result. No single bit of advice will pay off more handsomely than *follow directions!*

● Make sure plugs are in, fuses are not burned out, circuit breakers are closed, faucets are open, and cords do not have loose wires.

● Give your machines a chance to operate effectively. Any appliance that must overcome obstacles, such as partially clogged valves, packed dry bearings, etc., will break down sooner than a clean, well-maintained machine. Again, follow directions on cleaning, loading, and using your appliances.

● Check your state's Cooperative Extension Service for a book on servicing home equipment. Many of the faults that interrupt equipment service can be fixed quickly with little or no cost.

● If your appliance or equipment came equipped with a service manual and diagrams of parts and functions, study it to see if you can buy a part and install it yourself. Or, write to the manufacturer for information on servicing his equipment and to obtain parts. But, unless you *are* the handy type and know exactly what you're doing, don't tear out the innards of a machine and then call a serviceman to put them together again.

● Don't fall for appliance service contracts. A contract to handle all service calls for a set price per year may sound appealing, but if you have selected an appliance carefully in the first place, service calls will cost less on the average than the total of several years' contract costs.

Preventive Maintenance to Cut Costs—Nowhere is the philosophy "A stitch in time saves nine" more applicable than in home maintenance.

● Painting, inside and outside, should not be neglected. "Save the surface and you save all," the slogan says.

● Water leaks can cause damage that is costly to correct. If the leak is in the roof, get it fixed or do it yourself—but don't forget it. Caulk openings around windows, doors, and corners, around dormers, and at protrusions that allow water to enter. Inside, fill cracks between tub and tile or between tiles, to prevent water seepage.

● Floor maintenance performed regularly heads off costly refinishing or replacement. Keep a wear surface of hard wax on wood and tile floors and a resilient wax coating on flexible surfaces. Vacuum carpets with a beater-type machine to loosen the deep dirt that grinds away the base of fibers and cuts them loose.

● Yard and grounds maintenance can be a labor-saving device. Unless you spray or dig out weeds when they are small, they become a bigger chore to control later. Fertilizing a lawn to keep it healthy can save a complete rebuilding at a later time.

● Maintain home equipment regularly to prevent breakdown. Oil the ventilating fan, cover the window air conditioner in winter, oil the vacuum cleaner, washing machine, or dishwasher as noted in the operating manual, and keep traps, vents, and dirt-collection devices cleaned out.

FURNISHINGS

Saving 20% of your housing dollars is nowhere easier than in selecting and buying furniture, appliances, equipment, carpets, interior decorative materials, and home improvements. Planning pays off handsomely in timing purchases and in analyzing trade-offs. Using credit effectively or not at all can cut your costs another 12 to 18% as detailed in Chapter 9.

Appliances and Equipment—Your key to a long-lasting, service-free appliance is knowledge. You can't expect to test and evaluate many appliances on the market, but Consumers Union does. This independent organization reports monthly on their tests in Consumer Reports, a magazine available primarily by subscription.

Suppose you are about to buy a clothes-washing machine. If you shopped diligently, you could choose from nearly 100 models among at least 20 brands. Differences in cost, washing effectiveness, load capacity, water requirements, cycle versatility, and potential service costs become a confusing jumble. Instead of shopping blindly, study the test reports, select two or three models that will serve your needs, then shop a number of discount and department stores for the best overall price on the machine of your choice. When shopping for appliances, remember—

• Except for the listed catalog price by such mail-order sellers as Sears, Wards, and others, there is no such thing as a "list" or "retail" price. You may see some other term, such as "Suggested Retail Price." But the price you pay is the one you negotiate.

• Check prices in a number of stores. Even the big downtown department stores compete with discount houses, particularly when you include the value of delivery, unpacking, and installation in the price.

• Find out who is responsible for service and who will handle any claims under a guarantee or warranty.

• Note the terms of any warranty. Long-term warranties usually indicate a manufacturer's confidence that the appliance will last for at least the stated period—and probably longer.

• Watch the special sales for big price reductions, particularly by the large mail-order merchandisers. Listed prices by Sears and Wards are likely to be competitive with most discount houses (but not all). When these giants offer a 19% cut in price, they usually mean it.

• Time your purchases of appliances and equipment to take advantage of special promotions. Appliances are frequently marked down at least twice a year—immediately after Christmas and during July "parking lot sales."

• Pay cash for appliances. Some of the biggest bargains in appliances are offered by sellers who plan to make their profit on installment contracts. Merchandise simply becomes a medium for loaning money. Buying for cash from these credit sellers will save you money.

Wall and Window Coverings—Whether you paint walls or hang wallpaper, vinyl covering, some fabric, such as burlap, or grass cloth depends largely on your own taste. The colorful "shelter" magazines abound with ideas you can adapt. Analyze the cost of various alternatives, particularly in terms of maintenance cost. You might find it practical, for example, to hang a rough, nubby grass cloth along a wall to children's rooms to eliminate the constant finger smudges on a painted surface. Prepasted and pretrimmed wallpapers and wall fabrics have taken much of the work out of hanging these materials yourself. The water-mix, latex-base paints, easy and quick to apply with a roller, have taken most of the work out of painting.

Do-it-yourself interior decorating and maintenance really pays off:

● For most jobs, the cost of material runs as little as 10% of the total cost of a professional job. When you do these tasks yourself, you pocket the difference.

● Buy good-quality materials. Value and quality of paint and wall-covering materials frequently increase faster than price. You spend as much time applying a cheap paint as a really good paint that costs only a few dollars more. Or, a vinyl-coated wallpaper may cost more in the beginning, but if it lasts twice as long, you can pay twice as much for the paper and save one whole cycle of installation time.

● Adapt standard sizes of draperies and window curtains available in department stores, particularly the large mail-order houses. Next best is to measure your own window areas carefully and buy custom-made draperies or curtains during one of the two home-furnishings sales each year. Many times a store will charge only for the material, throwing in the labor of making the draperies free.

Furniture to Fit Your Family—Two philosophies prevail among families with young children. One family will purchase expensive, tasteful living and dining room furnishings—and then prohibit children in those rooms. Another family will recognize that children scrunch, bounce up and down, and wrestle on and off furniture enough to double or triple wear rates. These families buy reasonably durable furnishings with the idea of replacing them entirely when children become more civilized (grow up). Either way, you must be able to tell good furniture from bad, shoddy furniture. Check your state's Cooperative Extension Service catalog of bulletins for information on how to recognize quality differences among furniture offerings.

Buy what you have selected at one of the twice-a-year home furnishings promotions by a major store or have it shipped through a catalog sales outlet. Sales include reductions of at least 20% on practically all merchandise—a storewide sale. Items to be cleared may be cut by as much as 50%. Be ready to pay cash within 30 to 90 days.

The second low-cost way to buy furniture is from a catalog outlet for a number of small home furnishings manufacturers. These small manu-

---

53% Savings Idea

Another way to buy upholstered furniture is to rebuild a used piece. Sharon Franklin found a new divan that suited her living room for $475. She found that by waiting a few weeks, she could save 20% at a storewide sale. The same divan would cost $380 on sale—still too much. So, she shopped in a discard store and bought a used divan with a sturdy frame but with an old, worn covering for $25. She selected a fabric that would match her decorating scheme and paid an upholsterer to rebuild the old frame completely with her new fabric—cost $200. Sharon's new divan cost a total of $225 for a net saving of $250—with her pick of fabrics.

---

facturers elect to distribute a detailed, definitive catalog to many small outlets all over the country. Many times these catalog outlets will also sell the nationally advertised products of the giants in the business—at as much as 40% below normal retail price.

Refinishing and/or refurbishing wood furniture is a trickier proposition. How satisfactorily any refinishing job turns out depends somewhat on the damage or wear sustained. Clean-lined, modern pieces are easier to refinish than old heirloom designs with many rounded knobs, grooves, and curlicues. Only a thorough examination of each piece can tell you whether refurbishing will pay off.

Unfinished furniture usually means cheap furniture. Such pieces are usually suitable only for painting and are useful mainly for children's rooms. But consider the trade-off between buying new unfinished furniture for such interim use and buying used furniture that can be fully or partially refinished.

Before buying or refinishing your first piece of furniture, develop an overall plan, one you can implement in stages. Remain flexible and be patient. Be prepared to select one piece or another, depending on which may be offered at a sale. Paying cash will allow you to complete your plan at less cost and/or with better quality furnishings than doing the whole job and then attempting to pay it off in installments.

SUMMING UP

Probably the most important fact to remember about shelter expenses is they are not "fixed." Most budgets consider housing as a fixed cost, but the many ways open to you to manage shelter costs offer a wide range of cost levels. Some of the most important considerations to remember are to—

- Analyze, on a dollars-and-cents basis, the cost trade-off between owning and renting or between remodeling vs. selling and rebuying.

- Determine how much housing you can afford, not from a fixed rule of thumb or published guideline, but by how much of your income you really want to spend on shelter.

- Trade-off costs of commuting and house ownership to gain least cost or best value when buying a house.

- Learn the tricks of shopping for a house and buying the one you want at the right price.

- Shop around for financing.

- Find the lowest-cost way to pay for improvements to your property.

- Learn the kind of shelter insurance you need and how to buy the protection best suited to you for the best price.

- Keep operating costs at a minimum by following the many money-saving practices developed by thrifty homeowners over the years.

- Study the many types, brands, styles, and qualities of home furnishings and equipment, then buy the furnishings you really want at significant dollar savings.

6

LEARN WHERE AND WHEN TO
BUY CLOTHES AT BIG SAVINGS—
THEN CUT THE COST OF UPKEEP

Planning pays off handsomely in getting the most for your clothing dollar. Here, low price alone is a poor guide to overall buying strategy. Clothes quality, design, and maintainability often increase faster than price—up to a peak cost-effectiveness level. Points to look out for in managing your clothing dollar include:

- Learning to analyze the true, full-life cost of clothes as a part of your wardrobe planning.

- Recognizing the differences in quality and the relation of quality to appearance and wearability.

- Timing all clothes purchases for maximum dollar savings.

- Looking for the not-so-obvious sources for good clothing buys.

- Knowing how to care for clothing to extend wear life and improve general appearance.

- Using your talents to make or adapt your own clothes to cut costs and establish individuality.

Probably no part of a family's spending plan is so susceptible to good management as the money spent for clothing. Although one of the traditional three necessities of life, clothing represents a highly variable cost. During short-term financial stress, you can probably postpone most clothing purchases and live out of your closet. If you truly enjoy wearing clothes in a "best dressed" derby, you'll economize elsewhere. Shopping and buying information in this chapter will help you to dress smartly at moderate cost. But, if you buy a $495 one-of-a-kind suit at an exclusive fashion salon just to glow inwardly at a society lunch, you may have difficulty identifying with these suggestions.

WARDROBE PLANNING

The key to a low-cost, stylish wardrobe is—you guessed it—planning. To get up to twice the buying power from your clothing dollar, you need to plan—(1) to know what you need, and (2) to buy right. Knowing what you need will eliminate the same kind of impulse buying that can wreck your food budget. Buying right means timing and selecting purchases for best value.

Wardrobe planning begins by selecting dresses and suits that can be adapted for many occasions.

Children's clothing is something else again. Here, you buy as few individual pieces of clothing as practicable because children tend to grow out of clothes before they are worn out. Watch out for costly fads.

Men's clothing styles change slowly, so timing becomes important. For example, suppose a man buys a lightweight suit on sale in July instead of April. He still wears it for half the summer season that first year. If he wears the suit for 4 years, the half-season lag accounts for only 12½% of the time the suit remains in his wardrobe. Yet, by waiting 3½ months, he saves at least 20%, often as much as 35%. A suit that sells for $189.50 in April may be marked down to $144.95 by the middle of July for a 21% savings.

QUALITY DIFFERENCES

Style, fabrics, tailoring—all affect clothing quality and price. Certain lines of men's, women's, and children's clothing include a high "design" content that affects price. Fabrics include a wide range of natural and man-made fibers as cloth manufacturers attempt to find the right mix of rich appearance, low cost, and durability. A number of guides to quality can be used to relate value and price, as follows—

● Construction and tailoring details affect fit and comfort as well as durability. Good fabric quality usually accompanies high-quality detailing. A man's jacket, for example, may include many hand operations visible only under close scrutiny. However, these hand-tailored operations make a big difference in comfort and fit. A suitmaker who spends the extra time on these niceties of construction will almost invariably select a comparable quality of cloth—he won't spend extra labor on a cheap fabric and vice versa. One of the best guides to men's suits is a USDA bulletin, *Men's Suits—How to Judge Quality*, Home and Garden Bulletin No. 54. A similar publication, *Buying Women's Coats and Suits*, is also available from the USDA (Home and Garden Bulletin No. 31). While both of these USDA publications may include out-of-date styling, quality standards and construction details are still pertinent. Ask your Cooperative Extension Agent for other publications that will help you judge clothing quality.

● Consumer protection laws can help you judge quality if you read the label. A label is attached to all new clothes, detailing the fiber content. The law can't force you to read the label, but the information is there. The label not only protects you against buying an inferior mix of used wool, for example, that will wear out quicker than virgin wool, but also it provides exact washing instructions.

● Wear guarantees now accompany certain lines of clothing. Children's shirts, pants, and shoes, men's socks, and women's lingerie, for example, may carry a guarantee that the article will wear for a specific length of time. If the piece of clothing wears out sooner, the store will replace it with a new one. For example, acrylic fiber shirts for teens may be guaranteed to wear for 1 year. Technically, your boy could wear the same shirt every day all year. If it wore out before the year was up, he would be entitled to another shirt. Actually, your boy probably wouldn't wear one shirt every day even if you were to launder it at night. But, if you were to buy six shirts, each guaranteed for a year, any one shirt would receive the equivalent of only 2 months' wear. So, to use wear guarantees, buy as few garments as practicable and, if one wears out within the guarantee period, return it promptly for adjustment. The same is true of socks. If three pairs are guaranteed to wear a year, don't buy six pairs. Some stores bank on the fact that only a few housewives will keep the guarantee tag and sales record that are necessary for adjustment. If your children are hard on clothes, the few minutes necessary to note which shirts, socks, or pants are associated with the tag and sales slip can reduce your costs.

BUY CLOTHES RIGHT

With your Spending Plan as a guide (see Chapter 8), consider the yearly amount you set aside for clothing as a checking account to buy against. Plan to buy all your clothes for cash or on one of the monthly convenience charge accounts that add no service charges. Avoid, like the plague, the revolving charge plans that run up the cost of buying.

● Determine which merchandise is plentiful and which represents the best buys. Many stores will throw whole lines of merchandise on sale. Along with these big sales, they will clear out odds and ends of seasonal or slow-moving merchandise. For example, a few luxurious wool-cotton

---

40% Savings Idea

Buy all your clothes at sales. Department stores and mail-order houses feature many sales of clothing. Keep abreast of the sale advertisements so you won't buy hose at $1.89 a pair in one store when the same hose are on sale for $1.39 a pair at a store only a block away. Savings of 20% are the minimum you should settle for. Take men's shirts, for example. One nationally advertised brand sells for $12.50 regularly in a local store. It's a good shirt that will wear well and look fresh through 60 to 80 washings. Exactly the same shirt, not an alternative "just as good" shirt, can be bought on sale at $8.95. If you were to pay retail prices, you'd be paying 40% more than you need to because these shirts sell regularly twice a year at the $8.95 price.

Another alternative is to spend the same money but upgrade quality by timing purchases during sales. Suppose you have $150 in your plan for the year to buy a suit. You have the option of shopping early in the season and buying a $150 suit or waiting until you can buy a $190 suit on sale for $149.95. Either way you spend $150, but by buying on sale you get a better-quality and probably a better-looking suit.

---

knit sports shirts, normally priced at $19.95, were marked down to only $7.95 at a recent sale. By the end of the first "courtesy day," these good buys had been snapped up.

● Read the ads carefully to determine what kind of merchandise is on sale. You might see such wording as, "Large stocks purchased specially for this event" or "Special purchase," indicating that the merchandise offered was not part of the store's regular stock—and possibly, but not always, of lesser quality. Notices like "Store-wide clearance" and "Regular stock sale" usually indicate a true sale of the store's normal stock.

● Check the flyers that show up in the mail when you purchase regularly from the mail-order houses. There are at least two types— seasonal sale flyers that include pictures and descriptions of merchandise which may include selections from their regular catalog at a lower price, or clearance flyers that may simply list items by stock number and refer to a page in the company's big catalog. The seasonal flyers frequently offer substantial savings on merchandise when you need it. For example, they may include a number of good buys on school jeans just a few weeks before school starts. Clearance flyers, on the other hand, arrive after the flush of the season and aim to clear the company's stock of slow-moving merchandise. By knowing what you need in the future and by studying the big catalog for details, you can often effect savings of at least 50%. Check details carefully, however, because some of these clearance sales do not offer a choice of color or design.

● Note timing of sales throughout the year. Already mentioned are the after-Christmas sales. But most stores run these types of sales in two stages. First is the sale to compete with other stores offering merchandise that is related to Christmas. Fancy lingerie, men's ties, expensive sports shirts, and other such merchandise is thrown on the sale counters first and promoted widely in the newspapers, beginning, many times, on Christmas day. Several weeks later, when the stores have had time to recover from the burst of Christmas activity, they have their real after-Christmas sale. You might buy Christmas wrapping paper the day after Christmas at a real saving, but wait until the later sales for real buys on men's shirts, suits, shoes, and other furnishings. All kinds of women's wear are marked down 40 to 60% at sales several weeks after Christmas. Summer wear usually goes on the block during a rash of sales throughout July and early August. During the course of the year, you'll learn to watch for special promotions heralding Mother's and Father's Day, ski clothing in February, a particular store's celebration of it's birthday once a year, and many other similar occasions.

● Sales-minded stores will sometimes advertise a complete stock of salesmen's samples. Prices are usually half the intended retail price.

● Another ploy is to check certain stores for potential bargains that may be too small to advertise. One bargain-conscious husband, for example, regularly walked through a downtown department store on his way back from lunch because the store would throw marked-down merchandise on a special table to get rid of it. Prices were only one-third to one-quarter of regular retail price.

Play the Irregulars Market—All clothing manufacturers maintain some form of quality control. When an article fails to meet quality standards, it may be separated from first-quality merchandise and sold at a special price. When stocks of irregulars accumulate, a store may use their low prices as bait for a sale.

Take socks, for example. For some technological reason, sock-knitting machines seem to turn out many socks with small faults. Socks that might sell normally for $2.50 to $2.95 a pair could be sale priced at 89¢ for irregulars.

Similar savings are possible on a wide range of children's, women's, and men's clothing if you keep a sharp eye out for these promotions.

Check Special Outlets—Depending on where you live and the manufacturers in your area, you can sometimes buy directly from the factory. Instead of wholesaling their "seconds" to a retailer, manufacturers may operate an outlet for their own merchandise, much like the bakery "thrift store."

One manufacturer of jackets, for example, withholds jackets that do not pass final inspection. All of the rejects from one week's production are offered for sale on a Thursday morning. One week men's jackets may be on sale. The following week, boys' ski-type jackets may be offered. But, the important thing is the price. Jackets designed to sell for $49.95 may be sold for $24.95—a terrific sale. A call ahead determines what kind of merchandise is to be offered on the next "special sale" day.

Special merchandise offered at such outlet sales is almost always sold on an "as is" basis, so make sure the size is right. Check the zipper too, and make sure the seams are all well sewed; this is one of the more frequent reasons for a jacket failing to pass. If a seam is not sewed straight, you may be able to take a few stiches and make it right. Here is where your know-how of clothes pays off.

Check three sources for information to locate special outlets. First, look in the classified section of your telephone directory under "Surplus." Check also the classified section of your newspaper, particularly the fat Sunday editions, for leads. Or, ask your bookstore for a local buyers guide to factory outlets and discount stores. But, the best source of information is the word-of-mouth communications that spread quickly among bargain-conscious families.

Buying Quality Used Clothing—Many families turn up their noses at the idea of buying used clothing. As a result, many bargains, particularly for children's clothing or specialty sports apparel, are available to the sharp buyer. Take children's clothing, for example. You may buy a 10-year-old boy a sports coat and slacks to wear to Sunday school and for dress-up occasions. But how many times does he actually wear out the jacket? Many families are in the same boat, with the result that many good-quality clothes are outgrown each year. Unless your family is stair-stepped so that clothes bought for the oldest can be passed down, your children outgrow more clothes than they wear out.

Instead of buying a new suit for a 10-year-old boy, look around for the many thrift shops operated to raise funds by a hospital guild, church league, Swedish club, or other charitable organization. Some of the best outlets are the thrift shops run by the Junior Leagues in cities throughout the United States. They have found one of the best and easiest ways to raise money is to sell clothing donated by members.

Check out these used-clothing outlets for dress-up children's clothing, for sports clothing, such as stretch ski pants, for warm coats and jackets,

---

75% Savings Idea

Ellen Sutcliffe picked up the habit of shopping in the local Junior League Thrift Shop after she stopped in with a friend who was depositing her contributions. On one occasion, Ellen found a practically new spring coat priced at $25. From the store label in the coat, she figured the original price had been at least $99.50. Contributed clothes must be cleaned or the store will have them cleaned and deduct the cleaning from the contributor's credit. So, the coat was wearable with no additional expense. On another trip, Ellen found a dress-up coat for her 10-year-old daughter for only $7.50—again in like-new condition. She estimated the coat's original cost at $34.95. Ellen got the habit of stopping to look at the store's stock whenever she was in the neighborhood because the stock varied from week to week and according to the season. She shopped ahead of the season she needed clothing.

---

and for frilly dresses. You would probably not find such items as school jeans, wash-and-wear pants, shoes, or other items that wear out rapidly. However, girls' clothing is frequently in large supply because many well-to-do families buy for variety, and, with so many dresses to choose from, a girl seldom wears the dresses enough to show wear.

Women's clothing frequently can be picked up in these thrift and consignment stores, again because the original owner may have tired of the dress or coat rather than because the garment was worn out. Men's clothing in good shape is less likely to be available in thrift stores. While a woman with a modicum of talent for sewing can refit a dress purchased used, there is less opportunity to refit a man's jacket. Also, men tend to wear suits and sports jackets longer than women, and men's clothing in thrift shops may be heavily worn.

Buying Overseas—English woolens hand-tailored to your own size and taste can be bought by mail directly from England. Many of the major stores in London publish catalogs. Also available from overseas are beautifully hand-knit Scottish and Scandinavian sweaters and yard goods. Handmade sandals, slippers, and casual shoes in almost infinite variety are available from Belgium and Italy.

Another source for clothes from overseas are the hand tailors of Hong Kong. Most cities include an outlet which will measure men to a suit or sports jacket, then mail these measurements and your choice of material to Hong Kong. Even with the duty that is collected when the postman delivers your purchase, the price is 15 to 20% less, usually, than you would pay for an ordinary, ready-made suit or jacket. Cloth quality is likely to be superb because it is imported or woven directly in Hong Kong to British standards.

The popularity of custom-fitted, hand-tailored men's clothing from Hong Kong has spread to women's wear. Coats, exquisite silk dresses and blouses, beaded sweaters, and accessories with much hand labor involved can also be obtained directly from Hong Kong by mail.

Other possibilities for buying overseas are the Virgin Islands, Puerto Rico, and other islands of the British West Indies. While you are on vacation, shop the islands' duty-free stores, but check the prices that may be aimed at the tourist.

PROPER CARE EXTENDS CLOTHING LIFE

Like anything we own, clothing responds to care and maintenance to provide longer, better-looking service.

Hang and Store Your Clothes Right—Simple care every day requires only a few minutes and saves two ways—it extends the life of suits, jackets, dresses, and shoes, and it extends the time between trips to the cleaner, laundry, or shoe shop. Some of the ideas for better clothing life are—

● Change clothes as soon as the business or out-of-the-house day is over. Loose-fitting casual clothes are not only comfortable but save unnecessary wear of more expensive business or dress-up clothes.

● Alternate clothes and shoes. Never wear the same business suit two days in a row, for example. And never wear the same pair of shoes day after day. Instead, trade-off; allow a suit to hang in the closet for a day or two between wearings. Women seldom have this problem because of their penchant for variety. Wrinkles will hang out of a jacket gradually when hung on a hanger that supports it across its full shoulder yoke. Hang pants from the cuff end so the full weight of the waist and belt will pull wrinkles out.

● Protect out-of-season clothes from dust and chewing insects. Before storing a winter suit away for the summer, have it cleaned, then hang it out of the way in its cleaner bag to keep off the dust. A clean suit or other clothing is less appetizing for moths and carpet beetles. If these insects are a major problem in your area, have the cleaner mothproof the clothing before storing it away. Otherwise, hanging them in the sun and a thorough brushing will do the job.

● Brush clothes, shine shoes, and remove bulky objects from jacket and pants pockets. All kinds of extras in pockets can push clothes out of shape unnecessarily. Use shoe trees in shoes; otherwise shoes are warped progressively out of shape by wearing, particularly if they are shucked off wet. It's easier to keep shoes looking good by frequent cleaning and waxing than to try and revive a stained, dirty pair. Leather remains soft and weather resistant if you use saddle soap to remove dirt and old polish before applying a wax polish. Brush a hat frequently to remove accumulated dust and to turn up the nap.

● Keep clothes cleaned. Watch for specials at your cleaners and check the differences between cleaning prices. If one cleaner offers a special on slacks for $1.19, check which pair might be ready and save paying the regular price of $1.69 or more a few weeks later. Plan your shopping to take advantage of the cash-and-carry rates that are frequently 20% off delivered prices.

Do-It-Yourself Dry Cleaning—The success of the do-it-yourself laundry has spawned centers for dry cleaning clothing that cannot be washed. The availability of heat-treated and permanently pressed pants opens the way to further use of these do-it-yourself cleaners. Say a full load (8 pounds) of garments can be dry cleaned for $3. Depending on their weight, you might get a coat, two skirts, and two dresses cleaned for only $3.

Spot removers used in time can save a trip to the cleaner for the whole garment. Make sure you don't set the stain, however, before it is too late. Consult the USDA's guide for removing stains at home (*Removing Stains from Fabrics*. available from Government Printing Office, Washington, D.C. 20402).

Wear It Out, Use It Up—If you are one of those women with a closet full of clothes but who never has anything to wear, examine whether the cause is your clothes— or you. Women tire easily of clothes either because the wardrobe was not planned or because they use little imagination in wearing accessories. Mixing blouses with suits, adding a pin or a scarf to a basic dress, or mixing separates are all ways to achieve variety. And, as you develop fresh, varied outfits, you can wear the same basics longer without becoming tired of them. When you continually mix accessories to spruce up first one outfit and then another, you can save on clothing purchases and eliminate frequent discards. But, forward planning is the key. Look ahead when you're buying to see how many ways you may be able to wear one basic outfit.

Men's clothing is much the same. Mixing sports jackets with slacks is more and more acceptable for business wear, particularly in those offices where shirt sleeves are the accepted working dress. A good suit will outlast most men's taste. It's nonsense to discard suits and jackets before they are thoroughly worn only to buy others. The old Yankee advice, "Use it up, wear it out, make it do—or do without," applies particularly to clothing.

Maybe you have heard the saying, "He's hard on clothes." Most times applied to children, the comment also applies to men. For some reason, certain men wear clothes out faster than others. Several reasons may account for the difference: (1) They may exhibit poor posture, slumping, and constant wriggling, abrading the seat, elbows, and back against chairs. (2) They are likely to throw a crumpled jacket onto a chair when they come into the house. (3) They wear the same clothes much of the time without changing for casual wear or without alternating from day to day. Simple care and thought can extend clothing life at least 100%— and you will look better groomed during that time.

You don't have to be a tailor to keep clothes repaired, but here is where the maxim, "A stitch in time saves nine," originated. Sewing up a seam before it opens too far makes more sense than ignoring it until you must take it to a tailor for repairs. A few low-cost tips—

● Use the many ready-made parts and repairs that are available at notions counters. Iron-on patches for jeans, prefabricated white shirt cuffs, knitted cuffs for jackets, formed pockets for replacements, and many other aids for the homemaker simplify clothing repair.

● Use one of the new stain pens to hide worn spots or to mark out spots that won't go away. The corner of men's jacket sleeves, where they rub against a desk top, often wears through to expose the light gray or white of hair canvas underneath. Instead of being conscious about the light spot, use a stain pen to color the hair canvas. Use a stain pen also to hide light-colored sports on a dark suit or jacket.

MAKE YOUR OWN CLOTHES

When it comes to profitable hobbies, home tailoring of women's clothes ranks near the top. Many housewives tailor their own clothes because of special fitting problems, but most home tailoring is aimed at having a better-looking, more varied wardrobe for a fraction of the cost it would come to in a store. Today, home tailoring is a $4 billion-a-year business. Home-tailored clothes mark the seamstress as "creative." She wears her home-sewn creations proudly and may discuss the detailing with friends to display her knowledgeability. The best fashion designers are now developing the newest fashions in designer patterns to support the home-tailoring market.

77% Doing-It-Yourself Savings Idea

Anne Henderson spent an estimated 60 hours tailoring a new winter coat from a high-fashion pattern. But, the final product was equal to any coat priced at $299.50—possibly more. Costs were $3 for the pattern, $14.50 per yard for 3½ yards of heavy, imported wool fabric at a special sale, and lining, buttons, hair canvas, and thread, at $14. Anne's total investment in materials was $67.50. But, her high-quality handwork and the detailed finishing brought the value up to the equivalent of the $300 coat. She also enjoyed the recognition of her friends for her tailoring talents exhibited in the coat.

Women's fashions with the extensive hand operations are most likely to yield a good payout relative to ready-to-wear clothing. Few women are willing to tackle a man's jacket. Most children's clothing cost about the same ready-made as for materials, due to the large volume of production. Also, while most home seamstresses can sew a better blouse for the money than they can buy, the savings are relatively small compared to sewing dresses, suits, and coats.

Where to Get Expert Instruction—Tailoring is a skill that requires a bit of learning. You don't whomp up a suit the likes of which just came out of Paris the first time out. One low-cost source of expert instruction is your high-school or community college adult education program. As you develop skill, you move up into successively higher classes until you are making full-fashioned suits and coats. As in any skill, there are many "tricks of the trade" to be learned from the instructor.

Sewing schools may be sponsored by distributors of sewing machines either as a premium for purchasing a machine or to develop interest in sewing. However, stay clear of the sewing courses that cost several hundred dollars. A course sponsored by a reputable sewing machine agency may cost $3.50 to $4 per lesson. An evening course as part of your school system's adult education program may cost as little at $25 for ten lessons and seldom more than $50.

Where to Buy Materials—All full-service department stores sell yard goods in terrific variety, but look around at other sources too:

● Yardage stores run sales three or four times a year.

● Examine the stock of remnants when near the fabric section of your favorite stores.

● Special outlets or "fabric fairs" for yardage operate in some cities much like a surplus store. When you find fabrics that interest you, the price is usually small, sometimes as little as 25% of what you would expect to pay in a department store.

● Buying fabrics by mail sometimes has two advantages: access to a greater variety and/or higher quality of fabric than is available locally. One source of imported fabrics issues a catalog with small swatches keyed to fashionable designs and photographed on professional models to spark interest. These fabrics are costly—from $8.95 per yard for pure silks to $24.50 for wool suitings. Even higher prices are attached to specialty materials for high-fashion formal wear. A number of other sources featuring fabrics from around the world sell fabrics more reasonably. Many of these sources refund the price of the catalog on the first order over a minimum amount. Check the small "display ads" or classified ads in popular women's magazines for low-cost sources of English woolens, Thailand silks, or Hong Kong brocades.

Selecting the Right Pattern—The real key to building a wardrobe at home is your choice of design and pattern—

● "Easy sew" patterns may be as simple as a back and front of a dress sewed together with a zipper somewhere to allow you to get in and out. Clever designers have made it difficult to detect the difference between an "easy sew" dress and a draped, casual dress of high style. One tip on "easy sew" dresses—follow the pattern advice on selection of material. Frequently a patterned or textured fabric sews up better in one of these loose-fitting dresses.

● Stay clear of the "designers" patterns from Paris or Italy until you are skilled in tailoring. These expensive, high-style designs call for inner dresses or jackets to attain their style. As such, they are challenging for all but experienced home tailors.

● Select patterns for suits and coats that are reasonably conservative. Often the subdued lines of a suit reflect an easier layout of pieces and less difficult tailoring. Also, a reasonably conservative design will remain in fashion for several years.

● Examine the many new fashions and patterns offered each month by the women's magazines. Their editors keep a wary eye out for designs that both look good and are relatively easy to sew.

Knitting—A Hobby That Pays Off—Ski sweaters, decorative separates, shorty coats—even full suits—are being knitted these days as never before. No machine has yet been developed that can knit the variety or rich designs available to the hand knitter. Instead of paying as much as $99 for a patterned ski sweater, you can knit one for your son or daughter for $25 to $30 worth of yarn plus $1.00 for a book of patterns.

Knitting takes time, of course, but uses time that is frequently wasted. You may find hours for knitting while attending PTA or similar meetings, while riding in a car on short trips, at coffee klatches, and when relatives visit. Knitting is something you can do while talking and, on some patterns, without watching

Most shops that sell knitting yarns, patterns, and accessories run classes for beginners. Basic instruction is simple and takes little time. But, by knitting under the direction of the shop owner, the beginner can ask questions and have her work checked. One bit of advice, "As a last resort, even when you may not understand, follow instructions."

Yarns for knitting can be bought at considerable savings by following one or more of the following ploys:

Watch for the sales of knitting yarns at local stores. Special items or their entire stock may be offered at prices at least 20% less than regular prices. Stores may run as many as four sales a year, so why buy at regular prices? Look ahead to your next project while still knitting on your present one.

Note the special sales offered in the flyers from mail-order houses.

Buy yarns at specialty outlets that sell yarn remnants from knitting mills in balls or on spindles.

Look over the offerings of mail-order outlets. Note the very small ½- or 1½-inch ads in some of the women's magazines that offer yarns by mail, either by hanks or on spindles. Sometimes these mail-order houses are out of the country. Even with the duty, yarns from Canada or Ireland may cost less than locally purchased yarns. If you should get to one of the free ports or travel in Canada, use your duty exemption to purchase yarns from out of the country.

SPECIAL CLOTHES-BUYING TIPS

Bargains at the Lost and Found—People, particularly children, have the darndest habit of leaving clothes in busses, public waiting rooms, at school, and any other place they may pause long enough to shuck a coat. A transit company, for example, may hold a garment left on a bus for a month, then either give it to the employee who turned it in if he wants it or sell it at auction. Other organizations may do the same and you can benefit. Check airlines, bus companies, department stores, etc., for an idea of when they sell unclaimed clothing. Schools and some other organizations turn clothing over to one of the charity groups. Check these resources too for an opportunity to buy up-to-date clothing that is seldom badly worn.

Unclaimed Auctions—Clothing is only one of the many articles that turn up unclaimed in customs houses, post offices, and in police departments. Regulations vary, but after a set length of time, these goods are sold at public auction (see Chapter 12).

SUMMING UP

Although considered one of the so-called three necessities of life, clothing costs are highly variable. Your skill as a money manager quickly pays off in buying and using clothing with an eye toward cost effectiveness. When clothes mean much to your well-being, remember that the same number of dollars can buy more variety, style, and freshness if spent wisely than the same dollars spent without planning. The most important ideas to remember are—

- Recognizing the importance of selecting clothing to buy and timing the purchase of each item.

- Studying the relationship between price and the many elements of quality—style, fashion, appearance, wearability, and durability.

- Taking advantage of sales, inventory reductions, clearances, close-outs, irregulars, and special outlet opportunities to get the most for your clothing dollar.

- Saving on clothing by shopping two little-known sources—used clothing shops and overseas stores selling by mail.

- Maintaining your clothes to assure top appearance and long wear.

- Learning the creative satisfaction (and very real cost savings) that accrue from sewing or knitting some of your family's clothing needs.

7

ENJOY YOURSELF— HAVE MORE FUN MORE OFTEN WITH THE MONEY YOU'VE SAVED FROM OTHER EXPENSES—AND BY SPENDING IT RIGHT

"Fun," as used in this book, and in this chapter, covers a wide range of activities. You can find out how to—

- Enjoy many everyday opportunities for *free* fun.

- Help every member of the family participate in sports—at less cost.

- Spend more fun-time at home.

- Ride your hobby at a lower price.

- Serve liquor at home and for parties for fewer dollars.

- Take more trips and travel widely.

- Learn the money-saving tips that will help your children attend college.

- Buy books, magazines, and records at astoundingly low prices.

- Enjoy more personal care for you and your family—and still spend less.

- Give more to your church and favorite charities without increasing dollar cost.

Every day in every way, we should all do something we enjoy— something that's fun. Having fun doesn't necessarily mean whooping it up at a party, playing a game of touch football with the neighborhood dads and lads, spending every weekend fishing, or playing round after round of bridge with your friends. Fun may also include quiet reading, personal listening to records, attending movies, plays, and concerts, vacation trips, and travel. Also included in fun, as used in this book, are such activities as contributions of time and money to your local church, helping your children attend college, attending night school yourself for self-improvement or vocational courses, playing at hobbies that may or may not be profitable, and contributing services to your community. Another fun item is personal care to keep you looking young and attractive. Money spent for those visits to the hair dresser, for example, comes under fun—at least in this book.

Having enough fun is important in maintaining a balanced personality. We all need a fun break; that is, participation in a recreational activity that smooths the abrasions and offsets tensions of work. Whatever your course, you can get more fun per buck by managing your "Fun Fund." You may even find that, as the song says, many of the "best fun things are free."

FUN THAT'S FREE

Free Fun for the Taking—According to *Webster's*, recreation is " ... a refreshment of strength and spirits after toil." Notice that nothing in this definition mentions that recreation costs money. You can't say to your family, "Let's buy $25 worth of fun this weekend." Fun doesn't come in units or with a price tag. There are so many opportunities for free fun and recreation in most communities that your family would find it impossible to sample more than a fraction. Take a "wide look" to ferret out the free activities that are often more fun than the play-for-pay types, particularly while catching up with past spending (see Chaper 10). Just a few of the possibilities are—

● Public-library fun-and-educational activities include their film programs, which rival those shown in pay theaters. No charge, of course. Libraries also offer a continuing program of lectures and seminars on a variety of subjects, along with exhibitions of art and sculpture. And of course there is no end at all to the wealth of literature and the endless variety of magazines available for the asking with a library card. In addition to books, modern libraries now lend record albums you can play at home or, if you have no player, in one of their listening rooms. Some libraries also loan out films for home showing, either sound or silent, depending on your equipment. During summer vacations, many libraries organize reading sessions for children. In these sessions young children gather to hear books read to them, not only to while away the time but to encourage their interest in reading.

● Public recreation programs open countless opportunities for game play in teams, instruction in swimming and other sports, and an introduction to great music and plays. Plans vary widely across the country but some agency in most county or city governments spends a budget for community recreation. In some localities, a prominent newspaper sponsors free athletic programs in cooperation with local officials. You're likely to find city and county beaches, picnic areas, and playfields for Little League baseball, soccer, and basketball maintained for all to use. Recreation departments may also pay for band and symphony concerts in the park on summer Sunday afternoons, for Shakespearean plays performed free on outdoor stages, and for free lectures during the winter in public halls.

● Universities, community colleges, and private specialty schools offer a wide range of fun activities. Music students and faculty perform in recitals and concerts with admission free. School orchestras and bands provide many concerts that are open to the public. College drama departments or interested groups of students perform experimental plays or productions of old standbys for experience and research—many times for no cost. Although college football and basketball teams play for massive crowds at expensive prices, many of the other athletic contests are open to the public for no cost. Swimming meets, tennis matches, wrestling, freshman football, intramural games—all may be seen for no cost on many college campuses. Practice sessions for college and high school competitive sports offer opportunities for instructing your children in a game's fine points plus "man-to-man" time with your boy or girl. Watch too for the yearly "open houses" by various departments of a college that allow you to take your children on a truly eye-popping tour of research laboratories and instruction facilities.

● Art, science, and natural history museums in many cities are free. Others charge an admission so small in relation to the fun and educational value they provide as to be almost laughable. Look too for the small art dealers' showrooms and the historical museums maintained for public view by state, college, or private groups in your community. Here, take a clue from the tourist. Visit the Chamber of Commerce or your city's Tourist Bureau for free propaganda that lists museums, art galleries, local points of interest, and opportunities you may never have considered.

● Industry tours offer a wide range of activity for groups of Indian Guides, Cub Scouts, and others. But tours are not limited to children. Take a tour through a brewery, for example. You'll not only be shown how beer is made and bottled, but you'll be tempted with samples of their product. Set up your trip by calling the public relations office of the company. Or, contact the local Chamber of Commerce for opportunities you may not have considered.

● Free cooking schools are frequently offered by the local gas or electric company. Offerings range from special classes for young brides to

---

$50-a-Month Savings Idea

David and Linda Morrow found themselves on the brink of debt trouble (see page 218) and, being close to a university, decided to cut their spending on movies, plays, and evenings out. Linda asked to be placed on the mailing list for the University's BULLETIN, a calendar of events. They were overwhelmed by the opportunities—free music recitals and mind-stretching lectures and turned their attention from commercial events. David began attending practice sessions of the university's varsity sports. "I get more kick out of practices than I do out of the Saturday game. I'm even getting to know some of the players by their first name!" he told Linda. By substituting free fun for commercial fun, David and Linda found they were saving an average of $50 a month—dollars they needed to catch up with their debts.

---

gourmet classes for those learning to prepare "company" meals. Find out about these cooking sessions by calling your local utility company information service. Occasionally, one of the cookware companies will sponsor cooking schools in cooperation with one of the department stores.

● Don't overlook the multitude of recipe, party idea booklets, and an almost interminable list of pamphlets offered free. Companies produce these to help sell their product. If a flour company, for example, mails you a free booklet on how to bake a wide variety of cakes, cookies, and sweet rolls, you may be enticed into buying its product.

● Schools aid in a community's recreational program by allowing their playground facilities to be used after school and on weekends. You and your family can practice shooting goals on the outdoor basketball court or play a game of scrub baseball or touch football on the playground. Many schools also maintain tennis courts, swings, teeter-totters, sandpiles, pull-up bars, and climbing pyramids for play.

Sports for the Family—When it comes to equipping your family with skis, a boat, swimming pool, or the many other items needed to participate in recreational activities, don't forget the same business buying practices you have been using to cut expenses.

● Buy your boat for less either one of two ways:

(1) Buy a used boat that may require considerable elbow grease before it's fit for the water. When a boat is allowed to depreciate because the owner hasn't kept it painted and varnished, the hull tight, and the outboard motor in good operating condition, you can benefit. Usually, when buying a used boat, appearances deceive, and a boat looks worse than it actually is. One of the reasons a boat owner may be selling his boat

23% Savings Idea

Bob Bender was interested in a 24-foot outboard cabin cruiser that was priced in the spring for $6,995. By waiting until September, he bought the same boat for $5,395. The $1,600 saved during the 8-month period from September through April the next season amounted to a cash saving of 23%. Here's a case where borrowing pays off. Suppose Bob had borrowed the $5,395 on September 1 at 12% (see Chapter 10). Interest would amount to $431.82. His cost for the boat at the end of April would then be $5,827 ($5,395 plus $432), still allowing a saving of 17%—and none of his own money would have been tied up in a boat he couldn't use in the winter.

is the big maintenance bill or work load facing him. So, instead of fixing his boat, he sells it—usually at a loss. Boat owners also play a game called "trading up." A boater may start with a 12-footer, then buy a 15-footer with a bigger engine, only to trade up to a 17½-foot runabout, and so on until he owns a 34-foot cruiser with twin screws, radar, sonar, and ship-to-shore telephone. You can benefit from buying and fixing up the castoffs.

(2) Buying a new boat out of season can save you as much as 30 to 40%. Boat shows blossom out in late winter to spur interest in new equipment. You pay top prices and may even wait for delivery when you buy at the beginning of the season.

● Skiing is a fairly expensive sport, but timing your purchases again pays off handsomely. When you save money on equipment, you have more bucks for lift tickets and lessons. Rent skis, poles, and boots for a time or two first. Then, if you're bitten by the ski bug, plan to buy your own equipment either in late February or in August and September. Learn which skis are the ones for you and be ready to pounce on bargains that are marked down as much as 40 to 60% in February. In August and September, many sporting goods houses run ahead-of-season sales to clear out any equipment left from the previous year. They also sell skis used as rentals the previous winter. You may be able to find a pair of used metal skis that normally sell new for $169.95 marked down to $39.95. Irregulars in ski clothing—stretch pants, parkas, gloves and mittens, and after-ski boots—are frequently available on sale ahead of the season.

● Low-cost sports programs for children and adults are sponsored by adult education programs in local schools. Programs may include volleyball, badminton, handball, basketball, and body conditioning. Well-managed school systems allow the use of their gym, shower, and instruction facilities at night for adults at a modest fee.

50% Savings Idea

Anne Salton bought a $69.95 chair-length ski jacket for $34.50 by shopping in the bargain "seconds" basement of a local jacket manufacturer. She found the seconds outlet by calling the manufacturer and asking if they sold reject and sample jackets at their factory. The answer was an emphatic "Yes!" One loose seam was all that was wrong with Anne's jacket—a job she spent 10 minutes correcting.

Play the swapping game to cut the cost of outfitting young skiers. Many PTA's or other organizations arrange a ski swap where families bring in their outgrown equipment for trading. Many ski stores also take boots in trade for new or used boots. An alert family can get a bigger pair of boots for an average of $2.50 per season—sometimes less by constantly trading up. Use the same tactics for pants, parkas, and sweaters.

FUN AROUND THE HOME

Family entertainment formerly centered around the home. Within the last 20 to 30 years, the burgeoning of cultural activities, the promotion of such specialized recreation as bowling and tennis and the growth of spectator sports have moved the center of gravity of fun outside the home. Fun at home can benefit children and adults alike by teaching and/or learning while playing. For example, there are the—

Games for the Family That Teach—For beginners in school there's the *ABC Game* for teaching the alphabet; *Phonic Rummy* for learning letter and word sounds, and *The Winning Touch* and *Smarty* for beginning arithmetic. For older children and adults there is *WFF:The Beginner's Game of Modern Logic; Equations: The Game of Creative Mathematics; and Wff'N Proof: The Game of Modern Logic*. In between these fun and thinking games, you'll find many others at local bookstores and by mail. Card games, of course, are innumerable; all the way from "high card wins" to contract bridge.

Build Your Own Play Equipment—There's absolutely no substitute for an enormous sandbox to keep little children creatively occupied. Fix up a big one while you're at it; say, 8 feet square, bounded by 10-inch diameter poles dug into the ground and lined with 2-inch lumber. Then dump in plenty of washed garden sand.

Another inducement to play activity is an outdoor play court, a paved area big enough for badminton, volleyball, shuffleboard, hopscotch, paddle tennis, basketball, roller skating, and tether ball. When properly planned, most of the paved area also serves as driveway, turnaround space, guest parking, and/or patio. If you live along the northern tier of states where winters are cold, you can turn the play court into an ice-skating rink by rimming the area with 2x4's and tacking on a plastic liner. Just fill the enclosure with water and let it freeze.

More individually built play equipment, as distinguished from games, will keep the kids close to home too. Check your library for books on how to build play structures and games. Look too at such magazines as Popular Mechanics and Mechanix Illustrated for ideas on how to build climbing houses, slides, backyard roller coasters, and similar equipment.

Inside games and play equipment are just as varied as those designed for outside. For example, you can lay out a game plan on the basement floor with tape, so you can take it up later. Then there's a putting range on the floor for wintertime golf practice, darts, a bounce board for ping-pong balls, and small-scale adaptations of outside activities. The box game offers infinite variations. Bring home varied-size cardboard cartons from the supermarket, push in the tops to reinforce the upper edge, and turn the kids loose—with or without stain pens. Their imagination will turn the boxes into trains, covered wagons, spacecraft, and houses to occupy hours actively—as a contrast to being plastered in front of the evil eye, TV.

One additional point about building play equipment for your family. You will probably get as much fun out of the building as the kids do from the playing. And don't try to be too exotic in designing or adapting ideas for playthings. Often the simpler a plaything is, the better it stimulates children's imaginations. For example, one of the best play structures you can build is a simple climbing house, about 5 feet square and 5 feet high, with bars around the edge and space left for a door. Kids play inside, outside, on, and around such a simple structure, endowing it with all manner of imaginative trappings in vogue for the day.

Hobbies—The great tranquilizer for millions is a hobby. The hard-driving executive who pulls on rumpled clothes and retires to his basement workshop to build period furniture after dinner relaxes more thoroughly and with less damage to his health than the executive who wraps himself around a pitcher of martinis every night. Gardening, photography, microbiology, free-lance writing—all contribute to a change of pace and activity for men, women, and children. And there's nothing about a hobby that says it must cost a lot or even any money. Fishing, hunting, a workshop, photography, and hi-fi hobbies can cost as much or as little as you care to put into them. But, writing, gardening, stamp and all the other kinds of collecting, bird watching, reading, and the myriad of other activities cost little or nothing.

If you do take up a hobby that calls for an investment in equipment, buy smart—to give you the tools at the lowest cost. Suppose you are equipping a basement workshop. For $295 you can buy a reasonably well-equipped 10-inch table saw brand new and on its own stand. For the same $295 you can buy a table saw plus a 6-inch jointer-planer or a heavy-duty drill press—used, of course, but hardly worn. If you equip your shop with used tools, you can buy a greater variety and, as any workshopper will tell you, there's always just one more tool he *really* needs.

Similar buying tactics apply to other hobby equipment too. Buying an entire camera outfit plus darkroom equipment from someone who has grown tired of the hobby or from the estate of a practitioner who has died can save bundles of cash. A whole outfit may be wrapped up in a package and sold for $100 or $200—perhaps for 10¢ on the dollar of original investment. Keep a wary eye out for notices on company bulletin boards, ads in the company newspaper, the miscellaneous "for sale" column of the local newspaper, and any bulletins published by clubs or associations of hobbyists.

SAVINGS ON LIQUOR

Pay Less for Your Liquor—Partying these days usually calls for drinks before dinner—or simply a stand-around cocktail party. Depending on which state you may live in, liquor can cost as much as the dinner itself when you entertain friends. So, if you entertain a lot, look for ways you can economize on buying and serving liquor. Such savings enable you to entertain more often and enliven your reputation as a good host or hostess. Try some of the following ideas—

● Serve wine before, during, and after dinner instead of hard-liquor cocktails and after-dinner liqueurs. Bowery derelicts and habitués of skid rows in other cities long ago discovered the cost effectiveness of wine. Cocktails are relaxing; they tend to release the flow of conversation at parties. So, why not accomplish this "loosening up" at the least cost—and with a flourish? Reduced to pure dollars and cents, serving wine cuts cocktail hour costs about 50%. Wine punch before dinner, a sparkling glass of dinner wine during the meal, and a dessert wine will keep the party alive and brand you as an exciting hostess who dares to be different. For other ideas on serving wine, write to the Wine Advisory Board, 717 Market Street, San Francisco, California 94103.

● Buy duty-free liquor when you travel outside the United States. Low, low prices are available if you buy outside the United States and make use of your duty-free allowance.

50% Savings Idea

When Harry Sands looked at the cost of booze after the legislature raised prices in state liquor stores by 60¢ a fifth for gin, bourbon, and Scotch, he took another look at wines. At first he decided—"Wine may be okay with food, but I like mixed drinks—cocktails before dinner!" Harry's wife wrote to the Wine Institute Home Advisory Service, 717 Market Street, San Francisco, California 94103, and asked for help. She received a folder of recipes for cocktails mixed with wine—Vermouth Old-Fashioned Cocktail, Sherry Old-Fashioned, Wine Gimlet, Sheri-Tini, and others. Sure, the taste was different, but the price was right—about half the cost of drinks mixed with gin and bourbon.

● Don't play the "snob brand" game with liquors. Develop your own taste and serve good liquor—not necessarily the most expensive or the most frequently advertised. Obviously, some brands of whiskey are "better" than others; some tase "whiskier" than others too. The guest who drinks his liquor "neat" or with a minimum of water is likely to savor the taste and aroma of a really good whiskey. But, don't waste good whiskey in a mixed drink. Use one, two, or three qualities (read "price") of whiskey and serve drinks according to taste. Don't advertise brands—simply pour whatever whiskey you buy into a decanter. No one but you knows which is which.

● Watch the difference in proof content for price. Bottled-in bond whiskey at 100 proof costs more than 80 or 86-proof whiskey of the same brand. Similar differences in price exist between 100-, 90-, and 80-proof vodka. Mostly party drinkers will be just as happy with a second or third cocktail mixed from a lower-proof liquor. If the only purpose of serving drinks is to get everybody drunk—serve lots of wine.

TRIPS AND VACATIONS

"Getting away from it all" for 2 weeks, more or less, still occupies much of our thinking, dreaming, and planning. If travel to exotic, far-away places is one of your goals, you will already have begun to practice the many economies necessary to save money for a trip. But, careful planning can make the same travel budget go farther. Here's how—

Free Help for Trip Planning—Whether you go by car, boat, airplane, or railway, study the multitude of travel folders, booklets, and brochures available. Planning a trip is half the fun, so, use the following sources for reams of free information—

- Write to the Chamber of Commerce or Visitors Bureau at the major city in the area you plan to visit. Hotels and motels may respond directly, or the Visitors Center may bundle many folders describing accomodations, plus brochures on the many attractions in the area, and mail them together. Tourism is big business, and active Chambers of Commerce promote their areas by advertising and responding to mail inquiries. Write also to the state house, business and development commission, or other agency in the state. Such agencies gladly supply road maps and folders on attractions to visit. The Canadian federal government plus each of the provinces supply similar information to lure you across the border.

- Airlines actively promote tours and travel to exotic lands overseas and close to home. Visit or write to a local office for travel brochures. Pan American and TWA also make available detailed guides to Europe and other foreign countries for a small fee.

- Railroads, ship lines, ferry systems, and, particularly, travel agencies—all provide a tremendous variety of folders, booklets, and brochures. Only when you begin to look will you discover the wide range of free literature available to help you plan your trip or vacation.

- Travel books in your library are another good source of information. Look too, while in your library, for back issues of travel magazines. Examine the articles and study the ads, particularly the small inch-high ads near the back, for low-cost travel ideas. These small ads are a source of ideas for a vacation that's different—a week's sailing cruise of the Caribbean, a guided pack-mule trip into the rugged wild areas of Idaho, or a float-plane fishing excursion into unfished lakes of Canada's Rockies. A postcard will bring a raft of information to help you plan your trip. Spread these travel-planning materials all out on the floor of your living room and take your trip several times vicariously. You'll enjoy the planning even if you don't take the trip.

Get the Off-Season Habit—Play the game of tourism and vacation economics backwards to get more fun for your vacation buck. Habit conspires with the law of supply and demand to push prices up during the relatively short seasons most favored by crowds. Hotel operators along Miami's gold coast know they can get higher prices from December 15 through March because that's when frozen northerners descend on the area in mobs to soak up the sun. At other times, hotels scrape for business by lowering room rates and putting together package deals.

Similar price reductions attract skiers to resorts during weekdays instead of crowded weekends. A skier can get in twice as many runs on a Wednesday as on a Saturday—at a 20 to 30% lower lift ticket price.

Sure, you must plan a little to take advantage of off-season or off-peak periods. Instead of taking the usual 2 weeks' vacation in August along with everybody else, try taking 2 or 3 days at a time for skiing during the week when the slopes are practically deserted. Or, fly to Nassau in April instead of February and spend the difference at upgraded accommodations or on a ship cruising the out-islands. Possibilities are limited only by your creative imagination.

Camping as a Family Vacation—Spending your vacation in a leaky tent and cooking over a smoky fire may not be your idea of a vacation—but such a picture is out of focus these days. Travel trailers, truck coaches, fold-up tents, propane stoves, and fix-in-a-minute meals have taken most of the work out of camping and left practically all of the fun. A family can rent equipment to visit the state and national parks, forest areas, and privately operated campgrounds for little more than the cost of staying home. Instead of staying in one spot, tour the natural scenic spots, camping in a different area every night. At some of the best locations, use your camp as a base, then fan out and explore the country. Every state, including Hawaii and Alaska plus Canada, maintain excellent camp-grounds to attract out-of-state visitors. Nearly all campgrounds are close to swimming areas and some offer a round of entertainment from teen-age dances to nature talks by park naturalists. National Parks and National Forest camping areas formerly offered free camping, but now most areas are open only if you pay. State parks also charge for use of overnight camping facilities. Some of the best campsites are offered by private operators such as KOA (Kampgrounds of America). They offer transient facilities or terminal facilities where natural attractions encourage a stay of several days or more.

Take your choice—crowded main campgrounds in the widely known areas or off-the-beaten-track campsites that are seldom used. You can camp on ocean beaches or among tall trees of park areas.

Equipment rentals may run from $125 per week for a camping tailer you fold up to $35-$70 per day plus 10 to 18¢ per mile for a self-contained motor coach. With such equipment, you needn't worry about motels and their "No Vacancy" signs. And campers are among the most friendly folk on the road.

Tips for Economy-Minded Travelers—Regardless of where you go or the kind of vacation trip you take, you can save money without affecting your fun by studying the cost effectiveness of alternatives. A few tips to save you real money on vacations are—

• Evaluate the cost breaks on transportation. Trains and airlines price tickets for children differently. Amtrak, for example, allows children under the age of five to ride free. Airlines charge children half price from ages two through 12. So, if you have children from ages two to five, you save the ticket price by taking the train instead of flying. Family-plan rules also vary. Take time to evaluate the different air fares available. They include charters to Europe and vacations spots, excursion round-trip fares, different kinds of family fares, student and military standby rates, and lower fares after dinner or after midnight. A knowledgeable travel agent or airline reservations clerk who is not pressed for time will price out the differences.

You must check the days of the week that family plan fares apply and, in the case of some airlines, how long the tickets are valid. An excursion fare, for example, may require you to stay at least 7 days but not more than 22.

• Rent cars on vacation from those outfits that may be within sight of an airport, but do not maintain service counters opposite the baggage claim rack. Car rental outfits that include words like "budget, economy, low-cost" in their name will rent compact cars for as little as $10 or $12 a day with no mileage charge (you pay for gasoline), compared to the usual $15 to $18 per day and 12-18¢ per mile.

• Look into the room-rate structure according to location. Note the difference in rates for motels or hotels that may be a block or two from the beach. Along Florida's coast, hotels that front on the ocean or the gulf charge first-class rates. But just across the street or highway, similar accommodations rent for one-quarter to one-third less—including beach rights. A block or two back from the beach, rates may be as little as half those fronting on the water. Similar differences in rates apply at ski resorts, lake front spas, and hotels near the center of things in a city. Look too for differences between beach hotels that are brand new and those a few years older. Major savings in costs are available by picking your accommodations for cost effectiveness—remember, the water and sun bless large areas with little distinction.

• Look for the "Children Free" sign when stopping at hotels and motels. Usually this means that children are free when they stay in the same room as their parents. When traveling by car, two children can sleep on the floor in sleeping bags in a single room, or a family with three or four children can occupy a double room with one or two of the children sleeping on the floor.

• Traveling with children in a car for long distances with a number of stops en route for sleeping and eating can be trying for parents and expensive—but traveling by car can be less expensive than even the best family plans. Eating in restaurants along the way also runs into money fast. To cut the cost of eating, and to save time, consider eating cereal in your motel room out of the individual packages designed to hold milk right in the carton. For Mom and Dad, pack a little immersion coil to heat water for instant coffee or tea. Milk and sweet rolls picked up the night before plus an orange eaten later in the car complete a breakfast that can be eaten while packing up to save travel time. At lunchtime, construct sandwiches while driving and top them off with more fruit eaten out of hand.

EDUCATION

How to pay for college? With the cost of a college education spiraling upward even faster than the cost of living, worries about how to pay for children's college press heavily on families. While paying for an education is not "fun" in the strictest sense, a college education represents a desirable goal—one that parents actually take pride in—so it's fun—in my wide definition of fun. For children the time and money invested in a college education can be expected to return an extra $250,000 to $500,000 and up over a lifetime compared to graduation from high school only.

Paying for College—No single way is likely to be the answer for helping your children go to college. Consider these ideas for reducing the impact of college costs—

● Pick a college or university close to home, preferably one supported by the state or community. While the "name" universities concentrated in northeastern United States confer unique status on their graduates, achievement after graduation depends primarily on your boy or girl. For many jobs, a college degree is an entrée—and the basic education available at state institutions compares favorably with the most expensive private colleges. But costs can vary widely. Tuition alone in a private college is apt to cost up to six to eight times as much as tuition in a state school. You can figure that college costs, while variable and manageable within certain limits, will run from $4,000 to $50,000 for a 4-year course. The $4,000 cost is for the student who lives at home and attends a publicly supported school. For students who attend the posh universities and party it up after classes, the $50,000 figure may be low.

● Attend a 2-year community college before transferring to a degree-granting institution. Community colleges are springing up like mush-

---

75% Savings Idea

The same year Fred White's second boy was ready for college, layoffs in the aerospace industry cut Fred's income to $76 a week—unemployment compensation. Within a couple of months, he was working again—but at only two-thirds his former salary. Something had to give. So, Fred's second boy registered at a community college only 6 miles from his home—tuition plus books and fees cost $198 per quarter—about $600/year plus $200 commuting and live-at-home expense—compared to $2360 tuition plus $460 transportation and $1,850 for room and board at the college he had planned to attend. The oldest boy, already beyond the 2-year level, transferred to a state college and began "batching" it with two roommates instead of living it up in a fraternity house. The boys didn't drop out of college, but they learned quickly to live with the changes.

---

rooms after a damp spring to provide a start for students who can't get into a 4-year college or who can't afford living away from home.

● Apply for scholarship, fellowship, or grant-in-aid financial help. Along with increases in tuition has come a proliferation of financial-aid plans (exlusive of loans). Scholarships obviously go to students with good grades, and the competition for scholarships is keen, but other factors also affect grants. Financial need is one. An applicant from a low-income family is more likely to receive financial aid than an applicant from a well-to-do family—when grades are comparable. Special organizations, such as labor unions, fraternal clubs, and employers also make funds available for scholarships. The Federal Government and certain state governments make grants to aid in financing college costs. The important thing, other than having excellent grades, is to look far and wide at the myriad possibilities. Some schools grant a number of small scholarships to as many as three-fourths of their students while others grant big-money awards to a smaller percentage. Here, you must consider the total net cost. Total cost after accepting a small scholarship at a private school may be more than full tuition and other costs at another. Check with the college financial-aid counselor at the college you plan to attend for help in searching out scholarship and grant-in-aid possibilities or check out the following sources of information: *College Aid for Students*, Supt. of Documents, Washington, D.C. 20402 (includes a bibliography of other sources); *Need a Lift?*, The American Legion Education and Scholarship Program, P. O. Box 1055, Indianapolis, Indiana 46206; and *The Ambitious Student's Guide to 201 Sources of Financial Aid*, Octamaron Associates, Box 3437, Alexandria, VA 22302.

● Start saving early. Compound interest works wonders in multiplying even small savings over several years. If you start 5 to 10 years ahead, consider buying mutual funds or stocks. When your boy or girl reaches 12, help them to begin earning their own money to set aside for college. One helpful incentive is to set up a special savings account for each child. For every dollar he earns and deposits in the account, you match it with a dollar. A small but consistent program of savings for college practiced over a long period yields much more cash than a crash program of a few months.

● Train your boy or girl for part-time work. Work opportunities at colleges are sparse and competitive. One reason is that few college students offer any skill other than "brute force and awkwardness." Yet, in most communities there are crying needs for skilled typists, auto repair mechanics, appliance servicemen, business machine operators, etc. Instead of simply working at odd jobs or a low-skilled summer job, a boy or girl headed for college could better spend a summer learning an interim trade. A girl skilled in typing and taking shorthand or in operating billing, cold-typesetting, or keypunch machines quickly finds part-time work. Students working their way through college these days face three handicaps: (1) college is so competitive, even good students must spend more time studying to maintain their grades, leaving less time for work; (2) part-time jobs are hard to find because a student can work so few regular hours and so many students are looking for the few jobs available; (3) part-time work nets the average student a disappointing return for unskilled labor because they compete against the largest unemployed group in the country. One answer—learn selling, a high-paying, part-time job with unlimited flexibility.

● Reduce a student's "board bill" when he leaves home. Except for some private schools, a student's food bill may amount to more than tuition and books. So, in line with the business practice of cutting the big expenditures, look at ways to cut the "board bill": (1)Board jobs, where a student works in the kitchen or serves at a sorority house, lunchroom, or restaurant in exchange for meals, usually pay off better than working for money, then buying meals. Also, the time spent usually includes time for eating. (2) Several students can live in an apartment and cook their own meals. The one danger here is not getting a nutritionally balanced diet. Costs, particularly if the students practice many of the ideas in Chapter 2, can be less than half the price of meals at a college cafeteria or restaurant.

● Borrow money to get through school. Like so many reactions to a need for bundles of cash, many students are borrowing money for school and repaying after graduation. The Federal Government is now guaranteeing loans up to $1000 per year with a limit of $5000 for a full course of study. Furthermore, the interest and repayment of the loans doesn't begin until the student is out of school for a full year, and he has 10 years to repay. College loan funds and banks or other loan institutions are also offering money to finance education. There are several real advantages and a few disadvantages to such a program of borrowing: (1) Extended college programs, such as professional medical, dental, or law schools, can deplete normal sources for financing college. Also, in medical and other graduate schools, there is practically no time available for part-time work, and the costs for tuition, books, special equipment, etc., increase drastically. So, borrowing for the last several years may be the only way to finish a professional course. (2) Depending on the number of children a family tries to finance through college, family resources can be turned to repayment after children leave home. (3) Repayment of college loans by the student can be made from earnings at a higher rate than similar time spent at a part-time job while in school. (4) A momentous debt to be repaid right after graduation, while a young man or woman may be also interested in marrying and starting a family, can be like a millstone around the couple's neck. (5) Money that goes to repay a loan also costs interest; whereas, money saved ahead of time for college pays interest. The difference between interest paid and interest earned can amount to as much as the principal amount itself.

● Attend evening or correspondence school. Would-be students who find attending full-time college impossible because of family responsibilities or other reasons can register for correspondence courses. Schools offer instruction in vocational and academic subjects by mail or in evening classes, but few schools offer enough instruction to qualify for a degree equivalent to that gained after a 4-year college course. Evening and correspondence course work can lead to that all-important degree, but the road is a hard one.

SAVE MONEY ON BOOKS, MAGAZINES, AND RECORDS

Reading for fun and listening to records can be achieved at bargain prices by limiting impulse buying and by planning:

Buy Books for Less—The best way to buy books for less is to buy only paperbacks. So much of the worlds's literature is available in handy, soft bindings that, unless you are primarily interested in filling bookshelves with colorful books, you can build a library for a fifth to a third of the cost of hardbounds.

Hardbound books or volumes not available in paperback form can be purchased at 25 to 40% discounts through bookstores selling by mail. Also, for certain standards, like popular cookbooks, dictionaries, travel books, etc., local stores offer 20% discounts.

Book clubs offer savings on hardbound books two ways. (1) One or more books are offered as an inducement to sign up. (2) Volume buying or republishing by the clubs permits them to cut prices below regular list from the publisher. To gain maximum benefit, accept the premium for signing up, buy only the minimum number of books required, then resign from the club. For example, suppose a club offers any three books from a wide selection for $1 if you sign up to buy a minumum of four additional books within 12 months. First, you'll pick the most expensive three books from the selection offered, other things being equal. Second, you will buy only the four additional books you really want—not the ones that will come regularly, unless you advise the club not to send each month's selection. When you complete your contract, you will have purchased seven books and paid for only four plus $1. If you want to buy additional books, join another club or wait a few months and rejoin the first one and get the benefit of receiving premiums once again.

Used books, particularly those nontimely, expensive volumes promoted extensively by mail, are good buys too. The persuasive mailings sent out by publishers move many books into homes—and then into used bookstores. Browsing in stores that cater to used books is an eye-opening experience. Prices are seldom higher than half the original price. And, on the bargain tables, you can find books for 10% of their original cost. New books are also put on a clearance table to reduce overstocks. Good bargains are available, particularly after Christmas or at the beginning of summer.

Magazines for Less—Impulse buying of magazines from a newsstand is the most costly way of keeping up with the times. There are two sure ways to cut the costs of reading magazines—

● Subscribe at rock-bottom prices for the magazines you do want. Magazines can and do sell subscriptions at half their normal subscription price, which may be only 35 to 40% of the price you would pay for the same number of issues at a newsstand. One of the reliable sources for magazine subscriptions at a discount is Publishers Clearing House, 382 Main Street, Port Washington, N.Y. 11050.

● Library copies of magazines can be read at home like books. Most libraries now circulate copies of a wide variety of magazines, so it is no longer necessary to read issues only in the library itself.

Records at Big Savings—Discounting of records has reached such proportions that buying at the list prices is only for the inept shoppers or those who order obscure editions requiring special service. Look at these ways to buy the specific records you want at prices around half the so-called list—

● Buy single records only at the discount stores or record departments of cut-rate drug and department stores. Spectacular reductions in price are likely to go along with a limited selection of the most popular records—a practice known as "cherry picking." Be alert too for the regular clearance sales.

● Examine the offerings of the record clubs and mail-order record outlets. Record clubs are becoming more competitive as local sources discount records to lower and lower levels. For example, a leading record club recently offered a special introductory offer of "Any 8 Albums for only $1." The contract offered the eight albums for $1 to anyone who agreed to buy an album a month at the list price for 8 succeeding months. All prices included a small charge for postage. A contract calls for paying $1 plus 8 x $4.98 for 16 records. Total cost equals $39.84 plus $1 or $40.84. Divided by 16, each record album then costs about $2.55 each plus shipping and packaging costs. Be sure, though to stop your purchases when you have completed your contract to buy the eight albums; otherwise, you will be paying list price plus postage with one free album for each two albums bought. As a new member, you get one album essentially free (12¢) for each album bought. Instead of buying more albums through the club, resign your membership and join another club or rejoin the club later to get the sign-up premium.

● Special offerings of high quality records are made available through *The Reader's Digest* and other organizations. Prices per record average about $2 plus postage. The quality is high, but you may be getting only parts of classical selections. Also, when you buy a five- or ten-record collection, there may be a few or many duplications of selections you already own.

● Many companies offer a wide range of records at a regular price of $1.79, $1.98, or $2. Suprisingly enough, these cut-rate offerings are of good quality, some better than others. Children's records, often played on $19.95 players, are plenty good for the treatment they get. Many of these low-price records are sold through food markets and outlets other than established record stores. *Changing Times* magazine and *Consumer Reports* offer advice on which of these low-price records are of good quality, both as to reproduction and performance.

● Don't overlook the range of records available on loan from your library. Expensive classical performances of orchestras and entire operas are available for no cost.

Movies at Home—Often overlooked as a source of low-cost educational entertainment are the many movies that can be shown at home for the family or in groups. The only catch here is the need for a 16 mm sound film projector. A new projector can cost $500 to $800, but a used machine can be picked up for considerably less. Once you have a machine, however, you can take advantage of free films from your local library or borrow industrially produced films for the cost of return postage only. Many full-color films are produced every year for showing to Boy Scout, church, and club groups. You may even organize your own film-viewing group to qualify for group showing of industrial films.

PERSONAL CARE

In our affluent society, more and more money is being spent to retain the look and feel of youth, to achieve a glamourous appearance, and to buy professional personal care. Where money spent for personal care means more than money spent on some other fun-type activity, by all means spend it, but consider spending less while retaining the look you want—

● Housewives can barter for help in giving each other permanents, hair colorings, and hair stylings. Manufacturers have solved so many of the technical problems of coiffeur chemistry that many women handle these chores themselves. But, there's no getting around it, another pair of hands is a big help in putting up all those home permanent curlers.

● Buy cosmetics from mail-order houses according to basic type rather than the heavily promoted brands. Cleansing cream is, for all intents and purposes, pretty much the same. But prices vary within a range of 300%. Choose basic cosmetics, for example, from Sears or Wards. Hudson Products, West Caldwell, NJ 07006, also sells a line of low-cost basic cosmetics. A number of other companies supply cosmetics by mail at prices as much as 50% under highly advertised brands. Don't overlook, either, the discounts offered by drugstores and other outlets on brand-name cosmetics. Discount drugstores, particularly, offer loss-leader promotions similar to specials offered by supermarkets to bring in customers.

● Beauty and barber colleges operate in most cities. Here everything from permanents to haircuts and hair stylings can be purchased at piddling prices. While operators are students and you may get less than a professional job, most legitimate schools guard against real "butchers." First, only advanced students are allowed to operate on volunteers. Second, instructors watch every move to help students in their training and to make sure the job is acceptable. Many times, a student permanent for $9.50 is every bit as good as one costing $25 because the student and instructor take more interest than a bored operator in a beauty salon. Look in the classified pages of your telephone directory for leads to beauty and barber schools.

● Be your own barber if your family includes a number of boys. When they are small, it's no trick to cut boys' hair. Purchase electric shears for $7.95 from a mail-order house and you'll get a detailed step-by-step guide on how to cut children's hair. A little practice, a homemade cape to keep cuttings off clothes, and you're in business. Instead of paying $2.25 to $4.50 per haircut, line up the kids and cut their hair yourself—it's often easier than carting them off to the barber.

GIFTS—GIVE MORE FOR LESS

One of the great fun things in life is to be able to give things or services to others. Whenever you give something today, though, consider the tax effects. Sometimes you can give more with no increase in cost by doing it right. Sometimes you gain by giving goods rather than money. You almost always gain more if part of your gift is your own sincerity.

Gifts to Your Church—Fun can be described as doing something we *really want to do*. Giving to your church certainly falls within this all-inclusive definition. Suppose, for example, that you own 100 shares stock that has been increasing in value through the years. Say its current market value is $100 per share and you bought it at $30. If you sold the stock, you would gain $70 per share profit, and with the aid of the capital gains provisions of the income tax laws, you would pay, say 30% on 40% of the profit or $8.40 per share in tax. For every $100 worth of stock you sold, you would be able to give the church $91.60 and be able to deduct the same $91.60 from your adjusted income as a contribution. A better way is simply to give your church the stock and let the church sell it for $100 per share. They get the full $10,000 and you still get the full $10,000 as a deduction from your income tax. The same benefit accrues from giving some object of art or other item of value. Give the object rather than selling it and giving the money.

Maybe you're not in a position to give your church $100 shares of stock. Consider giving your time instead. If you could spend half a day in the church office regularly, the church could save the cost of hiring half a secretary. Or, perhaps you can handle the many mailings a church sends out by doing the work at home to save the cost of a mailing service. Husbands in the church membership can make similar contributions of their time and effort by helping on landscaping chores, maintaining the church itself, and taking on some chores that normally must be paid for.

Fund-raising drives for a church or charity are often something other than a straight canvass for money. Old standbys in this area are baked-goods and garden-plant sales. You, as a church member, can contribute your skill as a cook or gardener along with a minimum out-of-pocket cost and benefit your church considerably more than a simple gift of cash.

Give a Little of Yourself—Whitman wrote, "When I give, I give myself." How much more appreciated is the Christmas card that is homemade, that includes a picture of the family or children or includes a personal note rather than the coldly professional card imprinted with the name of the sender. The gift of homemade jelly or fancy cookies at Christmas produces a warm feeling, because the receiver knows that a part of the giver came with the gift. The cost of a gift is less important than the thoughtfulness and sincerity of the gift itself.

In a family situation, expensive toys, fancy clothes, and paid-for activities are a poor substitute for the time parents spend with their children. A child would rather spend an hour with his Dad than play for hours with a toy his father sent him. There is a two-way benefit from giving yourself to your children. First, of course, there are fewer cash outlays for toys and playthings. Second, and more important, a boy or girl knows when a Dad is giving himself. They sense that Dad's time is a precious commodity.

Buy Gifts for Less—When no substitute for a purchased gift will do, plan ahead for Christmas and birthdays. If Dad, a brother-in-law, or a nephew is a regular on your gift list, buy a shirt, socks, tie, or sports coat when they are on sale. Even if Dad's birthday is in May, buy him a shirt in the after-Christmas sale. If you plan to give your son a new pair of skis for his birthday in October, buy them during the spring after-season sales and store them away.

Buy gifts at the discount stores, even in season. Toys, particularly, are subject to widespread discounting. Kids couldn't care less if the gift they want came in a box with a posh department store's name on the outside. Your shopping acumen really pays off in selecting and buying gifts for all occasions.

SUMMING UP

Two ideas are linked into one as the basic philosophy behind this book—

1. You learn how to spend more on those activities you enjoy, those fun-type activities that make life interesting.
2. This is the chapter that tells how to spend the money you have saved to have more fun—to do the things you really want to do. And, like the other money-spending activities, fun can be had for less than you might suppose by—

- Taking advantage of the *free* fun opportunities in your community.

- Enjoying spectator and participation sports for less.

- Spending fun time at home and at hobbies.

- Learning the economics of partying and serving liquor—at a discount.

- Taking more trips and traveling widely.

- Putting your children through college.

- Buying books, records, and magazines at bargain prices.

- Spending less for personal care, beauty treatments, and the like.

- Sharing more of your good fortune with your church and favorite charities—with little increase in dollar cost.

8

USE A FAMILY SPENDING PLAN
TO GET MORE OF THE
THINGS YOU REALLY WANT

Sound management of a family's money, like the management of business finances, depends on a plan and at least a few records. Learn how to plan your spending to get even more benefits from your aggressive program of money management. Step-by-step, you'll develop your spending plan to—

- Establish family spending goals.

- Find your present total family income from all sources.

- Determine your present expenses in all categories.

- Plan where your family's money comes from and where it goes.

"We've got the best planned poverty in town," one wife commented in a conversation on budgets. If budgeting is a nasty word in your family, talk instead about a Spending Plan that lets you spend *more money*—not less—on the things *you want*.

First, let's see what a Spending Plan is *not*.

- It is not a cure-all for family money problems.
- It need not be tedious and time consuming.
- It will not, by itself, start a fight between husband and wife. But, if disagreements over money are already causing quarrels in a family, a Spending Plan may bring hidden problems into the open.
- It is not an iron-clad document that can't be changed—or even bent out of shape at times.

Second, let's see what a Spending Plan *is*. The important word is *plan*. Planned spending calls for thought and discipline. The opposite— haphazard, whimsical, impulsive spending from one pocketful of change to the next—leads families into money trouble. A Spending Plan is a form of discipline. Simply writing down the goods and services you want this year, during the next 5 years, or at retirement can be a powerful form of discipline. Goods and services, as used here, include attending concerts and a college education for your children, as well as a boat, a new washing machine, a winter coat, etc.

Goal planning is the key to eliminating impulsive and compulsive buying—the two big actions that wreck many family money plans. Goal planning through a Spending Plan emphasizes the positive action— spending rather than saving. You and your family will find planning *for* something simpler than saving.

ESTABLISH FAMILY GOALS

What Do You Want? All of us think we know what we want—and what others want. But, until you write out your goals, you may not be aware of conflicts in your family's ideas about how money should be spent. Begin with a family conference. No one likes to be shackled to a Spending Plan dictated by someone else. Bring teen-agers into the conference too. They don't like living under a dictatorship any more than you do. Brainstorming techniques help discover what each member of the family considers important—now and later. Call for ideas, then write them on a blackboard or large sheet of paper. Don't knock down any idea at this stage. Allow every family member to express his or her own wants and needs freely. Remember, until you develop a full range of alternatives, you can't begin to choose effectively. Don't limit your thinking to necessities; include fun things too—vacation trips, a new fishing rod, clothes, records, church, education, charities. Allow everyone to express ideas during the early stages.

Only when you run out of ideas should you begin to evaluate expressed wants and needs. Consider them as goals to be achieved. Some will obviously be impossible. Other goals begin to appear more reasonable as you think more and more about them. As you evaluate your ideas, consider these goal-planning concepts:

First—What is a goal? You may want a thing—a new car or new skis. You may want a service—regular hair styling, house cleaning by an outsider, access to a golf course—any number of desirable options. Basically, a goal is something you want. Whether you "need" it or not is unimportant.

Second—Goals may be tangible or intangible. Tangible goals are those we can see, feel, hear, or touch. They exist. You can measure them precisely in terms of cost, size, or some other physical means. A car is a tangible goal. A stereo system is a tangible goal. Intangible goals can be just as important as tangible goals, possibly more so. But intangible goals may be more difficult to measure or define. Acquiring more education, developing a more vibrant personality, learning to control one's temper, or becoming a dynamic public speaker are typical intangible goals. Tangible goals usually cost money. Intangible goals usually call mainly for expenditures of time and energy. Both tangible and intangible goals deserve a place in your goal-planning program.

Third—Time affects goal planning. Some wants may be short-range goals, those you want to achieve within two or three months. Intermediate goals might extend up to a year. Long-range goals are those that extend beyond one year. You'll notice a funny thing about goals. Long-range goals, such as saving for children's education, retirement, or building a cabin on a lake in the woods, are easy to set because they are usually far out in the future. You really don't need to do anything today. Short-range goals come harder because they demand action—NOW. You can plan a trip to Mexico next fall and not do anything today. But, if you plan to fly

GOAL PLANNING

SHORT-RANGE GOALS—One to Three Months		
Item	Estimated Cost	Priority*
Total		
INTERMEDIATE-RANGE GOALS—Less Than One Year		
Item	Estimated Cost	Priority*
Total		
LONG-RANGE GOALS—More than One Year		
Item	Estimated Cost	Priority*
Total		

*Priority Scale   1—Now   2—Needed but less urgent   3—Desirable—when money is available

FIGURE 8-1

halfway across the country next week, you'd better make reservations and get a ticket now. Timing affects both goal planning and goal-directed action. Actionize long-range goals by breaking them into numerous, scheduled short-range goals. To achieve a retirement income of X-number dollars, plan to put aside so many dollars every month. Each month's contribution then becomes a short-range goal on the way to achieving a long-range goal.

Fourth—Not all goals are equally achievable or equally important. Only by examining their cost in terms of money, time, and effort and evaluating the importance of each goal relative to the others can you develop a meaningful set of family goals. Use the Goal Planning Worksheet (Figure 8-1) to help you priortize your goals—to help you decide which ones are most important to you and to each member of your family.

Finally—Bring all these factors into focus by first estimating the dollar cost of each goal. If you find the dollar total staggering and beyond your means, as most families do, here's where you begin choosing. One system uses a 3-stage priority rating—1 for "Urgent," 2 for "Needed but Postponable," and 3 for "Desirable—When Money Is Available." Hopefully, not all of your goals will fall into the Urgent category. You may refine and rework your goals and priorities for achieving them for several days, weeks, or months. But, don't put off going on to the next step in developing your family Spending Plan.

Sources	Period	Annual Total	Monthly Total
Wages			
Husband	Weekly		
Wife	Monthly		
Interest			
Life Insurance Dividends	Yearly		
Savings Account	Semi-annually		
Investments			
Stock dividends	Quarterly		
Miscellaneous			
Craft sales	Irregular		
Garage rent	Weekly		
	Total		

FIGURE 8-2: What's Your Income? (A Sample List)

WHAT'S YOUR INCOME?

Lay aside your wish list for a moment and figure your total income. Most families depend on weekly, biweekly, or monthly paychecks for cash. But don't forget other income—interest on savings account, rent, dividends on stock investments, or extra moonlighting income from part-time work. Put down the gross amounts—before the deductions for income tax withholding, Social Security (FICA), and the seemingly endless other deductions (Figure 8-2).

Salesmen and others who depend on commissions, independent businessmen, or farmers whose income varies with the whims of the weather and the market will have to rely on estimates. Past earnings plus an educated look to the future, however, can help to develop a usable annual income. Even if your SWEG (that's *s*weeping, *w*ild-*e*yed *g*uess) should be off by 10—even 20%—you'll have a base to work from. Then, if your estimated income falls short at each monthly check point, you can adjust spending to compensate.

DEVELOP YOUR SPENDING PLAN

At this point you're ready to assemble the pieces and develop a Spending Plan that will help you manage your family's money and achieve your high-priority goals. If you find that managing your money is difficult *with* a spending plan, it's *impossible* without one. Developing your Spending Plan requires two steps:

First—Analyze where and how your family now spends its money. You'll see two major divisions on the Spending Plan Worksheet—Current Spending and Desired Spending (Figure 8-3). Work through the Current Spending first. If you keep some records of your spending, you should be able to fill in the blanks with little trouble. Examine check stubs, past bills, and installment contracts to help you account for big chunks of your current spending. For expenses you pay once or twice a year, divide the annual amount by 12 to reach a monthly figure. You should be able to read the social security and income tax deductions directly off your paycheck stubs. Convert these to a monthly figure. Hardest to define will be your out-of-pocket or cash spending. If you have no idea how to begin apportioning personal spending, keep a detailed record of your cash spending for one or several weeks—long enough to see a pattern. Each day write down the cash you spend for lunches, cigarettes, coffee—everything! At the end of the day, divide these expenditures into the categories noted on the Spending Plan Worksheet. Apply a SWEG if you must, but try to account for at least 95-98 percent of your total income. Ask every member of your family to help in figuring where all the money goes. You gain two benefits from this exercise—(1) Every member can contribute information that helps to account for all spending, and (2) Everyone begins to understand the principles of operating a Spending Plan.

When you finish estimating your spending (first column of Figure 8-3), compare total expenses with your income. If you are spending less, you are already putting money away. If your estimated expenditures exceed your income, look at your plan for leaks.

One help in matching a Spending Plan to your income is to look at what other families are spending (Table 8A). For example, compare the percentage of income you spend for food to that spent by other families. But use judgment in such comparisons. No family is exactly like yours. So, your family's spending will differ from the averages.

Now—you're ready to begin choosing and changing. If your spending is like most individuals or families, you'll find too little cash left to achieve important goals. You face the following options at this point—

● Expand income—But, earning more income may prove difficult over the short term. Also, you may keep only 80 to 50 spendable cents from every added dollar earned after taxes depending on your income.

● Continue doing without some or all of the desirable goals established in your family conference and goal planning sessions.

● Change your pattern for spending current resources. Changes may come hard, as we tend to cling to old habits. Every family needs to make its own decisions, as there are few meaningful guidelines. There is no reason why your spending pattern should conform to some other family's or individual's pattern or published averages. Neither is there reason to consider your present spending pattern as unchangeable.

If you and/or your family is typical, you will probably combine portions of all three of the above options. You may increase your income through merit or cost-of-living increases or by moonlighting at a part-time job. You may have to postpone some of your desired goals. But, your biggest opportunity may be to change your present spending patterns to gain more spending power from current income.

Examine every category in the Spending Plan Worksheet (Figure 8-3). When you allocate all income into categories (including savings), you can increase spending in one category only by decreasing spending in one or more other categories. Certain spending can be difficult to change—mortgage payments, for example. Organization dues, life

SPENDING PLAN ANALYSIS WORKSHEET°

	Spending Category	Current Spending		Desired Spending		
		Weekly	Monthly	Weekly	Monthly	%
MARKET	Food, including quantity purchases					
	Delivered milk and/or bread					
	Nonfood items (paper, cleaning supplies, etc.)					
	Subtotal					
HOUSING	Rent or mortgage payment					
	Taxes					
	Hazard Insurance					
	Utilities (water, heat, electrical, etc.)					
	Maintenance & repairs					
	Home furnishings ⎱ (Installment payments)					
	Home equipment ⎰					
	Subtotal					
TRANSPORTATION	Car owning costs (payments, etc.)					
	Car operating (gas oil, license)					
	Car maintenance, repairs, & tires					
	Car insurance					
	Subtotal					
CLOTHING	Purchases					
	Cleaning & laundry					
	Repair (shoe, etc.)					
	Subtotal					
PERSONAL SPENDING — **HUSBAND**	Recreation (movies, sports tickets, dinners out)					
	Beverages (alcoholic & other)					
	Cigarettes & tobacco					
	Bus fares					
	Personal care (haircuts, etc.)					
	Newspapers, magazines, etc.					
	Subtotal					
WIFE	Personal care (beauty)					
	Cigarettes					
	Lunches					
	Bus Fares					
	Miscellaneous					
	Subtotal					

FIGURE 8-3

	Spending Category	Current Spending		Desired Spending		%
		Weekly	Monthly	Weekly	Monthly	
MEDICAL	Physicians' and dentists' visits					
	Hospitalization & medical ins. premiums					
	Drugs, prescriptions & other					
	Subtotal					
FAMILY BETTERMENT	Education					
	Club dues & other					
	Vacations					
	Sports (other than tickets)					
	Hobbies					
	Subtotal					
GIFTS & CONTRIB.	Birthday & Christmas gifts					
	Church and other contributions					
	Subtotal					
MISC.	Life insurance					
	Dues & occupational expenses					
SAVINGS OR DEBT PAYMENTS	Bank, savings					
	Credit union					
	Savings & loan					
	Other					
	Subtotal					
	TOTAL SPENDING					
TAXES	Social Security (FICA)					
	Income tax					
	Other					
	Subtotal					
	TOTAL INCOME					

FIGURE 8-3 Spending Plan Analysis Worksheet (Continued)

TABLE 8A: Family Spending Patterns—Family of Four

	Lower budget	%	Intermediate budget	%	Higher budget	%
Total budget (Annual)	$11,436	100.0	$18,682	100.0	$27,571	100.0
Total family consumption	9,361	81.9	14,426	77.2	20,545	74.5
Food	3,491	30.5	4,484	24.0	5,645	20.4
Housing	2,248	19.7	4,365	23.4	7,109	25.8
Transportation	870	7.6	1,594	8.5	2,172	7.9
Clothing	855	7.5	1,221	6.5	1,787	6.5
Personal care	302	2.6	404	2.2	573	2.1
Medical care	1,073	9.4	1,088	5.8	1,280	4.6
Other family consumption	522	4.6	1,270	6.8	1,979	7.2
Other items	526	4.6	850	4.5	1,269	4.6
Taxes and deductions	1,549	13.5	3,406	18.3	5,757	20.9
Social security and disability	722	6.3	1,057	5.7	1,077	3.9
Personal income taxes	827	7.2	2,349	12.6	4,680	17.0

Price levels for December, 1978
Source: U.S. Bureau of Labor Statistics + update estimates

TABLE 8B: Spending Patterns for Selected Family Types

Family size, type, and age	Lower level*	Intermediate level*	Higher level*
Single person, under 35 years	$3,306	$ 4,980	$ 6,908
Husband and wife under 35 years:			
No children	4,626	6,979	9,317
1 child under 6	5,859	8,824	11,798
2 children, older under 6	6,797	10,255	13,695
Husband and wife, 35-54 years:			
1 child, 6-15 years	7,747	11,674	16,603
2 children, older 6-15 years	9,361	14,426	20,545
3 children, oldest 6-15 years	10,951	16,523	22,486
Husband and wife, 65 years and over	4,811	7,262	9,882
Single person, 65 years and over	2,640	3,986	5,482

*Price levels for December, 1978

insurance premiums, and payments on medical bills or installment contracts, such as car payments, will also be difficult or impossible to change over the short term.

As you look for ways to change the pattern of your spending, try to spend less on those elements that provide the least benefits. Your aim should be to spend less on necessities and more on desirable categories and "fun." Remember these ideas while you examine your spending critically—

● You can only save big money by attacking those categories that already account for major chunks of your income. Reducing a large expenditure by a small percentage will be easier than reducing a small expenditure by a large percentage—and the dollar results will be comparable.

- A small reduction achieved frequently will account for a considerable cash saving over a long period—say, a year.
- Examine possible investment spending to reduce continuing drains on current income. Installing insulation or any of the other energy-saving ideas in Chapter 4 can yield dividends of more cash flow every month. Often, an investment to reduce spending will yield more dollar benefits than interest or dividends from savings or stocks.
- No spending category should escape critical scrutiny.
- Take a sharp look at variable expenses. Food and clothing are two of the three necessities we can't get along without, but both are variable within wide limits. See other chapters for ideas to cut spending in one category to provide more dollars to spend in one or more other categories.
- Look at day-to-day expenses closely. Pocket-money items are often impulse purchases. Perhaps personal allowances are out of line. A 10% cut for every family member may develop their incentive to cut expenses other ways—to restore their personal allowance.

Resolve to stay within the limits for each major part of your Spending Plan. Don't worry too much if you fall short the first month. After all, if you are a skier, you didn't execute graceful parallel turns down a steep face at the end of your first lesson. And if you bowl, what was your average score after only a month's time? Don't be too discouraged if you must borrow from one fund to make up an overexpenditure in another. However, if you bend one fund out of shape to keep another solvent, borrow from one of the volatile ones—such as pocket money, recreation, clothing, or food. Having less to spend in the fun category can spur you to manage necessary expenditures more effectively.

But—let's suppose that, after a rigorous round of cost cutting, your expenses still total more than your income. By this time you recognize that your solvency is at stake. So, work through your plan one more time. Time payments often take big chunks of income. Chapter 10 details the costs and pitfalls of installment buying and provides data and plans to help you control overspending.

Analyze Your Spending Plan—A searching look at the cold written-out facts may bring to light one or more facets you may have been pushing aside. Let's look at several possibilities—

- Underspending, surprisingly enough, may be limiting the fun and pleasure you and your family get out of life. Are you setting aside too much money for retirement without considering the value of social security and company retirement fund benefits? Are you accumulating cash just for the sake of a secure feeling and denying yourself a fun-type vacation trip once or twice a year? Setting up safeguards against possible emergencies should be a part of any prudent person's Spending Plan, but oversaving, like overspending, can reduce the fun you get out of life.

● Overspending in total can only lead to personal bankruptcy if it continues. In the United States personal bankruptcies continue to increase and are running close to 200,000 a year. In one study, 83% of the bankruptcies involved persons in the 20- to 39-year age group. The first aim of any analysis is to bring spending into line with income over the long term. There are times when expenditures will exceed income, but these periods should be planned for ahead of time. Or, if an emergency strikes, current spending should be reduced to as low a level as possible, to keep borrowing to a minimum.

● Compatible spending occurs when you have matched your interests and desires with available income. Inherent in any such accord are realistic limits on desires. A Spending Plan enables you to shift emphasis from less important or less interesting areas to places where you and your family *agree* money spent can yield the most overall satisfaction. The important word here is *agree* as a family. A Spending Plan gives you *control* over spending to achieve family goals.

Regular evaluation, possibly as often as every 3 months but cerainly once a year, is desirable to see how your Spending Plan is working. If you must continually supplement one fund from either another fund or your savings allotment, increase the allocation to the fund that needs frequent transfusions. However, don't change your plan to fit your spending.

A Practical Planning and Saving Idea

Henry and Susan Deerfield wrote me after studying the First Edition. They commented, "We never really understood the value of a plan for spending before. Both of us were turned off by budgets. But, a Spending Plan is positive. We have already redirected our spending, cut out over $1000 of what had been frivolous, impulsive spending, and as soon as two unfortunate debts are paid, we're going to Europe for a summer. How's that for a goal? The thing about a Spending Plan is—when either of us starts to spend, we immediately think, 'Which account will I charge this to?' It helps to work toward a goal." Motivation through goal planning can become a powerful force. Plan to use it yourself to get what you want from your resources.

Control your spending to fit your plan. Don't change allocations to a fund without careful thought or until the amount allocated proves to be inadequate over a fairly long period, preferably at least a year, to reflect all seasons.

RECORD KEEPING

No business could operate in today's complex world without records. Bookkeeping has become incredibly sophisticated, with the assignment of computers and automated equipment to the assembly of payrolls and other accounts. Record keeping is one business practice that really pays off when adapted to family use too. All the record keeping you require for managing your money effectively can be done in less than 30 minutes a week—maybe only 15. A simple, efficient record system can even save you time overall when income tax time rolls around. Instead of sorting through envelopes of old receipts or check stubs, well-organized records provide the answers you need—and you won't miss several of those important deductions.

Any number of printed record systems are available. Some cost as much as $5 to $25 for a set of blanks that will last a year. Others are available free from Cooperative Extension Offices. But, you don't need fancy forms to keep family books. Start now to save on unnecessary spending by using the simple system detailed in Figures 8-4 and 8-5. This system lacks the precision most accountants require, but it eliminates much of the rewriting and refiguring each month that complicate many of the printed-book systems. Some of its advantages are—

● Uses simple ruled sheets in a loose-leaf notebook.
● Keeps records for years in one place.
● Provides a monthly record of how each category of spending relates to an overall Spending Plan.
● Keeps writing and rewriting to a minimum, thereby saving work.
● Provides a constant record of the spending status of specific categories of spending.
● Permits overdrawing a fund during certain seasons without upsetting the entire system.
● Regularly sets aside funds according to your Spending Plan.

Psychologists recognize a principle of behavior that states, "When you monitor spedific behavior, you effectively change that behavior." Thus, when you keep track of your spending, you tend to change your spending habits. Just keeping records helps you gain more of the goods and services you want—to actually achieve the goals you have defined as important. You can monitor your spending and change your money management behavior if you adapt the following Howgozit Charting System. This system fulfills the needs for a simple home record-keeping system like no other. The system derives its name from the function of tracking accounts and keeping information current on how each one is going—*How Goes It*—with each fund.

The Howgozit Charting System (Figure 8-4) includes two parts—

1. An accounting for checks and deposits in a bank checking account. This part is the familiar check register. You are probably already using the check register furnished as part of your blank checkbooks. You can continue to use your checkbook register or the separate worksheet labeled Check Register in the system.

2. A money Management Information System (MIS) to control and track spending by category. The MIS is an adaptation of the old and reliable envelope method of dividing and spending money in categories. Instead of placing currency and coins in separate envelopes marked "Food," "Rent," "Car," and other categories, the MIS sets up a separate fund for each category noted on the Spending Plan Worksheet. The MIS divides your overall money on deposit in your checking account into separate "envelopes" or registers by category. When you spend money, you write a check and deduct the amount from the balance just as you might have done by taking bills and coins from a specific envelope. The MIS includes a register or Howgozit Chart for each of the categories in your Spending Plan Worksheet. Each Howgozit Chart functions as a separate fund and operates on a monthly cycle. You play the Howgozit Charts like a game—every month you pass "Go" and collect that month's allocation for each of the named funds. As you pay bills throughout the month, you charge each fund or Howgozit Chart for that category of spending. An example helps to understand how you can use a typical Howgozit Chart—

One common fund is Transportation to account for car buying and operating expenses. With today's emphasis on car pooling, public transportation, and alternative modes of travel, your spending for Transportation could take several forms. Begin by examining your Spending Plan Worksheet. In the example it was decided to spend an average of $120 monthly for gasoline, repairs, insurance, and expendables such as tires, brake linings, parking, car washes, bus fares, and miscellany. The $120 might include a car payment too; it does not necessarily represent a desirable level of spending. The $120 is selected only as a round number for this example. You determine how much to spend on Transportation by working through your Spending Plan. If you are paying installments on a car, that money should be included in the monthly allocation for Transportation. Money for airplane tickets spent as part of a vacation trip should be charged to Family Betterment (recreation)—not Transportation.

At the first of each month, you would add $120 to your Transportation Howgozit Chart. (Later, you will see where the $120 for Transportation and similar allocations for other categories come from.) This allocation shows up as a $120 "Add" or credit on the Howgozit Chart for Transportation (Figure 8-4). Since the $120 is an "Add," it increases the "Balance" by $120. At the start of the MIS the $120 as a "Balance" represents money available for spending that month on transportation. As you write checks for items chargeable to Transportation, you note these amounts in the "Minus" or debit column and deduct the dollar amount from the "Balance." The "Balance" reflects the results of each transaction and will always tell you the number of dollars remaining available for spending. Each Howgozit Chart thus represents a not-so-subtle discipline on spending. The "Balance" may run into the red—indicating you have spent more than you planned to spend. The "red" balance may be written in a red pencil or may be circled to indicate an overrun. A "Balance" in the black indicates you are controlling spending for that category satisfactorily and the number of dollars remaining can be spent during the month without exceeding planned spending. The MIS presents information in the reverse of most systems because the "Balance" immediately tells you how many dollars remain—not how many dollars have been spent. Each month you increase the "Balance" or running balance by transferring money into each Howgozit Chart. Each time you write a check or note cash spending for each category, the "Balance" is decreased. The Transportatin Howgozit Chart receives cash notations and shows spending exactly the same way your Check Register shows deposits from a paycheck and spending with each check. The "Balance" always tells you how many uncommitted funds remain—not how much has been spent.

Each category in your Spending Plan rates its own Howgozit Chart. Slow-moving accounts may hold several years' transactions on a single sheet. Fast-moving funds may require several sheets each year. But, note these points—

● There is no rewriting or recopying from one month to the next. Each fund's running balance continues as each entry uses one line.

● The running balance indicates how you're doing compared to your planned spending rate. If you spend faster than your plan provides, your running balance will show an increasing red balance. If you are spending less, the running balance will gradually increase as funds remain to be spent in that category.

● The cumulative running balances of all Howgozit Charts should equal the balance in your checkbook or Check Register even though some of the Howgozit Charts (funds) may be "in the red." If the red balances exceed the black balances, your checking account will be overdrawn, if your arithmetic is correct.

● The running balance on each Howgozit Chart helps you pace or control your spending by category instead of attempting to control spending in total from the single balance in your Check Register. If Transportation is "in the red," you may decide to drive less, perform some of the maintenance yourself, elect to join a carpool, ride the bus, or find some other lower-cost alternative—even a bicycle. If you find that your planned spending for Transportation does not cover expenses for a six-month period or longer and no amount of cost-cutting can bring actual spending in line with planned spending, you should increase the allocation for Transportation. But, as part of your Spending Plan—if you increase spending on Transportation, you must reduce spending in another category, reduce savings, increase income, or go into debt.

For an overview of how the Management Information System works with the Check Register, check the system diagram in Figure 8-4. Not all of the Howgozit Charts are shown to conserve space, but the three—Housing, Transportation, and Market—provide examples for the total of 12 Howgozit Charts or spending funds that make up the full MIS.

As you will note from the system diagram, each deposit or withdrawal calls for two entries—once in the Check Register and once in the MIS or Howgozit Charts. Follow these steps that are keyed to the numbers in circles in Figure 8-4 to see how easily the MIS works:

Step No. 1—Starting with a paycheck, enter the net amount in the "Add" column of the Check Register. Increase the "Balance" accordingly.

Step No. 2—Enter the same paycheck amount in the "Add" column of the Allocation Fund (more about this fund later). Since you have added the same dollar amount to both the Check Register and the Allocation Fund, your system remains in balance.

Once a month, preferably at the first of each month, distribute each fund's allowance from the Allocation Fund as follows:

Step No. 3—Enter the total of monthly fund allowances in the "Minus" column of the Allocation Fund and decrease the "Balance" by the same amount. If the total exceeds the running balance of the Allocation Fund, simply show the difference as a "red" figure indicating an overdrawn condition. This is merely a bookkeeping maneuver, as will be explained later.

Step No. 4—Enter the allowance for each category of spending on the Howgozit Chart for that category as an "Add" and increase the "Balances" accordingly. The total of the allowances for the 12 categories must equal the total transferred out of the Allocation Fund in Step No. 3. Note that the system remains in balance because the amount transferred out of the Allocation Fund is distributed to the 12 Howgozit Charts.

Step No. 5—When you write a check, enter the amount in the "Minus" column of the Check Register and decrease the running balance by the amount of the check.

Step No. 6—Enter the amount of the check written in Step No. 5 in the "Minus" column of the Howgozit Chart representing that category of spending. Decrease the running balance accordingly. The system remains in balance because you have subtracted the same dollar amount from the Check Register and from one of the Howgozit Charts.

You may perform these steps each time you write a check or post all entries once a week to conserve time. Only when all transactions are posted will the balances of the Howgozit Charts equal the "Balance" of the Check Register.

The Allocation Fund serves two purposes:

1. When income flows in from several sources during the month, the Allocation Fund collects it—weekly paychecks from one or more persons, interest, dividends, etc. The Allocation Fund works much like a big bucket; all of the income pours into the bucket during the month. Then, at the beginning of the following month, you pour out the month's collection into the individual Howgozit Charts.

2. To start the Management Information System, you add a month's allowance to each Howgozit Chart and begin drawing on the running balance. But, most individuals or families do not have enough cash in their checking account to allocate a month's spending for each Howgozit Chart. Attempting to transfer funds when each paycheck or other bit of income is deposited becomes unwieldy. So, you can begin operation of your MIS by adding the balance showing in your Check Register to the Allocation Fund. Then, transfer the total of fund allowances as in Step No. 3 above and as shown in the example in Figure 8-4. This will leave a "red" or overdrawn balance in the Allocation Fund, but the total of the "red" balance in the Allocation Fund plus the other 12 Howgozit Chart

FIGURE 8-4: Management Information System (MIS)

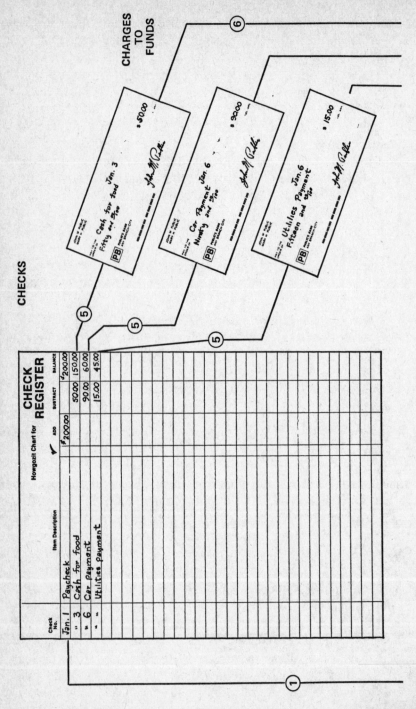

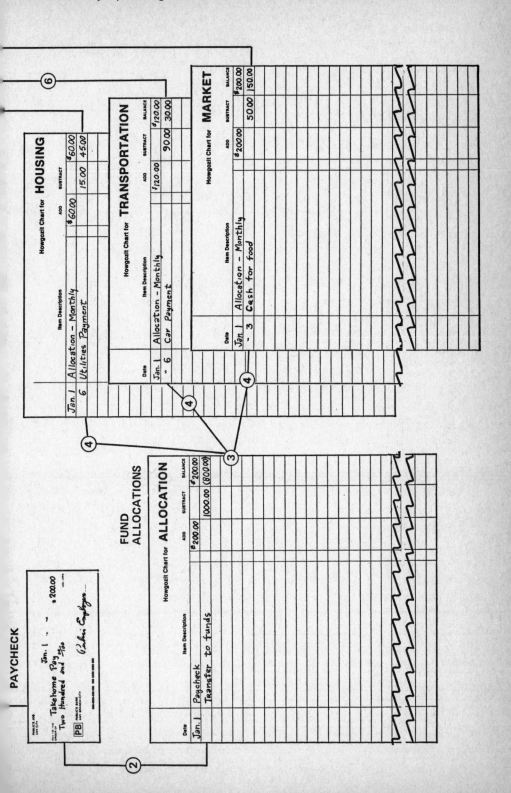

balances will still equal your balance of uncommitted funds in the Check Register. By using this system, you can begin operation of your MIS at any time.

During actual operation of your Management Information System, you will likely run into a few questions. The most frequently asked questions are:

● How do you account for pocket money? In the Spending Plan you will note two categories for Personal Spending. Simply allocate so many dollars each week or month for pocket money and don't bother accounting for each minor purchase. Account for the total spent by each person. If you are operating the MIS as an individual, simply ignore one of the Personal Spending categories. If you are operating the MIS as a family, include children's allowances, if any, in either the husband's or wife's Personal Spending allocation.

● How do you charge different funds when one check covers expenditures in two or more categories? Divide the check into each spending category. Here's how—First, record the check amount in the Check Register, as usual. Then, charge each of the funds affected by entering a portion of the check amount in the "Minus" column and adjusting the "Balance" accordingly. For example, if you wrote a check to mail-order house to pay for tires and clothing, enter the amount spent for tires in the Transportation Howgozit Chart and the amount spent for clothing in the Clothing Howgozit Chart. The total of the amounts charged to both accounts should equal the check amount; otherwise, you introduce an error into your records.

● How do I account for credit purchases? The Check Register and Howgozit Charts are affected only when you write a check. Credit purchases enter the system later when you write a check to pay for items bought earlier on credit. A simple way to keep track if you buy on credit only occasionally is to note such purchases in pencil as part of the "Item Description." These informal notations remind you that the "Balance" showing on the Howgozit Chart is really not fully uncommitted. When you write a check to pay for the previously charged items, cross out the informal notations. Two problems arise from this procedure when numerous credit purchases are involved: (1) Keeping track of credit commitments and payments informally can be clumsy and inaccurate. (2) Total credit commitments must be totaled separately when charges are spread out among several Howgozit Charts.

To correct these deficiencies and to avoid unpleasant surprises when bills roll in, set up a new Howgozit Chart for Credit (Figure 8-5). Using

Howgozit Chart for **Credit**

Date	Item Description	ADD	SUBTRACT	BALANCE
JAN. 16	SEARS — TIRES	$180.00		$180.00
JAN. 24	BON TON — DRESS	40.00		220.00
MAR. 1	PAID ON ACCT. --		$66.70	153.30

FIGURE 8-5

this separate Howgozit Chart allows you to track credit obligations in the same way you track individual spending categories. Tracking credit works this way—step-by-step:

Step No. 1—When you purchase anything on credit, enter the amount in the "Add" column on the Howgozit Chart for Credit. Carry the amount over to the "Balance" column. Note each additional credit purchase regardless of its normal spending category in the "Add" column and increase the running balance by the same amount. This way you know by looking at the "Balance" how many dollars you owe in total.

Step No. 2—When you pay for a previously charged item, enter the amount of the payment in the "Subtract" column and reduce the "Balance" by the same amount. Record only the principal amount—do not include interest charges when noting payments on the Credit Howgozit Chart. However, you will charge the total amount of the check to the appropriate Howgozit Chart to keep the Check Register in balance with the MIS. Paying interest increases spending for each category.

An example will help to clarify the operation of the Credit Howgozit Chart (Figure 8-5). Suppose you charge four tires at $180 at Sears. Enter the $180 in the "Add" and "Balance" columns of the Howgozit Chart for Credit. Later you buy a dress for $40 at a department store. Enter the $40 in the "Add" column and increase the "Balance" by $40 to $220. More than a month later you pay $60 to Sears and $10 to the store. Finance charges from both statements would total $3.30 (1½% of $220—

finance charges vary in different states). Instead of entering $70 in the "Subtract" column, enter $66.70 and reduce the running balance to $153.30. In the Howgozit Chart for Transportation, enter $60 in the "Subtract" column and reduce the running balance by $60. In the Howgozit Chart for Clothing, enter $10 in the "Subtract" column and reduce the running balance by $10.

●How do I handle small purchases for cash? The Howgozit Chart System is set up mainly for checks, but you won't want to write a check for every purchase. If you cash a check at a supermarket for more than the total of market purchases or if you write a check at the bank for cash, you should keep track of how and where you spend the cash. Ordinarily, you should deposit the full paycheck rather than deposit only a part and keep out part in cash. The two Personal Spending categories for husband and wife avoid having to track every small-change purchase. But, you might cash a check at a supermarket and use some of the excess cash to buy gasoline for the car. Unless you write yourself a note, you will charge the whole check amount to Market even though you spent part of the cash for a non-market item—gasoline in this case. When you buy gasoline for cash, mark the amount on a slip of paper. Later, when you are posting checks to the various Howgozit Charts, subtract the amount of the gasoline purchase from Transportation, just as if you had written a check, and add the same amount to Market. You can also charge gasoline purchases on an oil company credit card and pay in full each month with a check to avoid finance charges. Also, include repetitive spending items in each spouse's Personal Spending. If a husband regularly rides a bus to work, eats lunch out, and spends a certain amount for recreation for himself and/or the family, include that money in his Personal Spending. Don't make cash adjusting entries each week for his bus fares to Transportation, lunch tabs to Market, and movie tickets, a dinner out, or other recreational spending to Family Betterment. A little experience will help you avoid most of the cash adjusting entries. As for the cost of extra checks, remember you can get free check blanks from banks if you ask. Further, many banks offer free checking privileges if you maintain a minimum balance or keep your savings in the same bank. By using free checks and minimizing check service charges, you can afford to write more checks and reduce record keeping time.

●Why can't I keep money in savings where it pays interest? One of the categories in the Spending Plan is for paying off existing debts or for savings. There is no reason for keeping a large balance in your checking account. You might, however, want to maintain a minimum balance to gain free checking privileges. For example, one bank offers unlimited check writing as long as the customer keeps $250 minimum (not an average) in his checking account. The same bank offers unlimited check writing with no minimum balance for $2/month. Thus, by keeping $250 in the checking account, the customer loses interest on that amount if he had kept it in a savings account, but he avoids paying $2/month or $24/year. Result? Instead of interest earned, the $250 avoids a service charge of $24/year which is almost 10%—about double the interest the money would earn in a savings account—and, the $24 in service charges avoided is free of income tax. Any funds above a minimum can be transferred out of the checking and into savings immediately. Right after depositing your full paycheck, write a check to the savings institution where you keep your savings. A savings bank or savings and loan association will pay more interest on your savings than a commercial bank where you keep your checking account. Mailing a check is simpler than dividing your check if you must go to the bank. Other Howgozit Charts or funds may show higher than needed balances at some times throughout the year. If you pay your life insurance premiums annually, as you should to reduce costs, keep the balance in a savings account until the cash is needed. You do this by transferring cash out the same as for Savings. These "set aside" funds help you meet the succession of big payments throughout the year—house taxes, insurance premiums, and others. Keeping these funds in a savings account will earn a significant interest income—and you won't be tempted to spend the growing balances.

USING THE MIS TO CONTROL SPENDING

Recording each deposit and each check written twice, once in the Check Register and once in the Management Information System (MIS) requires only about 15-20 minutes per week extra—once you get the hang of it. But, there's little point in tracking expenditures and income through the MIS unless your efforts help you control spending according to your plan and help you and/or your family achieve the goals you have determined are important. The MIS works because you control spending by category. Instead of trying to control spending by using only the running balance of uncommitted funds in your Check Register, use the running balance showing on each of the Howgozit Charts as a guide. When a fund shows a "red" balance or your informal tally of credit purchases for payment later shows no uncommitted funds remaining, you are alerted to "go slow." Learn to pace your spending in each category according to the running balances of each fund.

Take personal spending, for example. When you run out of pocket money, what do you do? If you have already spent the cash allotted for that week's spending, examine your alternatives. You could exist for the rest of the week with no pocket money, borrow temporarily from your spouse, or draw an advance against next week's allowance by writing another check. If you draw an advance against next week's allotment, reduce the normal amount the following week to bring spending back into balance. Or, you might look ahead and see an expensive week coming up. So, you save part of this week's cash for next week. After a little experience, you learn to pace your spending to the planned amount. Another way to average out personal spending is to stash a $10 bill in a separate pocket of your billfold. This is your reserve. If you find yourself dipping into the reserve, you know you're overspending; that is, your spending pace is too fast. The following week, replace the $10 bill in its separate pocket and slow your spending to use only the cash remaining.

Develop a pace for spending with each of the categories. The Howgozit Chart system allows for overspending in one category as long as you balance it out later or, preferably, ahead by underspending in other categories. Don't expect uniform spending in each category every month. Clothing, for example, is a highly discretionary category. If you know you will be spending for outfitting the kids with school clothes in August or September, accumulate a surplus in the Clothing fund in anticipation. Or, if you overspent for school clothes, cut back on other clothing purchases until the Clothing fund is back "in the black." You'll find the Management Information System of Howgozit Charts will help you discipline spending to meet your Spending Plan.

If one or more funds constantly runs "in the red," you may need to revamp spending by juggling your Spending Plan. To increase spending in one category, you must decrease spending in some other category (including a reduction in savings) or increase income. If you attempt to increase spending in one category without figuring where the additional cash will be coming from, you will bankrupt the system—and yourself eventually.

Changing Your Spending Plan—About once a year and preferably not more often than every six months, re-examine your Spending Plan. An increase in income, a change in spending priorities, or completion of payments on a major debt, such as a car contract, are a few of the reasons for reallocating spending. You may find a first Spending Plan will be too tight in one or more categories. A reallocation of resources may be called for after trying your first plan for a few months. As you begin working with each category of spending, you'll find your priorities and goals changing.

$80 per Month Savings Idea

"What a bunch of nonsense!" was Guy Thiel's response to a suggestion that he keep track of every expenditure for a month. But, when his wife insisted, he grudgingly went along, noting each nickel, dime, and quarter spent in a pocket notebook. At the end of one month, totals showed he had spent $32.15 just for coffee. Other incidentals added up to a surprising total. "No wonder we never had cash to go out to dinner or do things with the kids," Guy remarked. "There's got to be a better way to spend our cash." Together Guy and his wife worked out a plan to control pocket change—a dollar limit each week. When it was gone—too bad! That was it! Soon Guy learned to pace his spending to last through the week—with a break for the Thiels' spending plan of $80 per month.

Changes in your Spending Plan are to be expected. But, learn to control your spending according to the plan rather than changing the plan frequently to conform with your spending pattern. As you become more and more skillful in controlling your spending you will find the pattern changing—less and less money will be going for unimportant spending. More cash will be available to achieve those goals you and your family have decided are important.

Forms for Your MIS—Howgozit Charts and the separate Check Register may be kept on plain notebook paper with the columns ruled in ink. Or, you can buy bookkeeping ledger sheets with the three columns for "Add," "Minus," and "Balance" already ruled. Keep the Howgozit Charts in a 3-ring binder for easy use and for reference.

A full starter set of printed forms and detailed instructions for setting up and operating the Howgozit Chart Management Information System are available by mail for $2.95. These are the same sets I use in teaching "Personal Financial Planning" at the University of Washington and in my regularly scheduled seminars. Send a check for $2.95 to Merle E. Dowd, P. O. Box 752, Mercer Island, WA 98040. Forms and instructions will be sent postpaid.

DEVELOP YOUR "MONEY SENSE"

Managing your daily expenditures through a simple record-keeping systems, like the one just described, accomplishes more than simply telling you where your money goes. Tracking expenditures and the discipline that grows from the systematic planning and allocation of money resources develop a "money sense." You'll find yourself recalling the available money in the Family Betterment (fun) fund before taking off for a ball game. If your family is like most, the money available for fun is all too small. If you run into these restrictions often enough, you'll soon look systematically for ways to cut other expenses in order to channel more money into Family Betterment. Your Spending Plan accompanied by regular record keeping are the tools you need to help you manage your money. But, several possible roadblocks may appear—

Managing Credit—No single item in most families' spending accounts for as big a leak as credit charges (see Chapter 9). Used wisely, credit and installment purchases can help a family get started or purchase items that would otherwise be unavailable. Home purchases, for example, would be almost impossible without long-term mortgage credit. Also, until you get complete control of your spending, you may need to finance a car. But, here you can, with good management and the ideas from Chapter 9, reduce credit expense. However, short-term credit for buying a continuing cycle of items is unnecessarily costly.

Emergency Spending—An accident or other unplanned major expenditure can wreck even the most effectively operating Spending Plan. Using your "money sense" will help to reduce the impact of an emergency: (1) assess the total impact; (2) check to see if one of your insurance plans covers any or all of the emergency; (3) if major expenses are imminent, develop a plan for handling them with the least effect on your Spending Plan.

Using the money in your Savings Fund is a first thought. Or, ask if a hospital and/or doctor bill can be stretched out without increasing the cost (that is, a charge for credit). You may need to reschedule your spending for a few months and warp your Spending Plan to channel more of your resources into the fund that skidded into the red because of the emergency.

Stopping Money Leaks—Many leaks occur in those supposedly "fixed" expense items. Even though an unnecessary expense may be small, if it is continuous, it mounts up by the end of the year. Turn back to Chapter 4, for example, and see whether housing expenses can be cut. Is you light bill too high? Develop a bloodhound's sense for sniffing out those small but continuing drains on your money resources.

Where Do You Stand?—At least once a year you should inventory your net worth. Much like the year-end Financial Statement most businesses issue, your family's net worth is the difference between your assets and your liabilities. Use a form similar to the one in Figure 8-6. Regardless of when you start operating your Spending Plan and keeping records, fill out a financial statement in detail. You'll probably be surprised at how much you are worth—even if you owe a mountain of debts.

At the end of the year, figure another Financial Statement. Most families will show an increase in their net worth over a year's time. However, if you suffered an accident; if a flood, tornado, or earthquake damaged your property; if a long sickness drained off a substantial amount of money; or you made many healthy payments toward a son's or daughter's education—your Financial Statement may show a net worth lower than the previous one. Analyze any difference, either up or down, to see if adjustments in your Spending Plan are in order. If your year-end statement shows only a minor increase at a time in your life when you should be adding materially to your net worth, make a New Year's resolution to adjust your Spending Plan to channel more funds into assets.

Investments, What Kind—Many books and a continuing flood of magazine articles offer advice on how to invest your money for the greatest return. It is beyond the scope of this book to go deeply into the many and varied avenues for investments. This phase of developing your money sense is a complex field all its own. The primary aim of this book is to make it possible for you to have money to invest. If you work diligently at getting the most out of the dollars you spend in order to save a portion for investment, you need to examine alternative investment possibilities in detail. No single avenue is likely to answer your requirements. Seek out the advice you need before committing the funds you have worked to accumulate.

SUMMING UP

A key function in any family's money management program is to set up goals to guide short-, intermediate- and long-term spending—a studied SPENDING PLAN. With this kind of a program, you plan for spending—not saving. You spend your money according to a plan that brings you and your family the most satisfaction and fun—and you spend or allocate all your income. To put such a Spending Plan into operation, you need to—

● Set up a series of short-, intermediate- and long-term spending goals.

● Find out what your income is and where it comes from.

● Calculate your regular and variable expenses according to category.

FIGURE 8-6: Financial Statement to Determine Net Worth

ASSETS		This year	Next year
Cash			
Checking account		_____	_____
Savings account		_____	_____
Credit union		_____	_____
	Subtotal	_____	_____
Securities & Investments			
Savings bonds (present value)		_____	_____
Stocks		_____	_____
Life insurance (cash value)		_____	_____
Annuity cash value		_____	_____
Notes or accounts receivable		_____	_____
Other		_____	_____
	Subtotal	_____	_____
Real Estate			
Home (net market value)		_____	_____
Other		_____	_____
	Subtotal	_____	_____
Personal Property			
Automobile(s) (cash value)		_____	_____
Boat, trailer, etc.		_____	_____
Sports equipment		_____	_____
Household goods		_____	_____
Furs, jewelry, etc.		_____	_____
	Subtotal	_____	_____
	TOTAL ASSETS	_____	_____
	Less TOTAL LIABILITIES	_____	_____
	NET WORTH	_____	_____

FIGURE 8-6: Financial Statement to Determine Net Worth (Continued)

LIABILITIES	This year	Next year
Current Bills		
Store charge accounts	_____	_____
Credit card accounts	_____	_____
Doctor bills	_____	_____
Utilities & telephone due	_____	_____
Insurance premiums due	_____	_____
Lodge or union dues	_____	_____
Subtotal	_____	_____
Installment Debts (Total owed)		
Automobile	_____	_____
Boat	_____	_____
Finance company	_____	_____
Credit union	_____	_____
Furniture	_____	_____
Appliances	_____	_____
Notes payable	_____	_____
Other	_____	_____
Subtotal	_____	_____
Mortgage Debt		
Balance due	_____	_____
Taxes		
Federal income (est.)	_____	_____
State income (est.)	_____	_____
Real estate	_____	_____
Assessments	_____	_____
Personal property	_____	_____
Other	_____	_____
Subtotal	_____	_____
TOTAL LIABILITIES	_____	_____

- Develop your own Spending Plan; then compare it with averages to see how yours stacks up.

- Organize a simplified plan for keeping records to make sure you either stick with your Spending Plan or know how to alter it.

- Develop your own "money sense" to help you manage debts, choose the best way to handle emergency spending, and stop the many little money leaks.

- Sum up your financial activities once a year to see where you stand.

9

INCREASE YOUR BUYING POWER
BY *NOT* USING CREDIT

Dollars you pay for credit are dollars you could use to buy
something you are now doing without. Used wisely, credit can help
you acquire specific "big ticket" items, such as a house. Used
unwisely and too often, credit can cut your buying power by 18%
or more. Before you climb on the credit merry-go-round, be sure
you—

- Know and understand the real cost of credit.

- Understand and use the information the government insists you
  get.

- Learn the various sources of credit and compare their cost.

- Know where and how to borrow money when you need extra
  cash.

- Protect yourself from unscrupulous practices sometimes used
  in the loan and credit business.

- Learn how to "earn" credit charges by setting up your own
  family small loan fund.

Credit is sometimes likened to drinking—it's great while you're on
the sauce, but the hangover is murderous. Credit, properly used, can help
a family acquire capital goods. When improperly used, credit can—and
does—lead to misery. One family, for example, with an income of $186
per week turned up owing $176 per week on a variety of time payments
and small loan contracts. Chapter 10 details alternative plans for reducing
one's debt load if overuse of credit has your family in a bind.

Business uses credit for its own purposes as well as to finance
purchases by consumers. When business borrows money, it expects to
earn a profit on the money. But, when you borrow money, your purchasing
power actually declines. When you borrow money to buy something, you
pay one or more added costs for the privilege of having it *now*.

The Consumer Credit Protection Act, popularly known as *truth-in-lending,* became effective July 1, 1969. Although it contained four parts, Title 1 affects all consumers. It requires that merchants and lenders disclose the full conditions about credit costs and terms before you contract or buy. Now anyone who extends credit must provide you with the amount of the *Finance Charge* and the *Annual Percentage Rate* of that Finance Charge. You no longer must calculate the dollar cost of credit or the annual interest rate. With this information disclosed to you, shopping for the best credit terms becomes a simple matter of paying attention.

Finance Charge, as defined by *truth-in-lending,* includes all charges a creditor may tack on as a part of the act of extending credit. In addition to interest, the Finance Charge may include loan fees, finder's fees or charges similar to initiation costs, service or carrying charges, price differentials due to time, investigation fees (credit worthiness or otherwise), the cost of any guarantee or insurance protecting credit extended against loss, and any points or other charges incident to extending credit. Premiums for life, health, or accident insurance must be included in the Finance Charge if required, to obtain credit. However, insurance premiums may be excluded from the Finance Charge if the insurance is not required to obtain credit and if you affirm in writing that you understand the added cost and wish to obtain the coverage.

Certain costs are not included in the Finance Charge, but they must be itemized and disclosed to you before you sign. Other charges in real estate transactions, such as title examination fees and others, are also not included in the Finance Charge.

Annual Percentage Rate must be disclosed for the Finance Charge. This constant-ratio formula calls for equal payments at equal intervals to pay off the principal amount and the Finance Charge over the term.

Additional requirements specified in *truth-in-lending* include disclosure of potential default or late-payment charges. You will note somewhere on bank-card statements and other revolving charge agreements the conditions under which late-payment charges will be imposed. Also, the conditions under which early payments may be discounted will frequently be disclosed, although such information is not required. One method of figuring rebates of unearned Finance Charges is the "Rule of 78" or the "sum of the digits" method. Here is how it works:

Fundamental to the Rule of 78 is a 12-month repayment schedule. If you add the digits 1 through 12 together, the sum is 78 and that becomes the denominator. For the numerator, add the sum of the months expired at the date of prepayment beginning with 12 and working backwards to 1. For example, at the end of the first month, the interest earned would be 12/78ths or 15.4%. At the end of the fourth month, the interest earned would be $12+11+10+9$ or 42/78ths. The remaining might be rebated by the creditor in case of full payment at the end of the fourth month. Similar rules apply to 24- and 36-month contracts.

The next time you receive a bill for a revolving credit account, note the elements disclosed. You will find such facts as the time period you have for payment to avoid payment of a Finance Charge, the amount of any minimum charge, description of the billing system used to determine the balance on which the Finance Charge is figured, the Annual Percentage Rate, a review of the transactions during the preceding period, and other interesting data. You will do well to review such information, particularly to avoid penalty payments and to reduce the amount of Finance Charges due. Unless you recognize and use the data *truth-in-lending* provides, you are not benefiting from its provisions.

THE COST OF CREDIT

Do you know how much credit *really* costs? What's the difference between simple bank interest, discounted, and installment interest? Knowing the difference can mean extra dollars in your pocket.

The cost of credit can be stated two ways: (1) the dollar cost of credit or the Finance Charge; (2) simple interest in percent or the Annual Percentage Rate.

Interest, as noted in Table 9A, is how much you pay to use borrowed money. But, there are different kinds of interest, and which kind you are being charged affects your dollar cost of credit.

TABLE 9A: Glossary of Credit Terms

"ANNUAL PERCENTAGE RATE"—the nominal annual rate figured on an actuarial basis for regular payments.

"BALANCE"—the amount you still owe on an account at any given time.

"BORROWER"—the person who buys something on time or borrows cash.

"COLLATERAL"—the property put up to "secure" a loan. If the loan isn't paid, the lender may get the property.

"CREDIT"—buying things and paying later, or borrowing money and paying later.

"CREDIT CHARGE"—is mainly interest but includes other charges such as cost of bookkeeping and investigation.

"CREDIT RATE"—the percentage that the credit charge bears to the average principal amount.

"CREDITOR OR LENDER"—the person, store, firm, bank, credit union, or other organization that lends money, or sells things or services "on time."

"DEFAULT"—failure to pay when due. Also failure to meet any terms of the contract.

"FINANCE CHARGE"—includes all charges imposed by a creditor incident to the extension of credit.

"INSTALLMENT"—one of a series of payments to pay off a debt.

"INTEREST"—how much you pay to use borrowed money.

"PRINCIPAL"—the amount you borrow or finance.

"REPOSSESSION"—the seller takes back goods when the buyer fails to meet payments.

● *Simple Interest* (sometimes called bank interest) is the percentage of principal charged for credit over a year's time. Suppose you borrow $100 at 6% interest. At the end of one year, you would pay back $106. Note that you have used the full $100 for the full year and that the $6 credit charge is added on.

● *Installment Interest* is the credit charge you pay when interest and principal are paid back on a regular basis throughout the year. For example, suppose you borrowed the same $100 and agreed to pay $6 over the year for the use of the money. Further, you agreed to pay back the total $106 owed in 12 monthly installments. For 11 months you would pay $8.83 and on the 12th month you would pay $8.87. While the dollar cost of credit is the same ($6), simple interest amounts to 11.1% because you had the use of an average of about $50 for the year.

TABLE 9B: The Cost of Finance Charges

Usual Finance Charges Stated	Dollar Charges	Annual Percentage Rate
4%	$4 per $100	7.4%
6%	$6 per $100	11.1%
8%	$8 per $100	14.8%
10%	$10 per $100	18.5%
1% per month	$12 per $100	22.2%

If Finance Charges are figured only on unpaid amount, then–

Charges					Annual Percentage Rate
3/4 of 1% per month on unpaid balance					9%
1% " " " " "					12%
1¼% " " " " "					15%
1½% " " " " "					18%
2% " " " " "					24%
2½% " " " " "					30%

● *Discount Interest* is subtracted from the amount of your loan at the beginning rather than being added on. For example, if you borrowed $100 and interest at the stated rate of 6% is discounted, you would receive only $94. At the end of the year, you would pay back $100. Note two things: (1) you pay $6 interest on $94, not $100, so your simple interest is nearly 6.4%. (2) to actually get $100, you must borrow $106.36 from which $6.36 is discounted immediately.

● *Discount Installment Interest* is subtracted from the total borrowed immediately and the remaining loan is paid off in installments. If you needed $100 installment credit, you would borrow $106.36, receive the $100 immediately, and pay back the $106.36 in 12 installments. Simple interest on such a transaction amounts to 11.75%.

● *Monthly Interest* on the unpaid balance is a popular way of stating credit charges and simply means that the percentage of the amount owed is charged each month. For example, if your unpaid balance is $100 for one month and credit charges amount to 1% monthly, you will be charged $1 on the following month's bill. Since simple interest states the percentage of principal charged over a year's time, monthly interest is multipled by 12 to get the yearly rate. In this case, a 1% charge amounts to 12% simple interest.

Table 9B notes the difference in simple annual interest rates of credit or Finance Charges stated in various ways.

Table 9C: Comparison of Credit Costs

Example: Color TV priced nominally at $499.50 with payment over 24 months (nothing down and no sales tax).

	Finance Charge	Annual Percentage Rate
Store A	$62.03	11.5%
Store B	96.08	17.5%
Store C	128.35	23.0%
Bank	81.75	15.0%
Loan Company	208.30	36%

Shopping for the same make and model of color TV in different stores turned up the results noted in Table 9C. Store A was representative of a first-class department store. Store B was a specialty appliance outlet. Store C advertised widely, "No Down Payment" and "All the Credit You Need." The bank was a regular commercial bank branch. The loan company made many small loans to consumers.

SOURCES OF CREDIT

Modern merchandising depends heavily on credit. You can use this credit conveniently and at little or no cost, or you can pay heavily for the privilege of "buying now—paying later." Protect yourself by knowing the differences and the costs of various sources of credit—

● *Regular Charge Accounts* are offered by department stores, mail-order houses, and others primarily for convenience. Usually there is no credit or service charge added when bills are paid regularly. Bills are totaled and sent monthly. If you do not pay within the 25 days allowed, a credit charge may be added on the next bill. Some stores permit regular charge-account customers to pay for large purchases (refrigerator, furniture, etc.) over a 90-day period without an additional charge for credit.

● *Revolving Charge Accounts* allow you to pay off big purchases over a period that varies by store. For this privilege you pay a Finance Charge, frequently at the rate of 1½% a month on the unpaid balance. From Table 9B you recall that 1½% per month runs into 18% per year. If you haven't analyzed how much this 18% cuts your purchasing power, follow this example: Suppose Store A sets up a revolving charge account limited to $600. Right away you spend the limit; that is, you buy goods totaling $600. As you pay off the balance, usually 5 or 10% each month, you can buy again up to the limit. For this privilege, the store tacks on its revolving credit charge of 1½% of the outstanding balance. On average that's $9 per month. So, each month you pay the $60. Out of this you can buy roughly $51 worth of additional merchandise. Keep this up for a year and you still owe the $600. During the year you have paid $108 ($9 x 12) for credit—enough to purchase the goods you bought during 2 months for free.

● *Bank Credit Cards, VISA,* and *Master Charge* are the biggest sources of credit. They permit bank customers to charge purchases at many stores. The bank pays the stores, consolidates the purchases, and bills the customer, adding a charge for the service. Finance Charges for such convenience run about 1½% monthly, similar to the revolving credit plans. Some states limit finance charges to .75%, 1%, or some intermediate percentage.

17% Credit Savings Idea

"Revolving credit has got to be the biggest put-on of the century," Jean Hastings exclaimed after studying the chapter on credit buying. "When I think of how much cash I have literally blown by charging and paying later, I wonder how I could have been so stupid! All this jazz about buying on credit now to increase your standard of living, why—" She was unable to go on for a moment. "When I think about spending $1 out of every $6 for a little time, somebody's standard of living may be going up—but not mine. From now on, cash on the barrelhead! That sixth dollar is mine—all mine." Jean's explosive comment probably made more of an impression on her friends than my book, because everything she said made sense.

● *Installment Buying* sets up a contract for a specific item, such as a car or television set. The contract calls for a down payment and payment of a set amount each week or month until the total is paid off. You pay more than the cash price for credit and service charges. Make sure you understand both dollar cost of the contract and the annual percentage rate (APR) being charged as disclosed in the required statement.

● *Credit Cards* are similar to the regular charge accounts offered by department stores. That is, you pay the total due each month with no credit charge added or pay a lesser amount plus a finance charge equal to 1½% of the outstanding balance in most states. All you need to obtain an oil company credit card is a good credit rating. Multi-purpose (travel and expense) credit cards, such as American Express, cost a flat sum each year regardless of how much they are used. In addition to the convenience credit cards provide, the monthly bills verify expenses for income tax deductions. A person who travels widely may very well benefit from the multi-purpose cards because he needs to carry less cash. But, credit cards should not be used in place of other sources of credit for big-ticket purchases.

HOW TO BORROW MONEY

Nearly every family occasionally runs into some short-term emergency when extra cash is needed. Where you obtain such a loan and how much it costs will depend on your financial know-how. You don't really have to be an expert, but you will need to consider various alternatives. Each case is a different problem—and probably the "best" solution will vary from case to case.

Let's suppose your refrigerator suddenly goes "kaputt." It can't be fixed economically, so you must replace it. Table 9D lists alternative costs of replacing your refrigerator. The first alternative is to buy the refrigerator on "time." Such a purchase could cost extra two ways: (1) the refrigerator may cost more at a store that provides easy credit, and (2) time-payment plans can be an expensive source of credit, sometimes running as high as 24%. Studies indicate that discount houses advertising the lowest prices often charge the greatest time-payment differential. That is, a store may sell appliances or other goods for very low prices and then set up a time-payment plan that brings in a high profit for the store. Many times, stores, auto dealers, and discount outlets use goods as a medium for selling debt. These stores don't make their money selling goods, they make their profit financing sales. However, other stores may charge less for credit but a higher cash price to push the total cost higher than a discount house.

A second possibility is to borrow the money and pay cash for the refrigerator. Suppose you can borrow from a bank at 12% Annual Percentage Rate (installment basis—Alternative #4, Table 9D). Or, on a secured loan, you may be able to borrow at 8% (simple interest basis). By combining a low cash purchase price and low-cost financing, you gain as much as $70.66, the difference between high- and low-cost alternatives.

TABLE 9D: Alternative Costs of Purchasing Replacement Refrigerator

Alternative	Cash price of refrigerator	Finance Charges	Total cost
1	$379.50	$51.12	$430.62
2	419.95	46.87	466.82
3	429.50	38.14	467.64
4	379.50	25.12	404.62
5	379.50	16.66	396.16

[1] All figured on 12-month basis

One axiom among lenders is: the less risk, the lower the interest. So, any kind of acceptable security you can furnish will lower the cost of borrowing money. You can construct a rising cost of credit sources that parallels rising risk, something like this—

Insurance loan	lowest
Negotiable collateral (passbook, stock, insurance policy)	close to lowest cost
Real estate loan	close to lowest cost
Installment or credit union loan	low
Signature loan at small loan company	high cost
Pawnbroker	next to highest
Illegal lender	highest

28% Savings Idea

Marilyn Foley discovered a two-way saving—with cash. About to buy a waffle iron at a hardware store, she inquired about which bank credit card the store accepted. "Any of three," the clerk replied, "but why don't you do yourself—and us—a favor. Pay cash, and we'll knock 10% off. That's about what it costs us to put your purchase on the books." Marilyn quickly figured a saving of 18% on the credit card plus the 10% discount for cash—28% total. She had to write a check, but the store accepted it the same as cash. You, too, can search out those stores in your community that are more interested in selling merchandise than selling debt. The cash you save is yours to spend.

• *Life Insurance Loans* offer a no-risk, low-cost source of funds. Nearly all cash-value life insurance policies include provisions for borrowing up to the cash value of the policy at its next anniversary date. Here, again, you are borrowing your own money, if you borrow directly from the company. Also, direct life insurance loans are usually "standing" loans; that is, they are due in a lump sum at the end of the loan period. However, insurance companies are perfectly willing to let you continue to pay interest on the loan once a year, usually at about 5 or 6 % (simple interest). Some G.I. government policies permit borrowing at only 4%. If you should die before the loan is paid off, the principal and accrued interest are deducted from the policy proceeds. You may also assign the cash value of a life insurance policy to a bank or other lender as collateral for a cash loan. Interest may be slightly higher and there may be a service charge, particularly if the loan is small. Insurance policies are a good source of low-cost credit. However, use them only when you have your borrowing tendencies fully under control or when a dire emergency presses, because such loans reduce your insurance protection.

• *Passbook Loans* offer almost perfect security; the money you are borrowing could be your own. The procedure is simple: You put up your savings-account passbook or certificate of deposit as security for a loan that does not exceed the balance in the account. Until the loan is repaid, you will not be able to withdraw funds from your account without permission. With perfect protection and no risk, the bank will make the loan for about 2% over the interest rate being paid on your savings. But why borrow money when savings are available? Ordinarily, if you have funds in a savings account, you should consider using them instead of borrowing. But many persons find they need discipline; they will pay back the bank when they wouldn't stick the same money back in their savings account. Where the temptation not to repay a savings account is too strong, the difference between loan interest and savings-account earnings may be a small price to pay for the necessary discipline. For example, suppose you borrow $100 and put up your savings-account passbook as security. You may keep the money for a year at a cost of $7 (with a 7% loan). During the same year, your savings earn possibly $5.00 in interest. You are then paying $2.00 for the discipline necessary to repay the loan.

• *Negotiable Collateral Loans* offer nearly as good security as a savings-account passbook, with a similar low interest. The most common securities posted as collateral are stocks or bonds. Here the quality of the stocks or bonds may have some minimal effect on the interest rate you can negotiate.

● *Real Estate Loans* secured by mortgages are another low-risk type of loan with relatively low interest the rule. Variations occur, however, according to the type of loan. A first-mortgage loan costs least. This is probably the type of loan you have on your house or condominium, if you own such property.

Second mortgages are considerably riskier for the lender—so his rates are higher, possibly up to 12 or 18%. Second mortgages can draw on the proceeds of a forced sale to satisfy mortgage holders only after all of the interests of the first mortgage holder have been satisfied. Rather than pay the cost of a second mortgage loan, consider the possibility of refinancing your first mortgage. Refinancing is practical only if you have paid down a mortgage for a number of years and the market value of your holding greatly exceeds the outstanding principal. Analyze the alternative costs of paying off the first mortgage in full and refinancing your real estate at a higher principal amount against the cost of raising money with a second mortgage. For example, suppose you owned a house and lot valued conservatively at $50,000. You still owe $10,000 on the first mortgage. If you should need $5,000 to pay for college or for some major emergency, consider arranging a new first-mortgage loan for $15,000 that would pay off the $10,000 owed and leave you the needed $5,000. The alternative would be to arrange a second-mortgage loan directly for the $5,000. Factors to consider are: (1) over-all dollar costs of the refinancing vs. the added interest of the second mortgage; (2) monthly payments required to either pay on the new refinanced $15,000 loan or the combination of payments on the first and second mortgages; (3) difference in interest rate for the old first mortgage loan and the new refinanced mortgage loan. Ordinarily, any kind of real estate loan or refinancing should be considered only when a large sum of money is to be raised. You would not, for example, float a first-mortgage loan on a lot just to raise $100. The service charges plus interest that normally go along with a real estate loan make a small loan uneconomical. You may very well do better, in terms of dollar cost, to arrange a signature loan for the $100.

● *Chattel Mortgage* loans are those with some kind of goods pledged for security. Furniture, a late-model car, a large boat—nearly any kind of personal property with some marketability and value can be used as collateral for small loans from certain lenders. The goods offered as security remain with the borrower and continue to be used. In every case, however, interest rates are higher than for the low-risk loans and may reach as high as 24%. Also, there may be an appraisal fee tacked on to cover the effort needed to place a value on the goods being offered as collateral. Despite the presumed value of the collateral chattel mortgages are seldom settled by seizing and selling merchandise. Rather, the chattel mortgage offers a means for "going legal." That is, with a mortgage contract established, the lender has ready recourse to the courts for the issuance of garnishments and wage assignments to pay off the loan in case of nonpayment (see Chapter 10).

● *Signature Loans* are made with no security other than the established reputation of the borrower. Usually, signature loans are made by credit unions (frequently with the provision that repayments be deducted from paychecks), banks, and small loan companies. Interest rates are seldom less than 12%, and may be as high as 36%. If your credit reputation is tarnished, you may not be able to get a loan without a comaker—a friend or relative who also signs the note. A comaker's signature attests that, if you don't pay the loan, he will. Naturally, few people are willing to be a comaker for anyone other than close friends or relatives. Because of their high cost, signature loans should be avoided like the plague. If possible, find some other source of funds or offer some kind of collateral.

● *Pawnbroker Loans* are among the most expensive available, primarily because the pawnbroker must not only act as a banker but as a warehouser and seller. Loans made on jewelry, cameras, sporting equipment, and other valuables are similar to chattel mortgages, except that, instead of simply pledging the property offered for security, the property itself is left as security with the pawnbroker. While the dollar cost of pawnbroker credit may be relatively small, true interest may be as high as 100% or more. Usually, an item left with a pawnbroker as security for a loan is retrieved quickly and the charges paid—or not at all. Because the pawnbroker seldom loans anywhere near the market value of the piece, he actually risks very little and charges are out of proportion to risk involved or the dollar value of the loan.

SHOP FOR YOUR LOAN

To assure getting the money you need for the lowest cost, look around for alternatives. Compare loan possibilities two ways—dollar cost and Annual Percentage Rate (APR). *Truth-in-lending* now makes comparisons easy. In today's market, money is a marketable commodity, just as much as a color TV set or any other goods. Competition affects money-lending rates just as it does appliance prices.

● *Look Before You Leap* When borrowing money or arranging for credit. Remembering these small points may save you embarrassment and dollars—

(1) Read the contract, particularly the fine print, before you sign. Provisions in contracts for installment buying protect the seller. You must assume the responsibility for making sure you also have some protection. Conditional sales contracts, for example, require that title to the goods remain with the seller. You should check to make sure the contract is not "open ended." Any new purchase should be the subject of a new contract; otherwise, you may have to return all goods purchased over a period of years if you should fail to make the last payment on your latest purchase. Examine the contract too for any waivers of wage assignments or other protection that is legally yours.

(2) Don't sign any contract unless the blanks are all filled in or crossed out. In some states, it is illegal for the seller to offer a contract with blanks not filled. However, you have the most to lose if a seller adds a higher interest rate or other charges to a contract you have signed "in the blank." Once you have signed a contract, you are legally liable to pay.

(3) Don't extend payments over such a long period that the item loses its value faster than it is paid off.

(4) Look for "balloon" end payments where weekly or monthly payments are unusually low.

(5) To reduce credit charges, pay as much as possible down and pay off the remainder in as short a period as possible.

YOUR OWN FAMILY FUND

One profitable way to reduce the cost of credit is to be your own banker. Lend yourself cash out of a revolving fund you keep current and enjoy earnings as high as 18 to 24% on your savings instead of the piddling 5 to 6% paid by many banks and credit unions. Such a plan keeps you on a cash basis, makes it possible to purchase large items, and keeps your borrowing power intact for emergencies. Here's how the family fund works—

Suppose you want to buy a new clothes washer and dryer. After shopping at a number of stores, you come up with an alternative choice between a low price at a discount house with a relatively high finance cost or a higher price with a more modest financing plan. Costs of the two plans look like this—

Plan A (Discount House)		Plan B (Department Store)	
Cash cost of washer	$249.95	Cash cost of washer	$279.50
24-month contract	317.16	12-month contract	307.51
Monthly payment	13.22	Monthly payment	25.63
Dollar cost of credit	67.21	Dollar cost of credit	28.01

Your best bet in this case would be to pay cash at the low discount price. But, you don't have the cash right off, so you start a fund to buy the washer and, in the meantime, continue using a self-service laundry. You may be surprised to learn how little you save on laundry costs by operating your own washer and dryer. A study by the U.S. Dept. of Agriculture in the Washington, D.C. area found that the cost per load at a self-service coin-op laundry averaged 57¢ per load. This cost included cost for use of the automatic washer and dryer plus supplies. Cost per load for laundry done at home in a washer and dryer varied according to the number of loads of laundry done each week. Total cost per load varied from 73¢ per load for three loads a week to 41¢ per load for ten loads a week. The breakeven point where home laundry costs just about equalled self-service laundry costs was at five loads a week, the point at which the home laundry cost was 55¢ per load. Home laundry costs included amortization of the washer over 10 years and the dryer over 14 years plus the cost of water, fuel to heat the water, electricity to operate both the washer and dryer, and supplies (detergent and disinfectant). Not included in the self-service laundry costs was the cost of transportation to and from the self-service laundry.

So, until the family wash reaches at least five loads a week, you save little by having a washer and dryer at home, except the convenience of not having to load up the laundry and drive it to a shopping center. So, during the time you are saving the $249.95 needed to pay cash for the washer, you continue using the self-service laundry. The trips to the self-service laundry are a weekly reminder that you need to put aside the $25.63 each month necessary to get your own washer. Note that the amount to be set aside is the lowest price for the washer plus financing charges—not the lowest cash price. When you have saved the $307.51, buy the washer. Immediately, the difference in your savings account gives you a head start on your next purchase. This difference ($57.56) represents the money you earned by waiting.

If you want a dryer to go along with the washer, repeat the process again. Except that, this time, the payments you set aside each week or month are about the same as the payments you would be making on the washer if you had purchased it on a time-payment plan.

The example of using cash instead of credit for buying major appliances is only one advantage of getting on and staying on a cash basis. Another study by the USDA found that to buy five major appliances, one after the other, would require 128.2 months, using the credit plan offered by a major mail-order house. Buying the same range, refrigerator, washing machine, clothes dryer, and dishwasher for cash would require only 107.6 months. This means that by saving the money to buy the first appliance for cash and then saving the money regularly that would have gone into credit repayments, a family could have purchased another major appliance, such as a television set or room air conditioner, with the money saved—plus having all five appliances on hand and paid for 20.6 months sooner.

Any family can set up its own finance fund to get on a cash basis. If your family is spending needless dollars for credit, resolve to tighten up your spending for a short period to: (1) pay off the high-credit-cost bills, and (2) set aside cash to use as a family revolving finance fund to permit paying cash for large purchases. A young couple just getting started in marriage, for example, can keep expenses low by living in a small apartment and eating simple food until they build their revolving cash fund. Such a fund is easier to acquire if the wife continues to work for a while after marriage. Perhaps all of her earnings can go into building the family revolving finance fund as part of the discipline of learning to live only on the husband's earnings. Then, should the wife become pregnant, the disturbances to their Spending Plan are less onerous. Another good source of cash to start a revolving family finance fund is the cash spent for monthly car payments. Instead of immediately trading your car off for a new one when your present car is paid for, resolve to drive it for another year. But, continue paying the equivalent of the car payments into your finance fund. Then, use the fund to buy things for cash or as a bigger down payment on a new car a year or two later.

Big-ticket items are not the only places to save on finance charges. With your revolving family finance fund, you can pay for clothes and household items that you may now be charging into a store or mail-order house revolving credit plan. As noted earlier in this chapter, such regular financing usually adds 18% to your cost of goods. By simply staying on a cash basis, your money instead of the bank's money earns 18%.

SUMMING UP

Probably no single money leak robs so many families of their optimum purchasing power as the unthinking and indiscriminate use of credit. You need to know the many facts and trade-offs of when and where to use credit wisely, if at all. Learn how to make the really tough decisions confidently on how your family uses credit by studying the—

- Real cost of credit and the various kinds of interest.
- Quick method for calculating the true interest of various types of installment loans or contracts.
- Various sources of credit and a comparison of the credit cost for each.
- How and where to borrow money for emergencies at the least cost.
- Ways to protect yourself from excessive credit charges and outright theft.
- Advantages, in terms of increased purchasing power, of setting up your own credit fund—and your collecting the interest.

10

A REDUCING PLAN FOR YOUR DEBTS

Spending aggressively, learning to save, and keeping track of family money may be great for those not in debt. But, how does a family get even with the board to start an effective spending program? If your family is struggling with a heavy debt load—

- Take a three-way test to find out just how deeply you may be in debt.
- How does your family's debt compare with other families' debts?
- Learn the four stages of debt—and how to cope with each stage.
- "Quick Check" for debt-paying ability.
- Outside sources can help with your debts.
- Chapter X111 Wage-Earner Plan vs. straight bankruptcy.

How much debt can you afford? When do debts become hazardous to your continued financial health? Nearly 200,000 personal bankruptcies reach the courts each year. Debt and credit counseling services for people in debt are scheduled weeks and months ahead. In this environment, how do you stack up? A three-step financial checkup can rate your family's financial health. See Figure 10-1.

First—how much cash could you lay your hands on to meet an emergency? Quick cash may be in a savings account, U. S. Savings Bonds, or the cushion in a checking account. But, measure the checking-account balance just before depositing a paycheck rather than just after. How much cash is a minimum reserve? Requirements for the families vary, of course but a survey reported that half of the families questioned could reach $200 or more quickly in an emergency. So, since this is a scorekeeping quiz, rate yourself this way: If you can count $200 or more in quick cash, give yourself a plus (+). If your quick cash totals less than $200, give yourself a goose egg (0).

FIGURE 10-1: Your Financial Health Score Card
(Copy on Large Sheet)

			Score
Quick cash availability			
Less than $200	0		
More than $200	+		
Time to pay off installment debts			
More than 12 months	0		
Less than 12 months	+		
Percent of disposable income committed to payments on installment debts			
More than 20%	0		
Less than 20%	+		
Rate your own financial health			
3 0's	Very poor		
2 0's, 1 +	Poor		
1 0, 2 +'s	Fair		
3 +'s	Good		
No debts	Excellent		

Second—How long will you be paying installment debts? How many months ahead is part of your income committed? Do not include house or rent payments or the monthly bills you pay in full. Installment debts are those which draw interest and which you pay over several months or longer. Payments on a car, revolving credit accounts, bank credit card balances, or a personal loan make up the bulk of installment debt. Total the dollars still to be paid (see Figure 10-3) and divide the total by the amount you are now paying each month. Some bills will be paid off quickly; others may run for a year or longer. Don't worry about variable times for this checkup; you're looking for total time. Your answer will be in months. Rate yourself with a + if you can pay off your installment debts in 12 months or less. If payments continue longer than 12 months, rate yourself 0.

Third—What percentage of your take-home pay do you shell out for installment debts? Take-home pay is that amount left after Federal income tax and Social Security (FICA) are withheld from your income. If your employer deducts union dues, credit union deposits or payments, insurance premiums, or others, count such deductions as part of your take-home total, even though you don't actually receive the cash. Total the dollars you pay for installment debts on a regular monthly basis. Then, figure that total as a percentage of your take-home pay. For example, if you pay $160 monthly on installment debts and your take-home pay is $800 monthly, then you are committed to paying 20% on debts. Score yourself with a + if you pay out less than 20% of your income on installment debts. If you pay out more than 20%, rate yourself a 0.

Now—how did you score overall? Use these guidelines to score your vulnerability to financial stress:

If you scored yourself with goose eggs on all three questions, your financial health rates very poor. Any financial setback from a layoff, illness, or change in income level could leave your family in a tight money position. If yours is a three-0 family, you can benefit from the ideas in this chapter on how to pull yourself back from the brink of bankruptcy. You should certainly hold off buying anything new on installments.

With two 0's and one +, you may still be in a vulnerable position—but less serious than if all three scores were 0. A 0 score on questions two and three indicates you have committed income far into the future. Taking on more debts simply pushes further into the future the time when your family will be free of debts.

With only one 0, you may be only mildly vulnerable to financial stress. With +'s all the way, score yourself a better-than-average money manager. You have exhibited firm control over your installment buying. If you owe no installment debts, consider yourself an excellent money manager—and skip the rest of this chapter.

How does your family compare with other families in debt? According to studies by the Survey Research Center at the University of Michigan, 51% of all families surveyed owed some installment debt. Average amount owed was $1540. Two-thirds of the families with incomes between $10,000 and $14,999 owed some installment debt, with the amount averaging $1940. Debt payments as a percentage of income varied according to age level. Families with incomes ranging from $5000 to $7500 were the heaviest credit users with 17% of this group paying more than 20% of their after-tax income on installment debts. Where the family head was under 25 years of age, 48% of those families had committed 10% or more of their after-tax income to installment payments. The older the family head and the higher the income—the less installment debt carried.

David and Linda Morris began this three-part test as a lark. They figured they were in no trouble. However, when their score ended with three 0's, they were mighty shaken up. They knew they owed a number of creditors—but, three 0's—that was too much! Immediately, they worked over their Spending Plan and pinpointed six places where they were spending more than they really needed to spend—food was one. And Linda decided to cut out cigarettes for a $5.50 saving per week. Linda remarked, "It never occurred to us that we were right on the brink of money troubles. You helped us catch ourselves— just in time."

DEVELOPING YOUR PLAN

You have already computed your family's net worth by completing the worksheet in Chapter 8. From this analysis, you know how much your family, as a small independent business, is worth. If you find that paying on debts is slicing a big chunk out of your income and you worry about what might happen if your income falls off or stops entirely, resolve now to develop a plan for bootstrapping your family back to financial solvency.

You'll find two good reasons for paying down your debts to a reasonable level— maybe all the way to zero. After all, 49% of the families studied in the survey noted above owed no installment debts.

First—You can buy more if you spend fewer dollars for interest and finance charges. Most states permit lenders and merchants to charge 18% interest—that's $1 out of every $6 that buys time and little else.

Second—Owing money can leave you vulnerable to setbacks and reduce your flexibility. When you commit your future income, you can spend less freely today.

There are differences between using credit and being "in debt." Examine these three stages and find where you fit—

● Bills for purchases charged flow in regularly and you pay them in full each month. Possibly a major purchase, such as a car, may involve an installment loan that is paid easily out of current income. Under these conditions, you are using credit wisely and as it was intended.

● Installment payments, current charges for utilities, and normal purchases exceed your cash available. So, you set certain bills aside to pay later. Or, you draw cash from a savings account to catch up with payments. Either way your spending exceeds income. Deep inside, a feeling of concern gnaws away because you are slipping into debt.

● Finally, bills and demands for payment on back accounts exhaust your ability to pay. You don't know where the money is coming from. You substitute worry for action because you recognize you are deeply in debt. Unfortuantely, like the increasing rate of inflation, once you get behind, added interest, late-payment charges, and loans at high interest to pay back installment debts accelerate your slide deeper into debt. Some families never escape, or they "take a bath" through the bankruptcy court.

If your family pays no installment debts, you can disregard the problems of committing future income. But, if you are concerned about debts and resent the drag of installment payments on your spending flexibility, you can do something now. Depending on your situation, you can—

● Develop your own do-it-yourself debt repayment plan and follow through with no outside assistance.

● Ask for assistance from an agency in your community dedicated to helping families in debt trouble.

● Consider bankruptcy—either the Chapter XIII Wage-Earner Plan or straight bankruptcy where some of your debts may be discharged in court. More about bankruptcy later.

ANALYZING YOUR DEBT POSITION

Rather than guess, take the time to look at all angles of your debt position. Determine how long it would take to pull yourself up even again. You can complete this analysis in three steps—

First—Cycle through your Spending Plan to determine how much money you can scrounge from your income to pay on debts. Use the analysis worksheet in Figure 10-2. You will note that spending categories are aligned differently from the Spending Plan in Chapter 8. Difficult-to-control spending categories are noted at the top because house payments, life insurance premiums, and taxes offer fewer opportunities for reduced spending. However, if you now rent, you could move to a lower-cost house or apartment. Total the cost for a full year and divide by 12 for a monthly figure.

Tackle the controllable expenses one at a time or in groups. Combine home furnishings with household operations, for example. Ordinarily, any savings you might wring out of utilities, maintenance, and spending for floor wax, fertilizer, and other miscellany for keeping your house in operation could be used for home furnishings. However, during your debt-repayment period, you should hold spending for new furnishings to a minimum. Look back over the ideas in Chapter 2 for ways to cut spending

FIGURE 10-2: Payment Income Analysis (Copy on Large Sheet)

	Available Income	Monthly
Disposable (After-Tax) Income		
Husband		
Wife		
Other		
Total Available Income		
	Controlled Spending Plan	
Difficult-to-Control Expenses	Yearly	
House payment or rent		
Insurance premiums		
Life		
House		
Medical		
Other (no car)		
Taxes–House, other		
Subtotal		
Divide Yearly Subtotal by 12		
Controllable Expenses Monthly	Planned	Reduced
Food		
House operations and furnishings		
Car and transportation		
Clothing		
Medical		
Personal care and "fun"		
Emergency fund		
Subtotal–Expenses		
Total Spending		
Payment Income*		

*Available income less spending.

for food. Remember, you can save on food two ways—by changing eating habits and by more effective shopping. Combining personal care and "fun" creates pressure to spend less for these two highly discretionary categories. Some families combine medical expenses with clothing; then, if the family stays well, there is money to spend for new duds. Examine each category and squeeze your spending to a new, reduced level. The difference between your Total Spending and Total Available Income can be applied to paying off your debts.

Second—examine all of your debts with the aid of the worksheet in Figure 10-3. List each of your installment debts and fill in the information under the headings noted. Under the Total Owed, indicate the amount of the outstanding balance—plus any accrued late-payment or penalty charges. Separate the Total Owed into principal and finance charge portions. The principal amount would be the total of a bank credit card balance you could pay and incur no additional charges, for example. Be sure to include all of your weekly and monthly installment payments, but do not include bills you normally pay in full each month, such as a telephone bill and other utilities. Include any doctor, hospital, or dentist bills outstanding. If you have not already listed all your debts, the total may startle you.

Third—Compute a Time Check with the aid of the worksheet in Figure 10-4. This Time Check repeats one of the quiz questions at the beginning of this chapter. But, now you are using detailed figures and, hopefully, a higher Payment Income. Dividing total debts by monthly payments tells you how many months will be required to pay your debts down to zero. If the number of months exceeds 36, you are in pretty bad shape. Three years is the usual maximum that will be approved in a Chapter XIII Wage-Earner Plan proceeding. You may also recognize that your debts are front loaded; that is, many debts fall due over a short period beginning immediately. You can usually deal with this situation, as we will see later. Almost any time for total payoff of debts under 36 months can be managed one way or another.

Now—develop your own "game plan." Decide whether you want to pay off your debts in 12, 18, 24, or 30 months. Decide when you and your family would like to breathe freely again—without the gnawing worry of debts. The sooner you pay them off, the sooner you can begin living your own life again.

Unless you can count on a windfall from a rich uncle (not Uncle Sam), you should reaffirm a few facts: You won't be able to borrow your way back to solvency. You won't steal the money to pay off your debts. So—that leaves the responsibility squarely on your own shoulders.

FIGURE 10-3: Installment Debts Owed (Copy on Large Sheet)

Creditor	Total Owed	Principal Amount	Interest or Finance Charges	Monthly Payments	No. of Months
1					
2					
3					
4					
5					
6					
7					
8					
9					
10					
11					
12					
13					
14					
15					
TOTAL					

FIGURE 10-4: Debt Repayment Time Check

Total Installment Debts Due   _____

Payment Income   _____

Time to Pay
Debts (Months) $\dfrac{\text{Debts}}{\text{Payment Income}}$ = _____
                                                         Months

Example $\dfrac{\$2750 \text{ (Debt Total)}}{\$125 \text{ (Payment Income)}}$ =
                                                         22 Months

Somehow you managed to get into debt and you are the only one who can pay your creditors back. Once you really make up your mind to reduce your debt load, you're on your way—and many others will help.

Debts have a way of accumulating with time. So, paying off debts will also take time. You may find the road back to solvency rough at times. You may even slip backward from time to time. But, unless some catastrophic medical bills or an accident put you deeply in debt, you spent more than your income. To get even again, you must spend less than you earn. You can figure on a period of holding down expenses to achieve once again the freedom from debt worries. Living free of debt can change your whole attitude; it's a worthwhile goal. Just prepare yourself mentally for a long haul back.

Changes in your life style may be necessary to get your financial ship back on an even keel. Seldom will reduced spending in only one or two categories pull your family back to solvency if you have accumulated a sizable debt load. How many changes in your style of living will be required depends, of course, on how deeply in debt you find yourself. But, let's look at several alternatives.

The answer to your Debt Repayment Time Check (Figure 10-4) sets a broad limit. To reduce the time for paying off debts, increase your Payment Income by cutting spending or increasing your available income—or both. One other alternative is available—return some of the goods on which you owe sizable payments. A new car, for example, may represent an unacceptable load when you examine your overall debt lineup. But, if you decide to return a color TV or a car, make sure you do not get stuck for deficiency payments. Get a clear release from the seller even if you must pay an additional amount of cash.

Bringing in additional income can speed up payment of debts. If a wife isn't working. even a part-time income helps immeasurably in paying off high-cost debts or bringing payments up to date to eliminate late-payment charges and penalties. Another income, even for a few weeks or months, can help solve front-loaded repayment schedules. You might try a moonlight job to bring in extra cash.

Crash reductions in current spending mine your richest source of cash—your current income. Resolve to cut spending drastically for as long as necessary to reduce the load of overdue bills. Once you catch up, payments reduce installment debts fast because fewer repayment dollars are wasted on late-payment charges. Except for food, postpone buying anything for a month or two in certain categories. Clothing purchases, for example, can usually be put off. Learn about the many opportunities for free fun in Chapter 7. Learn to barter for babysitting and save mainte-

---

Dropping a Payment Burden

Gary Hansletter had lost almost 10 pounds over a 2-month period mostly because he couldn't sleep from worrying about his debts. Without telling his wife, he had talked with a counselor in the credit union where he worked. He was in debt far over his head—and he knew why. His brand-new, imported, high-performance sports car was gradually sinking their financial ship. He had skipped payments on bills for 3 months to collect the down payment. Now, he couldn't keep up the payments along with the other debts they owed. But, the counselor had finally convinced him of what he already knew but refused to admit—he must turn back the car. It was a wrenching experience because he had dreamed of owning that car for years. Turning the car back left him loser overall—but he was free of payments that totaled $187.80 every month. With that cash, he could begin to get even with his other bills again.

---

nance costs by repairing your car or house yourself. Even food buying can be curtailed sharply for short periods. A quick way to pocket emergency debt payment cash is simply to eat out of your pantry for a week or two. Buy only a minimum of fresh food. Eat up the cans of food in your cabinets or use up the food stashed in a freezer or frozen food compartment. Quick cash can help to hold off creditors while you put your overall plan into action.

KEEPING A POSITIVE ATTITUDE

As you examine every element of your spending, don't overlook even the smallest opportunities for saving cash. Take a hard-nosed attitude for a time. Look at your debts as a challenge. Reducing your spending level will take some time. Each week and each month you will come up with new ideas for cutting spending. And, every dollar you save reduces your debt load by that same dollar. Remember—learning to spend less requires effort and a willingness to change. Pull every member of the family into the action. Explain your total situation to your children. Teen-agers, particularly, will react positively once they understand the problems. They may even contribute part-time earnings to paying specific debts, or will spend their own money instead of allowances for a time. Don't let cost-saving become a grim, penny-pinching, negative operation. And, don't let yourself become discouraged. Develop and maintain a positive attitude while you hone and sharpen your spending skills. Resolve to spend only for what you absolutely must have during your "crash" period. Practice the old maxim of: "Use it up, wear it out, make it do—or do without!"

Keeping track of your debts and repayment schedule calls for a separate bookkeeping system. Otherwise, you lose track and your plan falls apart. So, set up a Debt Repayment (DR) account like the worksheet shown in Figure 10-5. Schedule your Payment Income into the DR account just as if you were paying a bank. Any moonlighting income aimed at paying off debts also ends up in the DR account. Sale of unused furniture or other stuff around the house can generate additional Payment Income.

FIGURE 10-5: Debt Repayment Account

Date	Transaction	Accumulation	Paid Out	Balance
	EXAMPLE			
Jan. 5	Weekly Debt Payment Income	$25.00		$25.00
12	" " " "	25.00		50.00
19	" " " "	25.00		75.00
26	" " " "	25.00		100.00
Feb. 1	Total Paid on Debts		$100.00	0
2	Weekly Debt Payment Income	25.00		25.00
4	Sale of Baby Furniture	46.00		71.00

Once a month, mail checks for installment payments according to existing schedules or extended plans. The total paid out each month shows up as a "Paid Out" total in your DR account. Individual checks that make up the total are detailed in your Debt Repayment and Planning Record (DRPR) (Figure 10-6). Each creditor rates a separate column in your DRPR. Along with each payment, note two items in each creditor column—total remaining to be paid and the amount paid that month. This way you keep a running account of the money still owing to each creditor.

How much each payment decreases the amount still owed depends on the type of debt represented. In the example for Creditor No. 1, the amount owed on February 1 is decreased by a full $20, and the March 1 total drops to $284.17. These payments represent a time-payment plan where a part of the principal and finance charges are amortized with each payment. However, Creditor No. 2 is a revolving charge account where 1½% interest on the remaining balance is paid first out of any payment. Out of the $8 payment, $2.67 pays the month's interest, leaving $5.33 to

FIGURE 10-6: Debt Repayment and Planning Record

Date	Total Paid on Debts	Creditor No. 1 $20/Month 12% Add-On	Creditor No. 2 Revolving 1½%/Mo.	Creditor No. 3	Creditor No. 4	Creditor No. 5	Creditor No. 6	Creditor No. 7
	Monthly Total Distributed to Creditors	Total Due Amt. Paid	Total Due Amt. Paid	Total Due Amt. Paid	Total Due Amt. Paid	Total Due Amt. Paid	Total Due Amt. Paid	Total Due Amt. Paid
	EXAMPLE							
Feb. 1	$100.00	$304.17 20.00	$178.00 $8.00 5.33					
Mar. 1	$100.00	$284.17 20.00	$172.67 8.00 5.41					

reduce the principal. On March 1, the principal is reduced and the interest is less, leaving $5.41 for payment against the principal from an $8 payment. Payments to other creditors would be similarly recorded.

The Debt Repayment and Planning Record consolidates several bits of information on one piece of paper. It records—

● Outstanding balance remaining with each creditor.

● Contract or credit terms for each creditor (stated at top of column). From this information, you can decide which of the accounts costs you the most in interest and which, therefore, should be paid off as quickly as possible.

● Division between principal and interest for each payment.

● Dates and amount paid on each account.

TIPS FOR PAYING OFF DEBTS

Your DRPR will help to keep your plan on track, but paying off debts will be speeded if you follow these tips—

● Recognize which of the debts you owe are secured. Study the contracts and terms for each debt. If you fail to pay a secured debt, the creditor may repossess your car, washing machine, TV, or other goods. Legal remedies available to the holder of secured credit give these lenders more clout in collecting debts. Therefore, consider secured creditors' interests first in any plan you develop. You may decide not to pay them first because their rates may be less than unsecured credit. Arrange an extension with secured creditors if your repayment plan falls short of complete payments each period.

● Attempt to accelerate payments on debts carrying the highest interest rates. Now that *truth-in-lending* (see Chapter 9) regulations require complete disclosure of interest rates, this comparison is easier than formerly. The prime factor is the rate of monthly interest. But, you must also consider late-payment charges, collection costs assessed to your account, and prepayment penalties in case you try to clear out an expensive debt early.

● Hold off payments on accounts which carry little or no interest—mainly medical, utility, and professional fees. Pay on these accounts regularly, but pay only token amounts until expensive debts are paid.

● When one account is paid down to a small balance, pay it off completely, even if regular payments on other bills must be deferred.

● Avoid taking on new debts while paying down old obligations. New debts dilute your paying power and extend your debt-payment time. One way to avoid new debts is to build a small emergency reserve fund to handle unforeseen expenses. A reserve fund also builds confidence in your ability to handle money.

● When you pay off a major obligation in full, celebrate, even if it is only to take the family out for a hamburger at a drive-in. Such tactics will help you stick to your goals.

● Be wary of the inviting escape through a consolidation loan. Unless you can borrow "cheap" money to pay off expensive debts, consolidation loans merely postpose the day of reckoning. For example, a Credit Union consolidation loan at 1% per month to pay off a revolving credit account at 1½% per month makes sense. Study alternative costs closely before borrowing to pay off loans. The cash value of your life insurance policy is another inexpensive source of funds to trade against expensive credit. But, avoid the small loan company's offer to extend payments and pay off pressing debts with a consolidation loan. The cost of a small loan company's credit may be as high as 3% per month.

● Level with your creditors. If you develop a plan that makes sense, seek out the credit manager or loan officer with each creditor and ask his help. Surprisingly few debtors contact creditors. But, a creditor's main concern is to collect his money—sometime. He would rather collect it sooner than later, but later is better than never. You may be able to stretch out payment schedules of some bills with no added expense. Just knowing that you have a plan will ease his concerns and insure his cooperation.

OUTSIDE SOURCES OF HELP

Your debt problems can usually be managed yourself with the help of a plan and a determination to clear up or at least reduce your debt load. But, sometimes, debts grow to an overall size that precludes feasible do-it-yourself action. Then, you need outside help—counseling, fund distribution, or both. Look to these community sources for help—

● *Consumer Credit Counseling Services* (CCCS) operate in nearly 150 major cities to help families in debt trouble. Check the phone book for the location of one in your community. The CCCS is a nonprofit organization sponsored by the credit-grantors in a community. Most CCCS units charge a small fee and provide two levels of service. First, staff personnel may counsel consumers on their debt problems. Such counseling usually involves analyzing debts and developing a plan for paying off the debts similar to the steps followed in the first part of this chapter. Second, when debt problems exceed a family's capability, the counselor collects money from the family each week or payday. Once a month the CCCS distributes this collected money on a prorated basis among the existing creditors. Ordinarily, the money available fails to cover the full monthly payments due. But, counselors usually talk creditors into scaling down monthly payments with no penalty charge and, frequently, a reduction in interest. CCCS exerts no legal force. Counselors depend entirely on cooperative effort to help debtors inch their way back to solvency. Debtors using the fund-disbursement plan of the CCCS are not permitted to take on new debt or borrow money without specific permission from the counselor.

● Credit unions sometimes offer money management advice and counseling. The counselors may also loan credit union money to a member to pay off pressing debts as part of a plan worked out with the debtor.

● Company and labor unions may provide credit counseling services, but they do not offer fund-disbursement services. Ask at your company's personnel unit for help or contact the union business agent.

● Credit bureaus may offer financial counseling to families in those areas or communities without a CCCS unit. Credit bureaus were instrumental in establishing CCCS units in many communities because they were acutely aware of the debt problems of many families through their information-gathering activities. Sometimes credit counseling is offered by volunteers from the credit-granting institutions among the members of a credit bureau.

● Family service agencies include credit counseling along with their advice on other family problems. Money and marital problems are so closely related that they must often be resolved together. Few family service organizations are geared to disbursing funds from a debtor, although they may intervene with a creditor to forestall harassment or garnishment.

● Commercial debt adjusters appear to offer services much like those of the Consumer Credit Counseling Service—counseling plus debt prorating. Because of their contined victimization of persons in debt, commercial debt adjusters have been banned or their operations limited in 43 states. Commercial operators usually charge higher fees, operate with little cooperation from creditors, and frequently take their fee off the top of any money collected for disbursement. Going to a commercial debt adjuster for help usually adds one more debt onto a stack of existing debts with little, if any, gain. Your best bet—stay away from commercial debt adjusters.

BANKRUPTCY UNDESIRABLE

Federal statutes under the amended Bankruptcy Act of 1938 provide two avenues of relief for the overextended debtor. One is the Wage-Earner Plan, popularly known as the XIII or Chandler provisions. Under Chapter XIII, a debtor pays off legitimate creditors under court protection. The second is a straight bankruptcy where debts are discharged; that is, declared noncollectible.

Chapter XIII Wage Earner Plan—Often considered one step short of bankruptcy, the Wage-Earner Plan is open only to real persons who derive their income mainly from wages or commissions. With the approval of a court, a debtor pays off all or most of his debts through a trustee operating much like the CCCS. However, the Wage-Earner Plan operating under a court, provides legal clout to prevent creditor harassment and garnishment. Interest on debts is suspended during the collection period, and the debtor cannot take on more debt without the court's approval.

Full operating details of a Chapter XIII Wage-Earner Plan proceeding are beyond the scope of this single chapter. But briefly, you must use an attorney to prepare your case. The court must approve the plans developed by you and your attorney. Following approval by the court and creditors, a trustee receives a portion of your earnings for disbursement to your creditors. Your plan must provide for essentially full payment to creditors within a 3-year period. A Wage-Earner Plan must not take more than 25%

Frank's Wage-Earner Plan

Frank Trumbull already had one garnishment on his record at the plant. Now two other collectors were on his back, threatening. Another collector had picked up his car on the street because his payments were so far behind. Late charges, increased interest on two "flipped" contracts, and collection charges continued to eat up the cash he was able to scrape up without denting the principal. He and his wife had spent money on the basis of their combined income. But Beth lost her job, and a two-month strike ate up every dime of their savings. Now—if he were to be garnisheed again—well, he couldn't stand the worry. So, Frank went to an attorney to set up a bankruptcy. Instead, he was told about Chapter XIII. Paying off his debts under the protection of the court and getting rid of those collectors sounded great. By the time the court disallowed many of the penalty charges and one fraudulent contract, Frank found the Chapter XIII was costing him less than he figured. Interest payments stopped, and the "flipped" contracts were refigured under the referee's plan. It was a long pull, but Frank and Beth found themselves on their way back to solvency. And Frank began sleeping nights again.

---

of a debtor's take-home pay. Under a Wage-Earner Plan, you commit your future earnings to paying off debts. If you fail to pay the required money to the trustee or if you incur further obligations without approval of the court, the Wage-Earner Plan will be discontinued or your case will be converted to a straight bankruptcy. In addition to protection from collector harassment and garnishment, a Wage-Earner Plan opens up an escape route from the stigma of being branded as a bankrupt. Your case may also protect you from false or usurious claims because each debt is scrutinized by your attorney and the court.

Costs associated with a Wage-Earner Chapter XIII plan include court costs and attorney fees. The filing fee is $30. A bankruptcy judge assigned by the court to examine claims receives a standard 1% of the payments actually dispersed to creditors. The trustee charges a maximum commission of 5% of the payments collected plus up to 5 percent for actual and necessary expenses incurred. Attorneys' fees usually vary according to the amount of money handled and are controlled by the court. Generally, attorneys' fees range from $150 to $450 for a Wage-Earner Plan. In some districts, the attorney's fee must be paid over the life of the proceeding rather than in one chunk at the beginning. All in all, a

Wage-Earner Plan is not cheap, but it offers discipline and authority not available to any other organization.

Straight Bankruptcy—This is the last step for a debtor. While the Wage-Earner Plan is voluntary, a straight bankruptcy may be started by either a debtor or a creditor. The idea behind personal bankruptcy through Federal courts appears deceptively simple. A debtor with a heavy load of debts and little chance of paying them off petitions the court for relief. The court allows the debtor to retain certain possessions according to varying provisions of state laws. Provable debts are then divided into two categories—dischargeable and nondischargeable. The law specifically forbids the court to discharge such debts as taxes, alimony and child support payments, debts contracted fraudulently, and a few others. Any assets remaining after the exemptions allowed are divided among creditors on a prorated basis. Remaining dischargeable debts are then declared noncollectible. The aim is to allow the debtor to start fresh with few debts.

Although "taking a bath" appears simple, more than half of the bankrupts studied in one survey ended up living at a lower standard of living than before. Further, marital problems may increase as divorces among bankrupts occur at a greater rate than among non-bankrupts. Even if the legal requirement to pay a debt is discharged, the moral obligation remains. Further, a debtor cannot retain secured property to the detriment of the creditor, so possessions bought on credit must either be returned or the obligation reaffirmed after bankruptcy.

Bankruptcy proceedings are instigated through an attorney who files a petition for a debtor. The court then assigns a referee to assemble the data and work out plans with creditors. All court costs and the debtor's attorney fees must be paid first out of the available assets.

Costs for a straight bankruptcy begin with a $50 filing fee plus $5 for the recorder. An attorney may charge from $200 to $600 for processing a bankruptcy case. Nonexempt property will be taken by a trustee and liquidated for payment to creditors, although few assets remain for distribution in most straight bankruptcies. Overall, court costs run about 25% of assets handled. Nobody wins in a bankruptcy case, and the costs can wipe out most of the benefit to a debtor. Therefore, anyone with substantial property mortgaged or pledged as collateral will probably lose under a straight bankruptcy. Since straight bankruptcy really is the "last step," a debtor should consider every other alternative. Make sure you have all the facts, as they vary among states. If at all possible, change your way of life and figure a way out by using one of the other options for getting out of debt rather than declare bankruptcy.

SUMMING UP

Families in debt spent more than they earned for one reason or other, not necessarily in "living it up on credit." To pay off those debts, families need to spend less than they earn and apply the difference to pay off past bills. In this chapter, you learned about—

- Measuring how vulnerable you and your family might be to financial stress—a layoff, sickness, strike, or salary downgrade.

- Loss of living standards when late payment and collection charges plus compounded interest soak up scarce income dollars.

- Talking with creditors to extend payment schedules.

- Developing an overall debt repayment plan you can put into effect without outside help.

- Credit counseling services available in most cities.

- Court protection against creditor harassment while you pay off past debts under a Chapter XIII Wage-Earner Plan.

- Advantages, costs, and disadvantages of "going through bankruptcy."

11

BUY THE MEDICAL AND INSURANCE PROTECTION YOUR FAMILY NEEDS FOR LESS CASH

Families today are spending an ever increasing percentage of their income for more and better medical care. Part of these costs are prepaid through health and accident insurance plans. Unless you manage these expenses with an eye toward cost effectiveness, you and your family can easily suffer a real loss in total purchasing power. Some of the ideas for cutting these expenses or achieving greater cost effectiveness in buying protection include—

- Learning how to cut the cost of medical care by staying healthy.

- Keeping away from the doctor's office, except for cases of real need, and knowing how to recognize when such needs occur.

- Paying less for the drugs and nostrums you use.

- Taking full advantage of the free medical services available in many communities.

- Knowing the various kinds of insurance—and which is best for your family.

- Studying the trade-offs—to buy the most protection for the least cost.

Costs for medical and dental care plus the regular cost for insurance protection against a variety of emergencies and disasters carve a large chunk out of most families' income. One reporter has been quoted as saying, in effect, that the cost of medical care is one of the biggest problems facing families, and that an ever increasing proportion of after-tax dollars is going for medical care and associated expenses. You and your family have an opportunity to cut such costs drastically—even more than the 20% reductions noted for other major family expenses—and with no real loss in protection when you need it.

STAY HEALTHY TO CUT MEDICAL COSTS

There's no better way to reduce the cost of a service than to eliminate it altogether. So, if you stay healthy, there's little need for a doctor. The human body is a fantastically adaptable combination of functional organs, but even it breaks down under excessive abuse, improper care, and poor or inadequate feeding. Some persons are naturally more resistant to disease and sickness for a variety of reasons, mostly hereditary, but others can help themselves to better health by following all or even some of the following proved ideas for staying healthy—

Diet to Stay Healthy—One researcher into the relationship between health and diet stated simply—"We are what we eat." The relationship between obesity and diet is well known. Here the problem is usually one of simply eating too much. Medical evidence indicates that being overweight is a drag on our entire system. Medical researchers cite numerous statistical relationships between obesity and a long list of diseases. This relationship is so clear cut that life insurance companies many times charge extra when an overweight applicant buys a policy. So, if you are prudently cost conscious, you can save three ways on this score: (1) cut the cost of food by eating less; (2) stay healthier by keeping your weight down to optimum levels according to your build and age; (3) save on insurance premiums by not paying extra for being overweight.

An Apple a Day Does Help—The old adage, "An apple a day keeps the doctor away," has been proven effective in at least two different scientific studies. At Michigan State University, 1300 students participated in an experiment to test the apple's effectiveness. Over a 3-year period, the students who ate at least one apple every day, made significantly fewer calls at the student health center. The apple-a-day routine also keeps the dentist away. A study in England confirmed that eating an apple after meals cleans the teeth and helps to prevent cavities. One way to help keep children's teeth free of cavities is to give them an apple in their lunch. They benefit two ways—constitutionally from the apple and orally from mouth cleanliness.

Exercise Pays Off—Benefits to health from regular excercise are so many and so varied, it is difficult to note and comment on all of them.

As little as 15 minutes per day spent in a physically taxing activity can keep your body in tip-top working condition. Despite the appealing advertisements, you can achieve the needed exercise outside of health spas or sweaty gymnasiums. Some of the busiest men in our country find time to jog from a half mile to as much as 2 miles once a day to keep their whole system functioning—extending their lungs, asking the heart to pump extra quantities of blood, and generally exercising most of the muscles in the body. But, regardless of what kind of exercise you choose—do it regularly. And, the best part about the medical effects of exercise—it's free. For preventive medicine, there's little that compares in cost effectiveness with a *regular* exercise program.

Protect Your Family from Accidents—Accidents kill and cripple more children in the United States than the combination of the seven worst diseases according to the National Society for Crippled Children and Adults. Each year, accidents kill about 19,000 children, and from 40,000 to 50,000 children are permanently crippled each year. Another 2 million children are injured seriously enough by accidents to require medical attention. With costs in misery, suffering, and dollars like these, consider what your family can do to prevent accidents. Parents need to do two things: (1) eliminate as many potential hazards inside and outside the home as is physically possible, and (2) impress a mild, consistent, and logical discipline on children to help avoid accidents.

Prevent or Lessen Injuries by Using Seat Belts—Automobile accidents kill over 50,000 persons and cause injuries to more than 3 million others every year. Tests and statistical studies have proven that the use of seat belts in both the front and back seats of the family car: (1) reduces the number of injuries in car accidents; (2) reduces the severity of injury in accidents where injury or death cannot be completely prevented, and (3) prevents death in accidents that would not be survivable without seat belts.

Reduce Infectious Risks at Home—Despite our best efforts to develop immunity and reduce the effects of colds, flu, and other recurring diseases, infection sometimes catches up to a household. You can reduce the effects and spread of such infection by isolating the sick person and by following a strict plan for reducing the number of germs and virus particles around: (1) Keep dishes used by the patient away from the rest of the family and then wash them immediately in hot, soapy water. (2) Insist that the patient use disposable tissues for nasal secretions or sputum; then burn them. (3) During the cold and croup season, avoid crowds as much as possible. As soon as possible after being in contact with persons showing signs of colds, flu, or coughs, wash both the hands and face to remove as many germs as possible. (4) Teach children to wash their hands with soap and warm water after any toilet exposure, immediately after playing, before eating, and before going to bed.

Vaccines for Disease Prevention—Medical science has, over a number of years, developed vaccines for a number of communicable diseases. Vaccines cost very little, and your doctor will no doubt recommend at what age your children should receive them. However, many school systems around the country offer free vaccines to children. Local health departments (city or county) also offer free vaccinations. Make sure to keep a record of the type and date of each vaccination and when "boosters" are needed to retain a high level of immunity.

Save Your Family's Teeth—Probably the most preventable medical expense for any family is the cost of dental care. Most children start off with a reasonably good set of teeth. Care for them and they will remain healthy and serviceable for a lifetime. Any loss to permanent teeth can never be fully repaired and repairs are likely to be costly. Here's how to keep your family's teeth in top condition—

• Use fluoride to help build strong, decay-resistant teeth. If you live in an area where drinking water is naturally or artificially fluoridated, your children get this protection. If you drink water from an individual well or the community water system is not fluoridated, your doctor or dentist can prescribe sodium fluoride drops to be added to fruit juice or milk once a day. A frequently used solution requires that only 4 drops be added to a child's juice once a day to provide full protection—at a cost of about $3.00 per year. Fluoride treatment should begin before a baby is born and continue until the age of 12 to 15 for life-time protection.

• Use dental hygiene to keep teeth clean and healthy. Tests have proven, and the American Dental Association has concurred, that a regular program of brushing teeth with one of the approved toothpastes containing stannous fluoride helps to reduce decay in teeth. The effects of brushing with a fluoride toothpaste are additive to those from systemic use of sodium fluoride. If you or your children can't brush after every meal, teach them the habit of rinsing the mouth with plain water immediately after eating. Sugar, particularly, is harmful when left in the mouth. So, immediately after eating sweet desserts or candy, children and adults alike should take a mouthful of water, swish it around in the mouth vigorously, then swallow it. Already mentioned is the benefit from eating an apple to clean the teeth. Eating raw carrots or celery has similar beneficial effects. In addition to regular brushing, children and adults alike should learn to use dental floss once a day to remove plaque from tooth surfaces brushes miss. Ask your dental hygienist for a demonstration of flossing techniques.

• Visit a dentist for regular checkups. Catching a cavity early not only reduces the pain when it is drilled and filled, but the repair costs less. And, regular dental care pays off other ways. Keeping teeth clean and free of tartar accretions helps teeth and gums to remain healthy. Also, the dentist may apply fluoride to the surface of cleaned teeth as a further prevention of decay.

● Control sweets in the diet. If you reduce the number of times children indulge in sweets, you can cut tooth decay.

● Massage and care for gums at home. Regular exercise and massage of the gums will prevent loss of teeth among adults. Your dentist can show you how to massage your gums, but you must do it yourself.

Free Guides to Good Health—Promotion of good health is popular and generally accepted, like being for mother love and against sin. Insurance companies, the various medical and dental associations, local health departments, and the Federal Government— all distribute information promoting good health. Your local extension agent has a variety of pamphlets and booklets on how to keep healthy. Or, ask your doctor for guides to good health. Also, check your library for books and pamphlets on every conceivable application of good health practices. Information in these pamphlets can be useful, but only if you put the recommendations into practice. You can read about the benefits of exercise to you and your family, but unless you work at the exercises, you will achieve none of the benefits.

Prevention of health problems are highlighted in *The Encyclopedia of Common Diseases* by The Staff of Prevention Magazine, Rodale Press. This book stresses the importance of nutrition in preventing health problems. It also recommends varied vitamin therapy and the use of many organic and natural foods to prevent some problems and correct others.

HOW TO KEEP AWAY FROM THE DOCTOR'S OFFICE

Prevention of disease and accidents can only protect your family up to a point. At certain times, you will need help. Sometimes you can provide the help you need outside the doctor's office—and save a fee. At other times, prompt attention can reduce the cost of professional care. For example—

Learn and Use First Aid—Minor cuts, bruises, and injuries can often be treated effectively at home. First aid then becomes total aid.

Be Your Own Doctor—Up to a Point—Train yourself to treat common sicknesses and accidents in the home. A major part of the training is to know how to diagnose sickness and recognize which problems you can cure yourself and which require the attention of a doctor. Most of the common childhood diseases and many adult afflictions are self- limiting; that is, with reasonable care, the patient recovers by himself. Fevers, colds, flu, most headaches, many infections, and frequently occurring diseases simply require time for the body to cure itself.

Numerous books have appeared to satisfy the need for practical advice on how to handle medical emergencies and long-term care at home. One of the best is *How to Be Your Own Doctor (Sometimes)* by Dr. Keith W. Sehnert (Grosset & Dunlap, New York). Included within this volume is "The Self-Help Medical Guide" with specific instructions for coping with the 14 most common diseases, 13 most common injuries, and 9 most common emergencies. Dr. Sehnert is Director of the Center for Continuing Health Education at Georgetown University and developed the book material through classes for lay persons. Another similar book is *Take Care of Yourself—A Consumer's Guide to Medical Care* by Drs. Donald M. Vickery and James F. Fries (Addison-Wesley, Reading, Massachusetts). This book uses the algorithm technique of defining symptoms and causes of illnesses along with prescribed treatment.

A book that combines some preventive techniques with treatment is *A Country Doctor's Common Sense Health Manual* by J. Frank Hurdle (Parker, West Nyack, NY). Another similar book is *A Minnesota Doctor's Home Remedies for Common and Uncommon Ailments*, Second Edition, by Dr. John E. Eichenlaub (Prentice-Hall Reward Books, Englewood Cliffs, N.J.). Helping your body to heal itself through numerous, simple ways is the promise of *Doctor Morrison's Miracle Body Tune-Up for Rejuvenated Health* by Dr. Marsh Morrison (Parker, West Nyack, N.Y.). A more unusual approach is *Helping Your Health with Pointed Pressure Therapy* by Dr. Roy E. Bean (Parker, West Nyack, N.Y.).

Reduce the Cost of Drugs—One of the reasons for the sharply increased cost of medical service is the increasing reliance on so-called miracle drugs. Whether prescribed by a doctor or yourself (home remedies), check these ideas for cutting the cost of drugs—

● Buy drugs by generic name. Most of the drugs frequently prescribed by doctors are manufactured by several drug houses. The generic name of a drug is the basic or family name as contrasted to the trade name assigned by a specific manufacturer. So, ask your doctor to prescribe a drug by its generic name wherever possible rather than a specific trade name. But, pick your druggist for his integrity and professional approach in the same way you pick your doctor. Government hospitals buy drugs by their generic name and save millions of dollars. There's no reason why you can't also save. The first step is to ask your doctor to prescribe by generic name.

● Buy drugs at a discount. Shop for a local druggist who sells prescription drugs at 20% or more off the usual drug list price. Your

---

66% Savings on a Single Prescription

David Schotte had been troubled with high blood pressure for a number of years. His doctor prescribed one of the new drugs for controlling blood pressure. Under the trade name the pills cost $5.95 per 100, which amounted to about $82 per year. By prescribing under a generic name, the cost dropped sharply to $28.60 for a yearly saving of $53.40.

---

doctor may give you a clue, or ask friends who might know. A doctor's wife frequently knows of a low-cost source for drugs. Some drugs you obviously need in a hurry, but when there is time to order by mail, you can cut the price of prescription drugs as much as 50%.

Mail-order sources for drugs are: NRTA-AARP, 1750 K St., N.W., Washington, D.C. 20006. You must be a member of the National Retired Teachers Association or the American Association of Retired Persons to use this service. Membership fee is $3/year, and applicants for AARP must be 55 years of age or older. Pastors, 126 S. York Rd., Hatboro, PA 19040. Pharmaceutical Services, Inc., 6427 Prospect Ave., Kansas City, MO 64132. Federal Prescription Service, Inc., 2nd & Main Sts., Madrid, Iowa 50156. Getz Prescription Co., 916 Walnut St., Kansas City, MO 64199. These services offer prescription drugs at various prices; some prepay postage, but only the NRTA-AARP require membership in their organization. Write for catalogs and compare prices. You'll need to send your doctor's prescription along with your order, of course. Nonprescription drugs can also be purchased by mail at discounts, but local sources frequently match mail-order prices. Check the same sources for their catalog and prices on common drug items.

● Buy according to chemical name. There's little use in buying brand-name drugs for such common items as aspirin, buffered aspirin, APC tablets, antacid liquids or tablets, and the like. These products are almost identical, regardless of who makes them. Buy them by the actual drug name which is required on every package. Examine the label of nonprescription drugs and buy according to the specific contents. For example, you can compare the vitamin contents of branded vs. store-packed vitamin tablets or capsules. A number of competitive brands of headache remedies, other than straight aspirin, cold remedies, and various other specialized drug products can cut these costs in half or less.

● Limit sizes and variety of drugs. Aspirin for children costs more than four times as much as adult aspirin. The orange or other flavoring may also fool children into thinking the tiny pills are candy. So, protect

---

50% + Savings Idea

Jerry Lindsay became an avid label reader when he discovered the savings possibilites for his family of four. On only five products (vitamins, two cold remedies, pain reliever, and caffeine), Jerry figured he saved $51 in one year—more than half of what he had been paying for these products. Some of the products he bought from a mail-order source. The others he bought by comparing the detail ingredients listed on the label of nationally advertised brands and those packed by a local drugstore chain, under its own name.

---

your children against possible overdosing and save money by simply breaking a 5-grain adult aspirin into four parts for children. Add flavor or simply sugar (like the song) to make the plain aspirin go down. Or, suppose you take 50 mg of Vitamin C regularly. One mail-order source sells 50-mg Vitamin C tablets for 40¢ per 100. But 100-mg Vitamin C tablets cost only 45¢ per 100. You save almost half by simply breaking the 100-mg tablets into two parts at the score line.

● Stop buying useless pills. Again, the best way to reduce a cost is to eliminate it altogether. Take cold remedies, for example. The common cold causes so much misery and hits a family so often, it is a prime target for drugmakers, particularly those that advertise heavily on TV. The facts are, however, that no drug can cure a cold. The treatment doctors prescribe for themselves when they get a cold is rest, liquids, and protection from exposure. They take aspirin to help them feel a little better while the cold cures itself. At times when the misery of a running nose or a stuffy head gets too much, they will use a few nose drops of ¼% neo-synephrine to shrink nasal passages.

Use the Free Medical Services in Your Community—Cities, towns, counties, and states vary in their practices of supplying free medical aid to the people of their community. Families are unaware that many services are entirely free; some are paid for by their taxes, others are paid for by voluntary or business organizations. To reduce the cost of medical service for your family, check into the following—

● X-ray checkups for possible tuberculosis in a clinic may cost from $15 to $25. You can save this cost by applying for tests at county organizations in some states. They provide free tuberculosis diagnosis including patch tests and chest X-rays.

● Immunization shots for both children and adults are provided at many county health centers. Also, immunization against such diseases as poliomyelitis may be obtained at no cost through the combined services of the government and the polio foundation.

● Laboratory examinations of various cultures and tissues may be obtained free from a central county lab. Here, practices vary widely across the country. Some of these laboratory services are available only to welfare patients, but many county health organizations will prepare and examine a wide variety of materials at no cost. Most doctors will make the culture and provide the laboratory examination for a fee. However, many county health organizations provide similar service at no cost. If your taxes are already maintaining the service, why not use it?

● Factory and office medical services often provide routine advice that can save a trip to the doctor. They can advise whether an infection should be treated professionally, for example. Some plant medical services also supply cold remedies, routine flu shots, and temporary relief items, such as aspirin. Their interest is in keeping you and other employees productively on the job—not to substitute for a doctor's services.

● Medical and dental schools in many communities offer out-patient treatment on a no- or low-cost basis. Such services frequently provide experience to student doctors or dentists. Although a student may actually examine you, their work is closely supervised by a professor who is probably more qualified at the particular specialty than a regular practitioner.

● Treatment for mental illness, alcoholism, drug addiction, and special handicaps, such as deafness and blindness, is usually provided in most communities because these conditions are often considered to be a community problem rather than a single family problem. Since the treatment of these long-term, chronic conditions is unusually expensive, it makes sense to make use of whatever community service is available.

KINDS AND USES OF INSURANCE

Many, many kinds of insurance are being offered for family protection today. How you spend the portion of family income earmarked "Insurance" markedly affects the total value of that protection. The variety of insurance packages offered and the confusing manner in which they are sometimes promoted make valid comparisons and decisions difficult. Nowhere is the term "cost effectiveness" more applicable than in the purchase of insurance. So, before embarking on a cost analysis, a few terms and basic information—

Life Insurance—Despite the many catchy phrases and package names, there are basically only two kinds of life insurance. They are—

● Term insurance. You are probably already buying term insurance for your car or house. Term life insurance pays your beneficiary only if you should die during the policy period. Term insurance is pure insurance—there are no cash values and no part of the premium is used for investment or savings. Term insurance can be useful in some insurance programs because of its low cost, particularly when the buyer is young. However, there are some basic deficiencies with term life insurance: (1) Premium costs increase at each renewal. A $50,000 term insurance policy may cost $134 per year if taken out at age 25, increase to $285 at age 45, and to $656.50 at age 55. (2) Renewal may be denied for health reasons and leave you without protection. For a small extra cost, you can buy renewable term that guarantees renewal regardless of your health. Convertible term is also available. It provides for conversion to some other kind of nonterm insurance without a medical examination.

● Cash-value insurance. These policies cover a person for his whole life no matter how long he may live. The simplest policy calls for paying the same premium each year (no other period) for life, although progressively higher dividends may, for the participating company, reduce the annual premium. The age at which such a whole-life policy begins determines the annual premium, so the earlier you begin, the lower the premium. Limited pay policies call for payment of premiums only over a specified period, say until age 65, although protection is for life. You can also pay for whole-life policies over shorter periods—in one lump-sum payment of 2-, 5-, 10-, or 20-year chunks. Endowment policies provide protection plus a guarantee to pay the face amount in dollars after so many years or at age 65. A frequently purchased policy is one taken out for a child that guarantees to pay X number of dollars at an age when he will be ready to begin college.

In their attempt to develop salable "packages," insurance companies now offer a confusing array of policies that combine life insurance protection for the man of the family plus all kinds of special payout periods and endowment features. There are the "family" policies, for example, that include all members of a family, plus children that may not even be born at the time the policy is written. "Family income" policies pay a regular monthly income in case the breadwinner dies. Retirement income policies combine some of the features of an annuity with provisions of whole-life insurance. When you analyze the cost of various policies, there are just two elements to consider—the cost of insurance and the cost of investment.

Getting the Most from Your Life Insurance Dollar—The only *real* reason for buying life insurance is to provide for the family in case the insured person dies. Other benefits, such as building cash value as a resource to borrow against, building an annuity or retirement fund, providing cash for settling an estate, or using premiums as a means of forced saving, are all secondary to the function of protecting a family's welfare.

Don't depend on an insurance agent to analyze your needs and tailor a program that fits only you. An agent can be sincere, fully trustworthy, and possibly an old friend, but he is not a completely disinterested person. He is a salesman, and he stands to gain by selling you insurance—possibly more if he sells you cash-value insurance rather than term. Assure yourself that any permanent policy recommended fits you—and not the agent. Use the following ideas as a starter in your analysis—

● Insure the breadwinner. Any family depends for its continued existence as a unit on a regular source of income. Concentrate insurance protection on the wage earner or breadwinner.

● How much insurance is enough? Few families can afford enough insurance to provide the survivors with the same standard of living they enjoy when the principal breadwinner continues to produce a full income. Overbuying can reduce a family's current standard of living unnecessarily. But, to determine how much protection is needed, set down the facts on a chart. Note that money needs jump when the children enter college. A principal source of income, social security, also varies according to family status. Income from investments can be a considerable factor in planning any insurance program. Also, the surviving wife can be expected to earn part of her income, at least when the children are grown and particularly during the years when children are in college. In fact, one of the best insurance investments a family can make is for adults to acquire a marketable skill before an actual need arises. The difference between income provided from social security, investments, and part- or full-time work by survivors needs to be met with insurance.

● Buy term insurance for family protection. Since few families can buy as much insurance as they really need during the early years, it makes sense to buy as much protection as possible with the money available out of already-strained spending plans. Two points to remember when analyzing this recommendation are: (1) term insurance costs less when the insured is young; (2) cost of permanent insurance doesn't begin to rise rapidly until after the insured reaches the early forties. As you develop your insurance program, remember these additional points—

1. The difference between the cost of term and total premiums paid for permanent insurance is some form of saving. A favorite ploy of insurance agents is to compare the total premium cost of term insurance to the cost of permanent insurance. Over a 20-year period, the ordinary life policy may show a lower net dollar cost—if you forget the value of interest on the additional money paid year by year. Further, although the cost of cash-value insurance is sometimes presented as the difference between the total of premiums paid in and the cash value, remember—you do not get the cash value unless you terminate the insurance. If the breadwinner dies, the company pays off the death benefits, usually the face amount of the policy. But, the company keeps the cash value.

A comparison of the cost of term insurance plus investment and cash-value insurance shows the difference. In this example program, a young man age 25 buys annual, renewable, convertible term coverage for $50,000 to age 55. He would invest the difference between the term premium and the cost of cash-value insurance, also for $50,000, in Series E Savings Bonds. At age 55 after 30 years, the man would have paid $19,650 in premiums for cash-value insurance with a cash value of $18,750. Or, he would have paid $7,635.50 in premiums for term insurance coverage. By investing the difference each year in Series E Savings Bonds he would have acquired E-bonds with a total redemption value of $40,275. From age 55 to 65 he continues to buy term insurance but only for $10,000 face value because he has $40,275 in E-bonds for total protection of $50,000. Or, he would continue to pay level premiums on the cash-value insurance. At age 65 he would have paid $26,200 in premiums for the cash-value policy, and the cash value would have grown to $26,250. Or, using the term policy and investing the difference, he would have paid an additional $2,132.10 for term coverage for a total of $9,767.60 in premiums. But, he would have acquired a total of $72,132 in E-bonds.

At age 65 the man converts the cash-value policy to an annuity that pays $194/month a part of which is taxable. After 65 the other man would have no insurance, but the $72,000 in E-bonds remains. He may either cash them and spend the proceeds or continue to draw interest for income. They will be a part of his estate. No residue from the annuity remains for the estate.

2. Group life insurance, available through many employers, unions, fraternal organizations, and the government, provides major protection for the least possible cost over a number of years. Buy all the group insurance through such organizations you are permitted to buy.

3. Combination policies use term insurance to build the added protection for early years needed by young families. Family income policies, for example, build extra term protection onto a base of ordinary life. If the breadwinner should die during the few years when children are too young to care for themselves, the family income policy pays a substantial regular monthly benefit. When the need for such high benefits is past, the family income provisions (term insurance) drop and the long-term protection continues.

4. When buying term, make sure the policies are renewable and convertible to another kind of insurance. The renewal provision assures you that at the end of a 5-year term, for example, you will be able to buy another policy, even if you should develop some physical problem that would otherwise make you uninsurable. Group term insurance purchased through an employer or other group usually includes a provision that enables an employee to convert to a form of whole-life insurance within 30 days after termination without demonstrating insurability.

5. Add term insurance to an existing policy. Instead of buying a completely new policy, consider buying a term rider for an existing ordinary life or other permanent policy. A rider or endorsement can usually be put in force for less initial cost than setting up a completely new account.

● Develop a combination program of insurance plus investment to provide a college fund. A frequent reason for buying insurance is to make sure there is money available for the kids to go to college in case the father dies. Endowment policies bought for such a purpose fail on two counts: (1) growth of cash value and, hence, the payoff in 15 to 20 years is low because the interest on such funds is less than is available elsewhere, and (2) insurance pays a set number of dollars while college costs keep climbing faster than either incomes or investment yields. Rather than buy an endowment policy, consider buying term insurance for protection in case of death with an investment program that will probably grow with inflation.

TIPS ON BUYING LIFE INSURANCE

Pay least for the insurance you select by—

1. Paying premiums on an annual basis. The additional cost of paying for insurance two, four, or 12 times a year amounts to 4 to 16% more than the premium paid annually. See Chapter 7 for ideas on how to plan for the accumulation of annual premiums.

2. Buying insurance in large chunks, if possible. Permanent insurance bought in large face-value amounts will either cost less or will develop cash values at a more rapid rate than several small policies bought at different times. One company, for example, charges $12 to open a policy whether it is a $1000 term policy or a $100,000 ordinary life policy.

3. Selecting the best and cheapest insurance. Frequently these factors go together. New, small companies, in order to expand their volume of business quickly, may spend a large percent of the first 1 or 2 years' premiums for agents' commissions, advertising, and administration expense. Result—your insurance dollar actually buys less protection. An old, established company, however, may have grown inefficient and may also include many older policy holders with a resultant high payout of benefits. So, to find your best buy, compare costs to you.

4. Comparing costs. Not all insurance costs the same. An ordinary life or term policy from one company may cost you more dollars in premium or reduced cash value than a similar policy from another company. In one exhaustive study of insurance costs covering more than 50 of the biggest companies in the United States, the net cost of the highest-cost company was 84% more than the lowest-cost company. Results from this same study indicated that non-participating companies tend to be at the high-cost end of the list.

5. Questioning the value of "goodies" offered. Double indemnity and disability provisions as a part of life insurance coverage are not usually good buys. If you should buy a double indemnity policy, where the beneficiary receives double the face amount in case of accidental death, study the fine print to make sure the kind of accidents subject to the double payment are not so restricting as to be nearly worthless. Disability provisions may be more properly a part of your health and accident insurance program.

6. Using dividends to reduce the cost of premiums rather than allowing the dividends to accumulate. Instead of allowing dividends to draw interest, invest the difference in premium cost in a mutual fund or high-interest savings account.

Two excellent sources of more detailed information on the costs of insurance protection and how to figure how much you need for your family are available from noninsurance sources. They are: *The Consumers Union Report on Life Insurance: A Guide to Planning & Buying the Protection You Need,* available from Consumers Union, 256 Washington Street, Mount Vernon, N.Y. 10550, and "Life Insurance and Annuities from the Buyer's Point of View," published by American Institute for Economic Research, Great Barrington, Massachusetts 01230.

HEALTH AND ACCIDENT INSURANCE

Even more confusing than the variety of life insurance plans available are the many types and varieties of health and accident insurance coverages. Basically, these plans fall into specific groups, as follows—

Medical and Hospital Insurance—These policies, many of them group coverages, reimburse you for part of the expenses connected with sickness or accidents. A policy may cover hospital costs, doctors' fees, and the various laboratory or special associated services, such as anesthesia. Usually a doctor's plan is obtainable only in connection with a hospital plan. One of the fastest-growing types of medical coverage is the "major medical" plan that covers hospital, doctor, drug, and associated expenses—but only after the assumption by the owner of a fairly sizable deductible. Major medical policies protect a family against the staggering cost of a long-term illness, extended hospital stay due to an accident, or some other really big medical expense. After you pay the deductible of $100 to $500, all other costs are covered up to a maximum that may reach $250,000.

Prepaid Group Practice Medical Plans—Rather than buy insurance, another method for obtaining protection from major medical expense is for a family to belong to a health maintenance organization (HMO). HMOs are available in many metropolitan areas and may include their own hospital and dental groups as well as physicians. In addition to covering most sickness and accident expenses, group practice plans emphasize preventive care, regular checkups, and long-term diagnosis.

When comparing the cost of medical insurance coverage and deciding how much you can afford, consider these factors—

• Group insurance for health and accident is likely to cost less than similar coverage bought on an individual basis. If you do not work at a company or other organization that makes a group health and accident insurance plan available, look around for other groups that may offer such insurance. Labor groups, professional organizations, and fraternal lodges often make group health and accident insurance available to members.

• Group practice medical services, (HMO) with their strict control of costs and improved efficiency from initial doctor visit through hospital treatment, generally offer more medical service per dollar than reimbursement policies. Most of the policies for both hospital and doctor care include internal limits or fee schedules that define exactly how much will be paid for each condition. If the schedule rate is lower than actual costs, you end up paying the difference. Group practice plans usually cover all costs.

43% Savings for Medical Care

Edward Dougherty's family of six included four active boys ranging in age from 9 to 18. He had been paying $192 per quarter for medical and hospitalization insurance that covered most of his liability. However, he found that the $150 deductible for each family member per year (maximum of three persons or $450) plus the 20% of hospitalization costs over that amount was costing him an average of $785 per year. It seemed that, between broken arms or other bones, infections, an occasional tonsil or appendix operation, and others, at least three of the six members of his family entered the hospital at least once a year. In addition, he was paying about $280 for office visits, checkups for camp, and eye examinations, for a total bill—not including drugs—of $1,833 per year. Prescription drugs averaged another $16/month or $192 per year. Overall he was spending at least $2,025 a year for medical expenses. Then, he investigated a HMO prepaid medical plan available in his area. Total cost for his family was $97 per month or $1,164. Included were unlimited office calls, hospitalization, and prescribed drugs, plus eye examinations—but not the glasses. During the first year, he figured he saved $861 and received better care for two reasons: (1) he didn't hesitate to ask for help; (2) group health emphasized preventive care.

● Insurance that attempts to cover all possible sickness and accident potentials, from a runny nose to extended traction for broken bones, usually costs too much for the average family. In addition to actual doctor and hospital costs, such plans also include an overhead charge of 30 to 45% for running a succession of small bills through their system.

● Assume some risks yourself and insure against the budget-busting disasters that, hopefully, strike only occasionally. This reasoning has fueled the rapid growth of major medical coverage. Many companies and professional organizations are making major medical policies available on a group basis to cut costs even further. The deductible feature of major medical policies eliminates the many small claims for individual doctor visits and limits coverage to the really costly surgical or extended stay diseases or accidents. When shopping for a major medical policy, compare costs and coverages in detail. Analyze these points particularly—

1. Look first at the deductible amount. If the major medical plan pays only after the first $500, you may find little use for the protection, and you will need to budget yourself for medical service that costs less than the deductible. However, the higher the deductible, the lower the policy cost.

A $50-deductible major medical plan may be obtainable only through a group plan. Some companies offer a sliding deductible; for example, one company begins paying after the first $50 of cost ($50 deductible), and then pays only 80% of the cost for the next $500. After that, the company pays all costs up to the $25,000 limit of the policy. For a major expense that ran more than $550, you would pay $150.

2. Ordinarily, a broad coverage policy is better than one that offers a high maximum. Look into the exclusions and make certain of what is covered in a policy. Most major medical plans cover full costs up to their limit (after payment of the deductible), except for specific exclusions. Limited treatment for mental conditions may be provided, but most policies exclude dental care, maternity (except for complications), and plastic or cosmetic surgery.

Loss of Income (Paycheck) Insurance—When sickness or accident forces the breadwinner of the family off the job, income may stop just at a time when extra expenses hit a peak. Insurance can be bought to pay weekly cash benefits in case income is interrupted by some emergency. Variation in amount paid, length of payment period and how long after the breadwinner is off the job before benefits start, and the age of the insured—all affect the premium cost. Consider these factors when analyzing the cost and benefits of paycheck insurance—

● Types of Renewability—Noncan (for noncancellable) binds the company to keep the insurance in force as long as premiums are paid up to some specified age. Guaranteed Renewal policies bind the insurer to renew the policy, but changes in premium rates by class can be made. An Optionally Renewable policy is renewable at the option of the company and provides no renewabiltiy protection for the insured.

● How much paycheck insurance you buy should be related to other sources of benefits in case of long-term disability. Social security, for example, may offer substantial benefits. Sick leave frequently continues a person's full salary during the waiting period before paycheck insurance begins to pay off. Consider sick leave benefits in connection with a long waiting period because the longer the waiting period, the lower the premium. In case of a job-related accident or sickness, workmen's compensation provides benefits that vary from state to state.

Dread Disease Policies—Certain specific diseases, such as cancer, spinal meningitis, and polio, may be covered by a special policy that provides benefits in case any member of a family should contract an incurable or costly-to-treat disease. Special hazard policies for protection during skiing, hunting, playing football, etc., are also available on the same basis as dread disease coverage. These policies can be bought separately or they may be added as riders to already existing health and accident policies.

Dental Insurance—Dental care plans are not usually available alone but are generally a part of a hospital and doctor insurance program. Some group practice plans include dental care on a scheduled rate basis at less than normal cost. Dental care plans may be sponsored by a company for the benefit of its employees or a union for the benefit of its members. Unless you have access to a group practice plan or to some organization that sponsors a dental care plan, you may find it difficult to obtain such coverage.

SUMMING UP

Dollar-conscious analysis of expenditures and what the money buys is nowhere more important than in buying medical service and insurance protection for your family. As these costs may be increasing more rapidly than income, the need for good management of these costs is becoming greater each year. Adopt the principle of cost effectiveness—the planned, analytical approach to getting the most performance for the least cost. Several approaches are open to you and your family to reduce sharply the cost of medical care. Among the most important are—

- Staying healthy to cut medical costs. Obviously, the less medical care you require, the less it costs—when you plan it this way.

- Learning how to care for your teeth to cut the cost of dental care.

- Learning how to care for minor aches, pains, and cuts yourself—and when not to be your own doctor.

- Cutting the cost of drugs.

- Taking full advantage of the many free medical and dental services offered in many communities.

- Knowing about the two kinds of life insurance and how each might fit into a program of planned protection for your family.

- Deciding how much insurance protection you really need.

- Analyzing the advantages of insurance vs. some other program for protection against emergencies.

- Knowing how to cut the cost of insurance when you do buy.

- Evaluating the differences in coverage and cost of health and accident insurance—and how these plans fit into your overall program.

12

HOW TO STOP
THE MANY LITTLE DRIPS THAT
DRAIN AWAY YOUR SPENDABLE CASH

Pocket change and small cash amounts slip through the average family's fingers without thinking or control. Learn how to stop these little nips by—

- Reducing the cost of paying bills.
- Staying clear of door-to-door salesmen.
- Bartering services instead of simply buying everything.
- Cutting the cost of commuting to and from work.
- Buying bargains at surplus auctions.
- Renting tools and equipment when buying is too expensive.
- Shutting off the flow of small change.

Every day in many ways a trickle of small change disappears from our pockets—never to be seen again. Sometimes, the trickle may be as innocuous as several daily, habitual cups of coffee, or the few pennies charged for processing each bank check, or more than needed postage for personal or business mail, etc. The point is—the trickle of change can and frequently does amount to a significant total by year's end. Staunching the flow of these little trickles, the many seemingly insignificant nips from our income, follows the principle of controlling repetitive expenses. If you think about and plan for the many little nips, you'll have extra money at year's end to spend on some worthwhile purpose.

SAVE MONEY ON REGULAR AND FREQUENT EXPENDITURES

Save Money on Bank Charges, Paying Bills, Writing Checks—A convenient checking account usually pays for itself in time and money saved compared to paying bills with cash. Check these ideas for saving money at your bank:—

● Pick the right kind of checking account. Suppose you opened a "regular" checking account at a local bank. The charges might run something like this: Minimum per month, 75¢ plus 6¢ for every check and 4¢ for every deposit. If you are like many families, you may write 30 checks and make four deposits of your paycheck every month. Total charge for this service would run 75¢ plus $1.80 (30 x 6¢) plus 16¢ (4 x 4¢) or $2.71 service charge. This $2.71 is less than one of the many economy checking systems that charge a flat rate of 10¢ per check. But, suppose you only wrote an average of ten checks per month and made two deposits. A regular account would cost $1.43 while the economy system would cost only $1. Some checking account charge systems credit your account with 10¢ for every $100 left on deposit throughout the month. At this rate, $100 left on deposit in a checking account would earn $1.20 for a year—a piddling 1.2% interest. You would be better off to keep any extra funds in a savings account rather than leaving them in your checking account to reduce bank charges. Some banks, however, charge nothing for a checking account, regardless of activity, if the minimum balance maintained is $200 or more. If you compare this with the monthly service charges that accrue, you may find that the $200 on deposits avoids paying $2.71 (using the previous example of 30 checks and four deposits per month) every month. On a yearly basis, service charges amount to $32.57 or a 16 + % interest—a better return than the usual savings account interest.

● Paying bills by check. The cost of paying regular monthly bills by personal check may run 6¢ to 10¢ for the check plus 15 cents for a stamp. Suppose on an average the total cost is 22¢ each. While the time saved by writing the checks and mailing them in a bunch is worthwhile, consider keeping these costs to a minimum. One idea is to pay utility bills with one check at one of the many locations which accept payments for water, gas, electricity, sewer, and rubbish pickup. You may be walking past one of these spots every day or when you're out shopping. Paying five bills at once may cost 8¢ (using the same average figure) versus 80¢ for five checks and five stamps.

● Do you need a safe deposit box? The only reason for keeping items in a bank vault is for protection against their loss by theft, fire, or other means. Most of the stuff kept in a safe deposit box need not be there, so you can either drop the expense entirely or reduce it drastically by using a small box rather than a large one. Items you really don't need to keep in a box are wills (let your lawyer keep them), house deeds (your title is recorded officially in county records), savings bonds (government will replace destroyed bonds at no cost), insurance policies (company will replace at no cost), and such items as social security cards. While these valuable papers could be replaced, some at a slight cost, you should keep a record of the items at some location other than your home for protection against fire. Items you should keep in a safe deposit box are irreplaceable items; such as jewelry, IOU's, and original marriage, military discharge, or birth certificates. If you have the space, you can keep stock and bond certificates. These can be replaced if lost, but the procedure may cost as much as 1 or 2 years' rental for a safe deposit box.

BEWARE OF DOOR-TO-DOOR SALESMEN

No method of distribution costs as much as selling a product door to door. Yet, many companies follow this practice because it increases their volume of sales. In general the vacuum cleaner salesmen, magazine subscription solicitors, fire alarm peddlers, and the many, many others who daily tramp around neighborhoods hawking their wares should be avoided like the plague.

Particularly odious are the referral schemes and other actual or pseudo-frauds used by door-to-door salesmen. In the referral scheme, you may be offered a chance to get part of the purchase price for some item like a fire alarm system, if you furnish the names of neighbors and friends who also will buy the alarm system. Or, you may be offered what purports to be a special price for some kind of home remodeling in exchange for using your home as advertising. While the price may sound attractive, the usual result is either substandard workmanship and materials or a disappearance act with your cash. Any door-to-door selling scheme should be checked at your city's Better Business Bureau or peddler's license bureau.

BARTER INSTEAD OF BUY

Trading help, services, or goods instead of paying cash has been a hallowed tradition in this country since the days of barn raising and the quilting bee. Consider these ideas for trading your skill or extra time in exchange for something you need but can't buy—

Trade Baby Sitting—Daytime sitters are hard to come by, particularly in suburbia. Instead of calling an agency with a 4-hour time limit and a healthy fee plus transportation, why not work out an arrangement with a neighbor or friend. You keep her children at your house in exchange for her keeping your kids at her house. Surprisingly enough, the reason such

---

$504 Savings Idea

Trading baby sitting or child tending need not be limited to part-days or evenings only. Janet and Charles Nepard first broached the idea of a week's trade with their friends, the Whitsells, because both of the Nepards were ardent skiers. They longed for a week's skiing in Colorado. They could handle the long drive from Chicago, the accommodations, and the lift tickets with some cash left for aprés ski. But, the $36 a day cost of hiring a full-time sitter for their three children for 2 weeks kept swamping their plans. Janet knew that Emily Whitsell had longed to visit San Francisco when her husband traveled there on business. But, Emily encountered the same problem—who would care for their three children? When Janet suggested the trade, Emily was ecstatic. By caring for the three Nepard children, she could earn her trip without leaving the house. So, they agreed, the Whitsells would take the three Nepard children into their home—two of them sleeping on the floor in sleeping bags—while Janet and Chuck skied in Colorado sans children. Later, Emily would leave their children with the Nepards and accompany her husband to San Francisco—minimum cost by traveling family plan. Cost for child care—zero!

---

barter of babysitting time isn't practiced more is the supposed embarrassment of asking. Once the ice is broken, though, such exchange of services saves untold dollars over a year's time. Such trades need not be limited to daytime activities. The wife can actually spend an evening next door one night a week in exchange for a night out while the neighbors reciprocate. Or a teen-ager can sit one night a week in exchange for ski lessons or transportation to a ski area.

Exchange Skills—Suppose you are a struggling accountant. You may be able to keep a small builder's books in exchange for kitchen cabinets custom-made and installed in your house. The builder probably hates to work on books and you may be all thumbs with tools. Yet, if either of you had to pay for both services, neither might be willing to part with the cash. Or, a wife, handy with sewing machine and needle, could remodel clothes in exchange for children's music lessons. As a part-time business, you might find it difficult to market your services as a seamstress, but a piano or dance teacher would welcome the opportunity of getting her clothes expertly tailored. Only your own imagination can limit the possibilities for exchanging skills services that benefit both parties.

Exchange Board or Room and Board for an Extra Set of Hands—If you should happen to live in a college town, you can undoubtedly

Barry Edmonds was determined to get his college education despite his family's inability to help him financially. His father was unable to work much of the time due to an injury, so there was no cash left for Barry's education. Although he attended a community college and lived at home for 2 years, he could not get his degree without attending the state university out of town. By working during the summer, he saved enough cash for tuition, books, and clothes. But, he could not afford the dormitory fee. By working through the employment office at the university, he located a family with six children and a big house. He arranged to live in a basement room, care for the yard, help with the children, clean the kitchen, and do other inside chores in exchange for his meals and room. No cash exchanged hands, but Barry avoided paying the housing bill he couldn't afford. A bicycle furnished transportation to classes. When he left college with his engineering degree, Barry didn't owe one penny. He started his career from a no-deficit position—quite a change from many of his colleagues who borrowed every cent they could raise to stay in school.

exchange the extra room and a seat at your table for part-time help from a struggling student. Keeping the house clean and using the freedom a built-in baby-sitter provides may be a good trade for the room that may be used only for storage.

CUT THE COST OF COMMUTING

The cost of getting to and from work can take a big chunk out of your everyday expense money. Even the least expensive bus trip at 35¢ per trip aggregates close to $175 per year. A combination of commuter train and bus or private car can easily reach $500 per year—possibly as much as $1200. Also, the Internal Revenue Service allows you no deduction for commuting costs.

Stop Driving to Work—Biggest savings will accrue if you eliminate the supposed need for a second car just to get to and from work. Obviously, if you are a salesman or your job requires you to use your car during the day, this expense is necessary and is probably paid for by your company. But, for every person who uses his car in his work, there are at least ten who simply use a car to commute. Using the car operating expenses detailed in Chapter 3, figure out how much commuting by car costs, then look at these alternatives—

Use Public Transportation—Commuter train service is available in many large cities. While costs of commuter tickets have been increasing, their cost is only a fraction of the costs for operating a car. If you need a car just to get to a commuter station, check the possibilities of setting up a car pool for travel to and from the station. If this isn't practical, ask the wife to examine how she could use the cash that would accrue from not maintaining a second car—then ask her to drive you to and from the station.

Walk—With bus, subway, or streetcar fares on the rise (35¢ to 75¢ each way is common), analyze the trade-off in time required to walk from the station to your office versus the cost. Suppose your office is a mile from the station. When you get in shape, you can walk that mile at a brisk clip in 15 minutes. A bus ride, not counting the waiting time, will probably take at least 10 minutes. So, you may spend $1.00 per day round trip to save 10 minutes' time. Not only that, the walk will do you good—help to keep you in shape. The same is true for getting from your home to the end of a streetcar or bus line.

Save on Parking—If you live in a remote area where you must drive at least part-way to work, consider one of these ideas for cutting the overall cost of commuting by reducing the cost of parking—

1. Drive to a transit parking lot at the end of a streetcar or rapid-transit line and take public transportation the rest of the way. Your saving on parking pays the bus fare—plus your saving on car expense.

2. Drive to a relatively quiet area on or near a busy bus line. Park on the street and take the bus or streetcar the rest of the way.

BUY AT SURPLUS AUCTIONS

Every year the Post Office, local police and sheriff's offices, transit authority, Customs, and many others auction off their lost-and-found, confiscated, or unclaimed merchandise.

Post Office Auctions—When all means possible have been exhausted to locate the recipient and the sender, packages in the dead letter office are opened and the stuff is put up for auction. Everything from power saws to tiny bottles of imported perfume to feather dusters may be offered for sale. Post Office auctions are usually well publicized in local newspapers or on a bulletin board at the Post Office. Before the auction takes place, you can examine the merchandise to be offered and take down the lot number. Some Post Offices that do a brisk business in surplus print up a short catalog describing the stuff to be auctioned off. But, once you buy, it's

---

$384 Savings Idea

David Swett found himself in one of those boxes all too common for commuters. No public transportation served his remote, hilltop community. None of his neighbors drove anywhere near his office. So, Dave had to drive himself. Although the mileage wasn't great, downtown parking was costing him $50 a month. A public, metered area offered 12-hour parking at 10¢ per hour. The cost was low because the area was far down a steep hill. Dave counted the steps—141 plus four blocks to walk. By feeding the meter, he cut his parking bill by $32 a month—$384 a year. Climbing the steps was a chore, but he found the morning exercise stimulating.

---

yours; there are no refunds, exchanges, guarantees, or delivery. Some items may be noted as "in working order," which means they may be damaged, dented, or scratched, or "not in working order." You buy the item "as is." If you are interested in certain items, be prepared to bid quickly when the lot is offered—the action is fast when the stuff comes under the auctioneer's hammer.

Customs Auctions—Very similar to the Post Office auctions, Customs accumulates piles of merchandise from overseas which is either unclaimed or is undeliverable for some reason or other. Since the rapid growth of air freight, Customs houses are no longer limited to ocean ports. International flights are terminating in many inland cities, and with them—unclaimed surplus. Packages may be identified in foreign languages, so the selection of merchandise may be more difficult than at a Post Office auction. However, you are permitted to examine the stuff before auction time. Check with your local Customs Office for the time and place of their next auction for a chance to pick up German or Japanese cameras, imported liquor, perfume, jewelry, and oddments so varied it's impossible to list them.

Police and Sheriff's Auctions—Most of the stuff offered for sale by some unit of the police is used—abandoned bicycles being one of the biggest items. Sports equipment is another big item. A great variety of stuff (from hubcaps to transistor radios) is confiscated loot from burglaries or car stripping. Since much of the merchandise is used, few dealers are likely to bid. Here again, stuff is auctioned off "as is."

Transit Auctions—Most minds are incapable of imagining the wide diversity of stuff left on busses, streetcars, subway trains, or airplanes—and in the stations served by transit. Most transit companies collect and care for lost merchandise, but if it is not claimed within an allotted period, the stuff may be auctioned or it may be sent off to some charity organization for resale. Methods vary among different organizations and localities. Check with the airline or transit organization in your community to see if they hold regular auctions.

BUYING VERSUS RENTING

Equipment rental centers now service practically every community in the United States. Instead of buying some items, consider renting. For example, you might use a lawn roller twice a year. At $2.50 a day, you can rent one and save the space for storing it—as well as the price. But, how about a roll-a-way bed for visitors? Is renting one a good deal when it may be used once, twice, or three times a year? Figure the economics of renting versus buying this way—Suppose a good roll-a-way bed costs $95 and the rental charge runs $12 per week. If you used the bed once a year, your money would have earned 13%. But, if you should use it twice a year, your earnings increase to 25%. Not a bad investment.

Competition has forced down the rental on many items, such as floor polisher ($1.25 per day) and trailers (as low as $5.00 per day). Even at $1.25 per day, a floor polisher that sells for $69.95 might be a good buy if it is used ten times a year ($12.50 amounts to a return of almost 18%) plus the convenience of having it immediately available.

Ordinarily, renting versus buying pays off when either or both of two factors are present: (1) the article to be rented costs several hundred dollars; (2) the article is used only infrequently. Renting a travel trailer once a year would certainly pay off ($95 per week would earn 5% for a $1,800 trailer). But renting sleeping bags at $3 per week is less attractive if they can be bought for $15.95.

STOP THE LITTLE DRIPS

Do you spend 25¢ to 40¢ once or twice a day for coffee, 25¢ for a paper, an extra tip to a cab driver or the waitress at lunch, or ... The list could be endless, and the total at year's end could show a monstrous leak from your family's money pool. Consider these ideas for tightening up on minor money leaks—

Make Your Own Coffee Break—When you break for coffee, do you crowd into an elevator, then sit around a crowded table or counter to sip a half-full cup at 35¢ per? Instead of paying 70¢ per day (total $102.60 per year) for this doubtful privilege, consider these alternatives: (1) Bring your own coffee in a vacuum bottle. A streamlined pint bottle holds two honest cups of the kind of coffee you like and drink at home. Cost: about 20¢ per day. (2) Make your own coffee from hot water and a spoonful of instant that you keep in your desk. Many offices now sport a water "cooler" that also supplies near boiling water for tea, powdered soup, or coffee. A mug of hot water plus instant coffee builds a hearty cup for about 8¢. Dry cream substitutes even provide for those coffee drinkers who have not yet learned to appreciate the pure product. (3) Switch from coffee to tea and use either a hot water source at the office or heat your own with a small immersion heater. The Japanese make a useful heating coil that sells for about $1.29 on sale. A mug of cold water can be brought to a rolling boil in about 3 minutes.

Pick Your Papers—Some families subscribe and/or buy regularly as many as five newspapers per weekday, plus the giant Sunday editions. One excuse offered is the need for something to read on the bus or commuter train. If true, why not make it the only paper purchased? Or, suppose you read a specialty newspaper, such as the *Wall Street Journal*. Instead of buying it in addition, buy it instead of a regular morning paper. Also, newspapers printed for home delivery seldom contain the late afternoon news. So, the newspaper you buy for reading on the trip home also becomes the family's newspaper. Many families can save from 50¢ to $1.00 every day by examining their newspaper habits.

Too Much Tipping—There are no two ways about it, tipping is inescapable. But, overtipping and tipping where service is abominable are sheer follies. The word, tip, originated from the phrase, *To Insure Promptness*, and was meant as an extra compensation for better-than-average service. When one receives better-than-average service, a tip expresses your thanks. But, the decision is yours. When you receive surly, unresponsive service, no tip is required or even desirable. A tip is earned; it is not the inalienable right of every taxi driver, waitress, or dining hostess. Overtipping, more than 10% on most bills, or handing out folding money for carrying bags and certain menial services, is extravagant—and instead of being tagged the big spender, you may simply be considered a hick trying to buy his way in.

Split Allowances—Another spot where parents frequently get "taken" is the allowances bit. Children need and deserve some part of the family resources for spending money and to learn how to handle finances. But, paying too much money for allowances because "all the kids in our school get X number of dollars" is no way to handle this hot potato. Since part of the reason for handing out allowances is to teach children the value of and methods for handling money, set up a plan for splitting allowances;

that is, pay them about half price for some of their activities and then charge them half price for certain items. For example, instead of asking one of the children to sit with the younger ones for free while you are out for the evening, pay him or her half the going rate. Then, when he or she wants to buy something special, like an oddball pair of shoes or a ticket to hear some long-haired singing group, split the cost—you pay half and they pay half.

SUMMING UP

Miscellaneous spending of pocket change and small amounts of cash can wreck even the most carefully thought-out spending plan. Even more troublesome is the fact that these little dibs and dabs of cash can be spent with hardly a thought. Specific ways to staunch this flow of pocket change include—

- Saving a few pennies regularly on such items as bank charges, writing checks, and safe-deposit-box rentals.

- Staying clear of the wily promotions of door-to-door salesmen.

- Trading time and services for baby sitting, specialized skills, and room and board for household help.

- Analyzing how to reduce the cost of getting to and from work— plus the high cost of parking.

- Buying almost any kind of bargain goods at Post Office, Customs, police, and transit auctions.

- Learning when to rent equipment instead of buying—to save cash.

- Reducing the flow of pocket change for miscellaneous expenditures.

A FINAL WORD

Planning—a final word as well as one of the first. If there is one thing and one thing only you can take away from this book, it should be the idea of looking ahead, planning what you want to do, and taking steps in time to make those things happen.

In business, planning has become a major reason for the continued growth of some companies. Lack of planning has been the frequent reason for the gradual demise of other small and large firms. A family can and should plan ahead like a well-run business. You, in conference with all members of the family, can set goals, plan how to achieve each of the goals agreed upon, and work as a group to make your plans come true, Few worthwhile things are likely to fall into your lap without some form of planning, even if your plan is only something hazy in your head. So, to get more out of your life, to use your resources to the fullest, and to eliminate much of the stress and strain of everyday living, set up a plan and work toward its fulfillment.

INDEX